WHITE ON RED

Kennikat Press
National University Publications
Literary Criticism Series

General Editor
John E. Becker
Fairleigh Dickinson University

WHITE

ON

RED

IMAGES OF THE AMERICAN INDIAN

Edited by

NANCY B. BLACK

and

BETTE S. WEIDMAN

National University Publications
KENNIKAT PRESS   //   1976
Port Washington, N. Y.   //   London

Manufactured in the United States of America

Published by
Kennikat Press Corp.
Port Washington, N.Y./London

Library of Congress Cataloging in Publication Data
Main entry under title:

White on red.

    (Literary criticism series) (National university publications)
    Includes indexes.
    1. Indians of North America—Addresses, essays, lectures.
2. Indians of North America—Literary collections. 3. American literature. I. Black, Nancy B. II. Weidman, Bette S.
E77.2.W45   970'.004'97   76-17831
ISBN 0-8046-9084-7

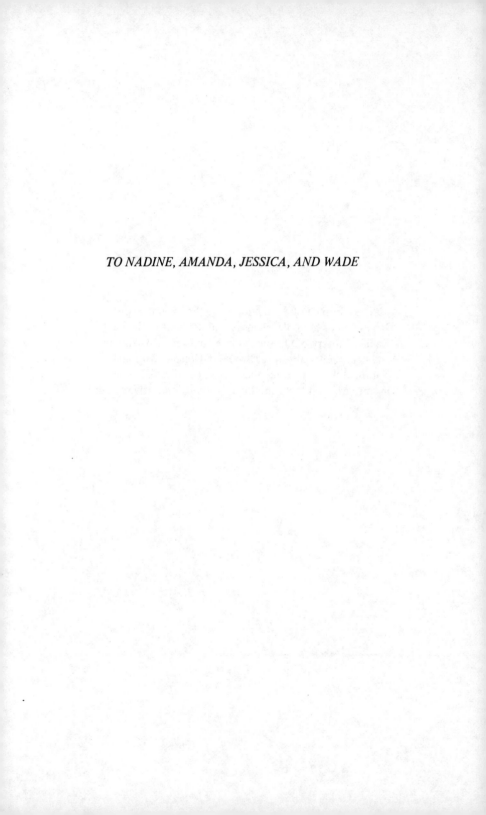

TO NADINE, AMANDA, JESSICA, AND WADE

ACKNOWLEDGMENTS

The editors wish to acknowledge the assistance of Olive James and of Mimi Penchansky and her staff at the Paul Kapper Library of Queens College, and Jenny Allenberg and her secretarial staff at Brooklyn College. We thank Thurman Wilkins for his encouragement, Lewis Leary for his interest, and Mike and Burt for their supportive criticism.

CONTENTS

PART ONE: FROM THE DISCOVERY OF AMERICA
THROUGH THE EIGHTEENTH CENTURY

INTRODUCTION   5

CAPTAIN JOHN SMITH (1579-1631)
From THE GENERAL HISTORIE, 1624   14

ANONYMOUS
From A JOURNAL, 1622   21

THOMAS MORTON (1590-1647)
From NEW ENGLISH CANAAN, 1637   28

DAVID PIETERZEN DeVRIES (1592c.-1655)
From VOYAGES FROM HOLLAND TO AMERICA,   32
    1632-1644

BENJAMIN TOMPSON (1642-1714)
From NEW ENGLAND'S CRISIS, 1676   36

MARY ROWLANDSON (1635c.-1678c.)
From A NARRATIVE OF THE CAPTIVITY AND   40
    RESTORATION OF MRS. MARY ROWLANDSON, 1682

WILLIAM PENN (1644-1718)
From A DESCRIPTION OF PENNSYLVANIA, 1683   49

COTTON MATHER (1663-1728)
From MAGNALIA CHRISTI AMERICANA, 1702   56
From DECENNIUM LUCTUOSUM, 1699   64

EBENEZER COOK (fl. 1708)
From THE SOT-WEED FACTOR, 1705   71

JOHN LAWSON (d. 1711)
From A NEW VOYAGE TO CAROLINA, 1709   74

ROBERT ROGERS (1731-1795)
From PONTEACH; OR THE SAVAGES OF AMERICA, 1766   79

JOHN WOOLMAN (1720-1772)
From THE JOURNAL, 1774   89

MICHEL GUILLAUME JEAN de CRÈVECOEUR (1735-1813)
From LETTERS FROM AN AMERICAN FARMER, 1782   95

BENJAMIN FRANKLIN (1706-1790)
*REMARKS CONCERNING THE SAVAGES OF
NORTH AMERICA*, 1784   101

THOMAS JEFFERSON (1743-1826)
From NOTES ON THE STATE OF VIRGINIA, 1784   107

WILLIAM BARTRAM (1739-1823)
From THE TRAVELS, 1791   113

PHILIP FRENEAU (1752-1832)
*LINES OCCASIONED BY A VISIT TO AN OLD INDIAN
BURYING GROUND*, 1788   120
From THE NATIONAL GAZETTE, 1792   122

PART TWO: THE NINETEENTH CENTURY

INTRODUCTION   127

CHARLES BROCKDEN BROWN (1771-1810)
From EDGAR HUNTLEY, 1799   138

JAMES NELSON BARKER (1784-1858)
*From THE INDIAN PRINCESS; OR, LA BELLE
SAUVAGE*, 1808   149

ALEXANDER HENRY (1739-1824)
*From TRAVELS AND ADVENTURES IN CANADA AND THE
INDIAN TERRITORIES*, 1809   156

WASHINGTON IRVING (1783-1859)
From A HISTORY OF NEW YORK, 1809   161

LYDIA MARIA CHILD (1802-1880)
From HOBOMOK: A TALE OF EARLY TIMES..., 1824   166

CONTENTS

JOHN AUGUSTUS STONE (1800–1834)
*From METAMORA, OR THE LAST OF THE
WAMPANOAGS*, 1829   **172**

WILLIAM GILMORE SIMMS (1806–1870)
From THE YEMASSEE: A ROMANCE OF CAROLINA, 1835   **176**

NATHANIEL HAWTHORNE (1804–1864)
From THE DUSTON FAMILY, 1836   **185**

ROBERT MONTGOMERY BIRD (1806–1854)
*From NICK OF THE WOODS; OR THE JIBBENAINOSAY,
A TALE OF KENTUCKY*, 1837   **191**

EDGAR ALLAN POE (1809–1849)
From THE JOURNAL OF JULIUS RODMAN, 1840   **197**

LYDIA HUNTLEY SIGOURNEY (1791–1865)
From POCAHONTAS, AND OTHER POEMS, 1841   **205**

MARGARET FULLER (1810–1850)
From SUMMER ON THE LAKES, 1844   **209**

WILLIAM CULLEN BRYANT (1794–1878)
From POETICAL WORKS, 1883   **214**

FRANCIS PARKMAN (1823–1893)
From THE CONSPIRACY OF PONTIAC..., 1851   **218**

HERMAN MELVILLE (1819–1891)
From MOBY DICK; OR THE WHALE, 1851   **222**

HENRY WADSWORTH LONGFELLOW (1807–1882)
From THE SONG OF HIAWATHA, 1855   **236**

WALT WHITMAN (1819–1892)
From LEAVES OF GRASS, 1855   **243**
*From THE HALF-BREED: A TALE OF THE WESTERN
FRONTIER*, 1846   **245**
From AN INDIAN BUREAU REMINISCENCE, 1884   **247**

JAMES FENIMORE COOPER (1789–1851)
From THE WEPT OF WISH-TON-WISH, 1855   **250**

HORACE GREELEY (1811–1872)
*From AN OVERLAND JOURNEY FROM NEW YORK
TO SAN FRANCISCO...*, 1860   **257**

ANN SOPHIA STEPHENS (1813–1886)
*From MALAESKA; OR THE INDIAN WIFE OF THE
WHITE HUNTER*, 1860   **261**

CONTENTS

HENRY DAVID THOREAU (1817–1862)
*From A WEEK ON THE CONCORD AND MERRIMACK
RIVERS*, 1849   265
From THE MAINE WOODS, 1864   269

RALPH WALDO EMERSON (1803–1882)
From CIVILIZATION, 1870   272

MARK TWAIN (1835–1910)
From ROUGHING IT, 1872   276

FRANK HAMILTON CUSHING (1857–1900)
From MY ADVENTURES IN ZUÑI, 1882–1883   280

HELEN HUNT JACKSON (1830–1885)
From RAMONA, 1884   285

AUTHOR INDEX   291

TITLE INDEX   291

PREFACE

Our purpose in this volume is to draw together literary treatments of the North American Indian, written by whites in the course of a three-hundred-year period, roughly from the settlement of Virginia, in 1607, to the Battle of Wounded Knee, in 1890. During this period, the Indian threat to white hegemony flared, smoldered, and was extinguished. The events of these years and the pressures that produced them defined cultural beliefs for many white writers. In their prose narratives, poetry, drama, and fiction, they tell us little of importance about Indians, but much about themselves and their transplanted civilization.

Because we want to show the ways in which whites transformed the human beings they met on this continent into images that served their own hopes and fears, we have not used the scientific criteria of ethnologists. We have made our selections from among an enormous number of possible sources, keeping in mind the inherent interest of each piece and its representative qualities. We have included some little-known selections from major authors, as well as a number of passages from the works of popular writers who more artlessly reflect the attitudes of their audience.

Since American poetry, drama, and fiction did not begin to develop fully until the early nineteenth century, most of the excerpts in the first section of the book are from volumes of nonfiction prose. Conversely, in the nineteenth-century section, the editors sought to represent drama, poetry and fiction as fully as possible, and so had to limit autobiographical narrative and journals of exploration; the long semiscientific works on the Indian that began to appear during the nineteenth century make an interesting study, but had to be eliminated for reasons of space. Romantic novels of the nineteenth century include such revealing images of the

Indian that they were too valuable to omit; we chose excerpts from them in the belief that, despite their unfashionable style, they deserve renewed attention. Throughout, headnotes place the excerpts in the contexts of the whole works from which they are taken.

The chronological order of the book offers the reader varied images in juxtaposition and discourages reductive stereotype-hunting; the editors invite the reader to consider the literary treatment of the Indian for him-or herself. Further, we offer this work as a sourcebook for critical commentary on the influence of the West and the idea of civilization. This anthology does not pretend to substitute for a thorough critical or sociological study, nor does reading it substitute for the experience of reading complete texts; rather, it assembles a thorough sampling of essential texts, each of which offers possibilities for further study.

The editors believe in the necessity of this study; cultural health is achieved only through our ability to regard ourselves and our versions of history critically. It was no surprise to us to find that Indians are a pervasive presence in white American literature; the relation of white to Indian, in this country, has been and remains a national obsession. This is only human and fitting, since whites bear so large a burden of guilt. These literary portraits supply evidence of the tragedy behind our American optimism. As Frank Waters writes, "It was not enough for us here in the United States to almost exterminate the red race in our sweep across the continent. Its ghosts still walk the land, and in our unconscious the Indian is a potent symbol."

A NOTE ON THE TEXT

The texts used in this anthology are acknowledged in the source note at the start of each selection. Spelling and punctuation have been modernized for greater readability; unnecessary capitals and italics have been eliminated.

PART ONE

From the Discovery of America

Through the Eighteenth Century

INTRODUCTION

When Christopher Columbus met his first "Indian" on Friday, October 12, 1492, he appeared unaware of just how important his meeting was; to a modern reader his reporting of the event is remarkably low-keyed:

It appeared to me to be a race of people very poor in everything. They go as naked as when their mothers bore them, and so do the women, although I did not see more than one young girl. All I saw were youths, none more than thirty years of age. They are very well made, with very handsome bodies, and very good countenances. Their hair is short and coarse, almost like the hairs of a horse's tail. They wear the hairs brought down to the eyebrows, except a few locks behind, which they wear long and never cut. They paint themselves black, and they are the color of the Canarians, neither black nor white. Some paint themselves white, others red, and others of what color they find. Some paint their faces, others the whole body, some only round the eyes, others only on the nose. They neither carry nor know anything of arms, for I showed them swords, and they took them by the blade and cut themselves through ignorance.[1]

Although Europeans had met with members of primitive races before the 1492 journey to America, and other travelers had been to America before Columbus,[2] there was something unique about Columbus's confrontation: with it began a seemingly endless struggle between white men and red men, a struggle which constantly beset the early settlers and which by 1800 had led to the destruction of Indian culture in the East. Although early colonists sometimes questioned their right to settle in foreign lands and felt compelled to formulate treaties before encroaching on Indian lands, as white men became more numerous and more firmly settled, the question of their right to the land ceased to be an issue. Despite the increasing callousness of political attitudes toward Indian affairs, the Indian himself—often a generalized conception—always piqued the curiosity of white men, and he became an object of fascination for anthropologists, novelists, poets, scientists, missionaries, and for ordinary readers of Indian captivities and Westerns for the next five centuries.

Long before Columbus, Europeans had conceived of and described races of men vastly different from themselves. From Pliny's *Natural History* in the first century to Mandeville's *Travels* in the fourteenth century, there existed a considerable tradition of peopling countries outside the perimeter of established shipping routes with strange races of men; this tradition reflected an early European curiosity to hear about people with unusual appearances and remarkable customs.[3] But these descriptions of one-eyed Arismaspians or men with goat's feet were more fanciful than factual, more like our modern science-fiction stories than scientific reporting. What is unique about the early reports of explorers of America is the degree to which, in comparison to medieval travel reports, they approach accurate reporting. The fifteenth and sixteenth centuries were better prepared to discover and analyze a hitherto unheard-of race than were the thirteenth and fourteenth centuries. What more natural accompaniment to the flurry of scientific discovery in the Renaissance than the discovery of a new race? Thomas Hariot's sixteenth-century description of the Indians of Virginia displays an attention to details of Indian life typical of a more scientific age. The rapid settlement of North American shores in the seventeenth century gave sufficient opportunity for firsthand observation and analysis of Indian customs to satisfy the most curious European.

Later descriptions of red men by white men, written after the first colonies were established in America, adopt an increasingly scientific approach to the red men. There is an awareness, even in George Alsop's *A Character of the Province of Maryland* (1666), of the necessity to record for posterity the customs of the red men.[4] As the white man became more powerful and the Indians were decimated, the white man felt the urgency to record details of a vanishing race, and—no longer threatened by physical attack by the Indians—he could afford the luxury of viewing the Indian from a less prejudiced viewpoint. The format by which red men are described by Thomas Morton, Daniel Denton, and Robert Beverley is that of the encyclopedia. The description of the Indian is divided into set topics such as "Of the Diseases, and Cures of the Indian" or "Of the Indian's Apparel." It is not infrequent to find, as in Thomas Jefferson's *Notes on the State of Virginia,* a chapter devoted to the recording of the names of tribes in the area or an estimate of the population of each.

Another impetus to the writings of white men about red men was economic: the desire to advertize and propagandize for the new land. An explorer's success depended upon discovery, and the Indian was the obvious symbol of discovery. Not only were Indians described minutely in letters to patrons, but they were frequently kidnapped and taken back to Europe as proof of discovery. Columbus's *Journals* and *Letters* are among our earliest examples of propaganda, for many of his remarks about the gentleness of the "Indians," their knowledge of gold, their pliability, or their physical strength were designed to advertize their future usefulness for the Spanish crown, whether as guides, as workers, or as slaves. At a later period descriptions of the colonies, designed to advertize the favorable prospects of settling in a new land, included descriptions of Indians for another reason: the Indians symbolized a new settler's fears about America. To allay such fears, the author would play down, or even mock, the fierce, warlike Indian.

The theological and philosophical movements of the sixteenth and seventeenth centuries provided the most powerful stimuli of all to writers about the Indians. Many of the religious groups which came to America, but none more dramatically than the Puritans, incorporated the Indian into their theology. The Puritans experienced the New World allegorically: worldly trials and tribulations were but stages on the spiritual road to salvation. Mary Rowlandson peppers her account of her captivity by the Indians with biblical references; their mere number indicates just how closely her actions were guided by religious precepts. When she is restored finally to her husband, she quotes the Puritan's favorite prophet, Jeremiah:

Now hath God fulfilled that precious scripture which was such a comfort to me in my distressed condition. When my heart was ready to sink into the earth (my children being gone I could not tell whither) and my knees trembled under me, and I was walking through the valley of the shadow of death, then the Lord brought, and now has fulfilled that reviving word unto me. Thus saith the Lord: *Refrain thy voice from weeping, and thine eyes from tears, for thy work shall be rewarded, saith the Lord, and they shall come again from the Land of the Enemy* . . . .
I have seen the extreme vanity of this world. One hour I have been in health, and wealth, wanting nothing, but the next hour in sickness and wounds, and death, having nothing but sorrow and affliction.[5]

Within such a view, the wilderness becomes the symbol of worldly temptation, trial, and hardship. The Indian, the natural inhabitant of the wilderness, is the instrument of the devil, or the devil himself, who labors to devise new and more horrible forms of suffering to tempt the Puritan soul. No virtue can be assigned the Indian. If the Indian seems to show kindness, the Puritan interprets it as a sign of God's grace. When, during the Third Remove of Mary Rowlandson's captivity, one of the Indians brings her a Bible, she takes notice not of his kindness, but "of the wonderful mercy of God to me in those afflictions in sending me a Bible."

The Jesuits, like the Puritans, used the Indian as a road to salvation but in quite a different way. While the Puritans had little interest in missionary efforts—except in the case of John Eliot—the Jesuits used their mission to accomplish their personal salvation. By becoming a missionary in an outpost in the New World and laboring to convert Indians to Christianity, the Jesuit practised the ultimate form of self-sacrifice for the love of God. A comparison of the captivities of Mary Rowlandson or John Williams to that of Father Jogues illustrates the difference (see Supplementary Reading list). It is inconceivable that Mary Rowlandson or John Williams would elect to stay in the wilderness. The priest, given the chance to escape, chooses to remain with his fellow captive, offer him Christianity, and labor to convert the very Indians whose captive he is. Among the Jesuits the act of self-sacrifice sometimes became more important than the success of the mission. Many of their "conversions" of natives were unaccompanied by theological understanding.[6]

Another important religious group—the Quakers—had no missionary goals at all; the Indian did not provide a road to their salvation. The Indians did, however, confirm their religious beliefs, particularly in "that of God in every man." If even a heathen could be found to be virtuous and tame, then all men must have "that of God" within. En route to visit the Wehaloosing Indians, John Woolman, while spending the night in the house of an Indian, chances to open the door to a tomahawk-wielding Indian. His reaction best illustrates the Quaker way:

Perceiving there was a man near the door I went out; the man had a tomahawk wrapped under his match-coat out of sight. As I approached him he took it in his hand; I went forward, and, speaking to him in a friendly way, perceived he understood some English. My companion joining me, we had some talk with him concerning the nature of our visit in these parts; he then went into the house with us, and, talking with our guides, soon appeared friendly, sat down and smoked his pipe. Though taking his hatchet in his hand at the instant I drew near to him had a disagreeable appearance, I believe he had no other intent than to be in readiness in case any violence were offered to him.[7]

Although the Quakers had little or no effect on the Christianization of the Indians (the Indians John Woolman visited were already Christian) their way for a time influenced politics in Pennsylvania and resulted in the most comprehensive system of treaties created among the early colonies. The Quaker way did much to influence the political and philosophical attitudes of one of the most eloquent later defenders of Indians—Benjamin Franklin.

The philosopher viewed the Indians differently from the theologian. Depending on how he valued white civilized society, the philosopher saw the Indian from either of two extremes. If European society was viewed as

basically good, then the Indian incorporated all values threatening to civilized society and he was depicted as a wild man. If European society was
viewed as corrupt, then the Indian incorporated all those qualities lacking
in European society and he was depicted as a noble savage.[8] The wild man
is the older of the two concepts and is a tradition which extends back
through the Middle Ages and beyond, back even to Herodotus.[9] Although
this older tradition of the wild man was by the sixteenth and seventeenth
centuries outdated or at least relegated to a subconscious level in the writings
of philosophers, it continued to exert strong influence on laymen and less-
educated observers of the American scene. The "wild" Indian may be seen
in descriptions of Indian methods of warfare and torture techniques, a
common topic for white writers. The "wildest," most savage Indians
described prior to 1800 occur in contemporary accounts of wars between
white men and red men. None perhaps is so extreme as Benjamin Tompson's
depiction of Philip, written at the height of King Philip's War.[10]

The newer philosophic view current in the sixteenth and seventeenth
centuries concerning primitive races is represented by Montaigne's essay
"On Cannibalism," which insists that the Indian lives in a better society than
what is usually thought of as "civilized" because his primitive society is
simple and natural. In America those individuals most oppressed by "civilized" society were likely to adopt a noble savage view. Thomas Morton,
twice banished from the New World by the Puritans, wrote of the Indians:

I found two sorts of people, the one Christians, the other infidels; these I
found most full of humanity, and more friendly than the other. . . .[11]

Because the white men who first arrived on the North American shores
and established initial contacts with the Indians were motivated by so many
impulses—philosophic, religious, scientific, as well as the desire to get rich—
it is dangerous to make any generalization about the attitudes of the early
settlers toward Indians. The variety of attitudes which flourished at the
start of white-red relations in this country can be appreciated only by
reading representatives of each: both Captain John Smith and Thomas
Jefferson; both Thomas Morton and Cotton Mather; both Mary Rowlandson
and Robert Rogers.

One generalization, an historical one, can be made: nearly all early
settlers arrived in America with a politically pragmatic attitude toward the
Indians.[12] If they could live with the red men peaceably, that was obviously
the better route to adopt. Finding food and shelter in the American wilderness was difficult enough without adding the fear of Indian attack to those
difficulties. Pennsylvania and Maryland were not the only colonies dedicated
to a system of treaties and fair treatment of Indians; they were simply the

most effective in their adherence to these principles. Even the Massachusetts Bay Colony, which has perhaps the worst record among eastern
settlers for dealing peaceably with the Indians, lived in relative peace with
the Indians for the first fifty-five years of its existence,[13] a surprising example of the triumph of secular expedience over religious principle. The
passage from *Mourt's Relation* selected here records one of the earliest
peace treaties between red man and white.

Despite the good intentions in each colony to consort peaceably with
Indians, it was not long before disagreements, disputes, and conflicts arose
between white men and red. By 1675, the Puritans were involved in full-
scale wars with the Indians in Massachusetts. Even in Pennsylvania, Quaker
influence waned, and by the middle of the eighteenth century warfare had
broken out on the western frontier; during raids of the Paxton boys (1764)
the conflict came within forty miles of Philadelphia.

Roy Harvey Pearce, in his admirable study of the white man's concept of
the savage,[14] views the white-red hostilities as symbolic of the failure of
the premise with which white men arrived in America: the only good life
was the ordered, "civilized" life of the Europeans, and the wild, "savage"
life of the Indian existed only to be ordered by the European. When he
failed to civilize the Indian, the European had to destroy him to maintain
the "rightness" of civilized life.[15]

Valid as Pearce's theory is, there are other reasons, perhaps more obvious,
for the eruption of hostilities between white men and red men. Seldom
before had two cultures so different from one another been placed side by
side to fight it out in Darwinian fashion or live together peaceably. The
task was made more difficult by the language barrier and by the rigidity
with which Europeans, especially those influenced by religion, clung to
their own ways. There were but few exceptions among Europeans: the
Quakers had none of the rigid biblical mythology of the Puritans; the
French, partly because of their dependence upon trade with the Indians,
learned the Indian languages quickly. *Mourt's Relation* best illustrates the
problems in establishing contact between the two cultures. The Pilgrims
arrived with guns at the ready for their first encounter with the Indians; in
their early days exploring the coast, they dug up Indian stores and graves
without a thought to the effect it might have on the Indians. The Pilgrims,
like the Puritans later, left interpretation of the Indian language to God,
and indeed He seemed to answer their prayers by sending as the first Indian
to face the Pilgrims Squanto, an Indian who had been to England and who,
miraculously, spoke English.

It is in nonfiction prose that we see the greatest interest in the Indian
prior to 1800; the Indian was a central figure in semiscientific, propagandistic,

religious, and philosophic writing. Not until the nineteenth century does the Indian become central to American fiction, poetry, and drama. That is not to say that there were no beginnings prior to 1800. There is some early poetry, represented in this volume by Benjamin Tompson and Ebenezer Cook, but even these poems are but one step from being versified history. One play on an Indian theme, Robert Roger's *Ponteach,* was written before 1800, but the Indian theme in drama did not truly flourish until later.[16] The seventeenth and eighteenth centuries were too preoccupied with survival to devote much attention to poetry, fiction, or drama, and the Indian was too close at hand to be fictionalized. There are the beginnings of significant American myths—the Indian maiden, Pocahontas, the vanishing American, the Indian chief—and these beginnings are represented here by Bartram's encounter with nymphlike Indian maidens, Captain John Smith's story of Pocahontas, Freneau's mock Indian orator, and a scene from Roger's *Ponteach.*[17] But the actual development of these concepts into myths occurs in the nineteenth and twentieth centuries.

The captivity is the only significant literary form depicting the Indian prior to 1800. The captivity as a genre began in the seventeenth century, flourished, and, by the end of the eighteenth century, was outworn. Roy Harvey Pearce notes the variety of forms the captivity takes, and he summarizes the development of the genre.[18] First came the religious captivities, mostly Puritan, like those of Mary Rowlandson and John Williams; these are characterized by "vivid immediacy" and "religious intensity." With a realization of the propagandistic value of the captivity came a loss of the directness essential to the success of the early examples. Cotton Mather exemplifies this stage. By the mid-eighteenth century, propaganda and stylism had taken over. The undisguised purpose of the captivity was to evoke hatred for the Indians. Sensationalism took over, as in the nineteenth-century captivity of Fanny Kelly.

It was not until the Revolution that the Indian assumed major importance as a theme in American literature outside of nonfiction prose. With the Revolution came a pride in things American and a search for uniquely American themes. There was no more natural theme to seize upon than the Indian. Freneau, at the end of the eighteenth century, is the earliest representative of this search for American themes, a search continued in the following century by Washington Irving, Henry Wadsworth Longfellow, and James Fenimore Cooper.

INTRODUCTION

NOTES

1. *The Journal of Christopher Columbus,* trans. Clements R. Markham (London, 1893), pp. 37-38.

2. Samuel Eliot Morison, *The European Discovery of America: The Northern Voyages, A. D. 500-1600* (New York, 1971).

3. Pliny, *Historia Naturalis,* trans. H. Rackham (London, 1938), V, 1, 8, 34; VII, 2. Mandeville's *Travels,* ed. P. Hamelius, EETS, O. S. (London, 1919-23), pp. 133, 187ff. See also Aelian, *De Natura animalium;* St. Isidore, *Etymologiae;* Hrabanus Maurus, *De Universo; Li Livres dou Tresor de Brunetto Latini;* Bartholomaeus Angelicus, *De rerum Proprietatibus;* Vincent of Beauvais, *Speculum Naturale.*

4. Scientific theorizing about the Indian is evident also in James Adair's *History of the American Indians* (1775). Adair argues that the Indians represent one of the lost tribes of Israel. Although such a theory was possible in an earlier century, the detail with which the theory is argued reflects the new scientific spirit.

5. "A Narrative of the Captivity and Restauration of Mrs. Mary Rowlandson," in *Narratives of the Indian Wars, 1675-1699,* ed. Charles H. Lincoln (New York, 1913), pp. 164, 166.

6. See, for example, the "Letter from Father Biard to Reverend Father Christopher Baltazar, Provincial of France, at Paris" (1611), in *The Jesuit Relations. . . . ,* ed. Reuben G. Thwaites (Cleveland, 1896-1901), I, pp. 163-75.

7. *The Journal of John Woolman* (Boston, 1871), pp. 145-46.

8. Hayden White, "The Forms of Wildness: Archeology of an Idea," in *The Wild Man Within: An Image in Western Thought from the Renaissance to Romanticism,* ed. Edward Dudley and Maximilliam E. Novak (Pittsburgh, 1972), p. 28.

9. Richard Bernheimer, *Wild Men in the Middle Ages* (Cambridge, Mass., 1952).

10. See pp. 36–39.

11. Thomas Morton, *The New English Canaan,* in *Publications of the Prince Society,* XIV (Boston, 1883), p. 123.

12. Howard Peckham and Charles Gibson, eds., *Attitudes of Colonial Powers Toward the American Indian* (Salt Lake City, Utah, 1969).

13. Alden T. Vaugh, *New England Frontier: Puritans and Indians, 1620-1625* (Boston, 1965).

14. Roy Harvey Pearce, *The Savages of America: A Study of the Indian and the Idea of Civilization* (Baltimore, 1965).

15. *Ibid.,* pp. 3-6.

16. See pp. 79–88.

17. The word "myth" is used here in the sense in which Leslie Fiedler uses it in his book *The Return of the Vanishing American* (New York, 1968).

18. Roy Harvey Pearce, "The Significance of the Captivity Narrative," *American Literature,* XIX (March, 1947), 1-20.

INTRODUCTION

SUPPLEMENTARY READING

OTHER PRE-1800 VIEWS OF THE INDIANS

Adair, James. *The History of the American Indians.* 1775.

Alsop, George. *A Character of the Province of Maryland.* 1666.

Beverley, Robert. *A History of Virginia.* 1705.

Bleecker, Ann Eliza. *The History of Maria Kittle.* 1797.

Bradford, William. *Of Plymouth Plantation.* 1620-1647.

Colden, Cadwallader. *The History of the Five Indian Nations.* 1727.

Denton, Daniel. *A Brief Description of New York . . . .* 1670.

Dwight, Timothy. *Greenfield Hill.* 1794.

Filson, John. *The Discovery, Settlement, and Present State of Kentucke. . . .* 1784.

Franklin, Benjamin. *A Narrative of the Late Massacres, in Lancaster County, of a Number of Indians, Friends of the Province, by Persons Unknown: With Observations on the Same.* 1764.

Folger, Peter. *A Looking Glass for the Times.* 1676.

Hariot, Thomas. *A Briefe and True Report of the New Foundland of Virginia.* 1588.

Jogues, Father Isaac. *The Captivity of Father Isaac Jogues among the Mohawks.* 1643.

Seaver, James E. *A Narrative of the Life of Mrs. Mary Jemison . . . .* ed. Allen W. Trelease. New York, 1961.

Wheelock, Eleazar. *Plain and Faithful Narrative of the . . . Indian Charity School at Lebanon.* 1763.

Williams, John. *The Redeemed Captive.* 1707.

Williams, Roger. *A Key into the Language of America.* 1643.

SCHOLARLY WORKS

In addition to those noted in the introduction, the following works discuss pre-1800 views of the Indian:

Aldridge, A. O. "Franklin's Deistical Indians," *Proceedings of the American Philosophical Society,* XCIV, No. 4 (August, 1950), 398-410.

Keiser, Albert. *The Indian in American Literature.* New York, 1933.

Sheehan, Bernard W. "Paradise and the Noble Savage in Jeffersonian Thought," *William and Mary Quarterly,* XXVI (July, 1969), 327-59.

Slotkin, Richard. *Regeneration through Violence: The Mythology of the American Frontier, 1600-1860.* Middletown, Conn., 1973.

CAPTAIN JOHN SMITH
(1579-1631)

The story of Pocahontas, as related by Captain John Smith in the 1624 revised edition of his *Generall Historie of Virginia,* is the first document in the development of one of America's most significant myths. Whereas the early settlers soon became aware of their initial naiveté in assuming they could mollify, civilize, and Christianize the Indian warrior, the Indian maiden might yet be attracted to civilized society through the white man's physical virtues and gentle charms. John Barth's twentieth-century parody of Captain John Smith's *Historie* recognizes and plays upon the vanity of the white man's presumption of superiority inherent in the myth of Pocahontas, the Indian maiden who fell in love with John Rolfe and created a hit upon visiting London and obtaining an audience with the Queen.

As with most legends, it is impossible to say where fact ends and fiction begins in Smith's account of Pocahontas. Scholars have made much of the fact that Smith never mentioned his rescue by Pocahontas in the earlier 1608 edition of his *Generall Historie.* Actually Smith's own dealings with Pocahontas are only briefly mentioned. The focus of his 1624 account is Pocahontas' marriage to John Rolfe and her subsequent visit to London, events which occured in 1613-1616, well after the publication of the first edition. What seems likely is that Smith, living is disgrace in London in 1624, added the sections on Pocahontas to play upon popular interest of the day in Pocahontas and to ride on the shirttails of her popularity.

14

From **The Generall Historie, *1624***

And now the winter approaching, the rivers became so covered with swans, geese, ducks, and cranes, that we daily feasted with good bread, Virginia peas, pumpkins, and persimmons, fish, fowl, and divers sorts of wild beasts as fat as we could eat them, so that none of our Tuftaffaty humorists desired to go for England. But our comedies never endured long without a tragedy, some idle exceptions being muttered against Captain Smith for not discovering the head of Chickahominy River, and taxed by the Council to be too slow in so worthy an attempt. The next voyage he proceeded so far that with much labor by cutting of trees asunder he made his passage; but when his barge could pass no farther, he left her in a broad bay out of danger of shot, commanding none should go ashore till his return. Himself with two English and two savages went up higher in a canoe; but he was not long absent, but his men went ashore, whose want of government gave both occasion and opportunity to the savages to surprise one George Cassen, whom they slew, and much failed not to have cut off the boat and all the rest. Smith, little dreaming of that accident, being got to the marshes at the river's head, twenty miles in the desert [wilderness], had his two men slain (as is supposed) sleeping by the canoe, whilst himself by fowling sought them victual, who finding he was beset with 200 savages, two of them he slew, still defending himself with the aid of a savage, his guide, whom he bound to his arm with his garters and used him as a buckler. Yet he was shot in his thigh a little, and had many arrows that stuck in his clothes but no great hurt, till at last they took him prisoner. When this news came to Jamestown, much was their sorrow for his loss, few expecting what ensued. Six or seven weeks those barbarians kept him prisoner, many strange triumphs and conjurations they made of him, yet he so demeaned himself amongst them, as he not only diverted them from surprising the fort, but procured his own liberty, and got himself and his company such estimation amongst them, that those savages admired him more than their own Quiyouckosucks. The manner how they used and delivered him is as follows:

The savages, having drawn from George Cassen whither Captain Smith was gone, prosecuting that opportunity they followed him with 300 bowmen, conducted by the King of Pamunkey, who in divisions searching the

John Smith, *The Generall Historie of Virginia, New-England, and the Summer Isles* (London, 1624), pp. 46-49.

15

turnings of the river found Robinson and Emry by the fireside; those they shot full of arrows and slew. Then finding the Captain, as is said, that used the savage that was his guide as his shield (three of them being slain and divers others so galled), all the rest would not come near him. Thinking thus to have returned to his boat, regarding them as he marched more than his way, slipped up to the middle in an oozy creek and his savage with him; yet durst they not come to him till being near dead with cold he threw away his arms. Then according to their composition they drew him forth and led him to the fire where his men were slain. Diligently they chafed his benumbed limbs. He demanding for their captain, they showed him Opechancanough, King of Pamunkey to whom he gave a round ivory double compass dial. Much they marvelled at the playing of the fly and needle, which they could see so plainly and yet not touch it because of the glass that covered them. But when he demonstrated by that globe-like jewel, the roundness of the earth and skies, the sphere of the sun, moon, and stars, and how the sun did chase the night round about the world continually, the greatness of the land and sea, the diversity of nations, variety of complexions, and how we were to them antipodes, and many other such like matters, they all stood as amazed with admiration. Notwithstanding, within an hour after, they tied him to a tree, and as many as could stand about him prepared to shoot him, but the King holding up the compass in his hand, they all laid down their bows and arrows and in a triumphant manner led him to Orapaks, where he was after their manner kindly feasted and well used.

Their order in conducting him was thus: drawing themselves all in file, the King in the midst had all their pieces and swords borne before him. Captain Smith was led after him by three great savages, holding him fast by each arm, and on each side six went in file with their arrows nocked. But arriving at the town (which was but only thirty or forty hunting houses made of mats, which they remove as they please, as we our tents), all the women and children starting to behold him, the soldiers first all in file performed the form of a bissom [Spanish, *bisoño,* for "squadron"] so well as could be, and on each flank, officers as sergeants to see them keep their orders. A good time they continued this exercise and then cast themselves in a ring, dancing in such several postures and singing and yelling out such hellish notes and screeches; being strangely painted, every one his quiver of arrows and at his back a club; on his arm a fox or an otter's skin or some such matter for his vambrace; their heads and shoulders painted red, with oil and pocones [blood root] mingled together, which scarlet-like color made an exceeding handsome show; his bow in his hand and the skin of a bird with her wings abroad dried, tied on his head, a piece of copper, a white shell, a long feather, with a small rattle growing at the tails of their snakes tied to it, or some such like toy. All this while Smith and the King stood in the midst guarded, as before is said, and after three dances they all departed. Smith they conducted to a long house where thirty or forty tall fellows did guard him, and ere long more bread and venison was brought him than would have served twenty men. I think his stomach at that time was not very good; what he left they put in baskets and tied over his head. About midnight they set the meat again before him; all this time not one of them would eat a bit with him, till the next morning they brought him as much more, and then did they eat all the old and reserved the new as they had done the other, which made him think they would fatten him to eat him. Yet in this desperate estate, to defend him from the cold, one Maocassater brought him his gown, in requital of some beads and toys Smith had given him at his first arrival in Virginia.

Two days after, a man would have slain him (but that the guard prevented it) for the death of his son, to whom they conducted him to recover the poor man then breathing his last. Smith told them that at Jamestown he had a water would do it, if they would let him fetch it, but they would not permit that, but made all the preparations they could to assault Jamestown, craving his advice, and for recompence he should have life, liberty, land, and women. In part of a table book he wrote his mind to them at the fort, what was intended, how they should follow that direction to affright the messengers, and without fail send him such things as he wrote for and an inventory with them. The difficulty and danger, he told the savages, of the mines, great guns, and other engines exceedingly affrighted them, yet according to his request they went to Jamestown in as bitter weather as could be of frost and snow, and within three days returned with an answer.

But when they came to Jamestown, seeing men sally out as he had told them they would, they fled; yet in the night they came again to the same place where he had told them they should receive an answer, and such things as he had promised them, which they found accordingly and with which they returned with no small expedition, to the wonder of them all that heard it that he could either divine or the paper could speak. Then they led him to the Youthtanunds, the Mattapanients, the Payankatanks, the Nantaughtacunds, and Cnawmanients upon the rivers of Rappahannock and Potomac, over all those rivers, and back again by divers other several nations, to the King's habitation at Pamunkey, where they entertained him with most strange and fearful conjurations:

> As if near led to hell
> Amongst the devils to dwell.

Not long after, early in a morning a great fire was made in a long house and a mat spread on the one side, as on the other; on the one they caused him to sit, and all the guard went out of the house, and presently came skipping in a great grim fellow, all painted over with coal, mingled with oil; and many snakes' and weasels' skins stuffed with moss, and all their tails tied together so as they met on the crown of his head in a tassel; and round about the tassel was as a coronet of feathers, the skins hanging round about his head, back, and shoulders, and in a manner covered his face; with a hellish voice and a rattle in his hand. With most strange gestures and passions he began his invocation and environed the fire with the like antique tricks, painted half black, half red, but all their eyes were painted white, and some red strokes like Mutchato's along their cheeks. Round about him those fiends danced a pretty while, and then came in three more as ugly as the rest, with red eyes, and white strokes over their black faces; at last they all sat down right against him, three of them on the one hand of the chief priest and three on the other. Then all with their rattles began a song, which ended, the chief priest laid down five wheat corns; then straining his arms and hands with such violence that he sweat and his veins swelled, he began a short oration. At the conclusion they all gave a short groan and then laid down three grains more. After that, began their song again, and then another oration, ever laying down so many corns as before, till they had twice encircled the fire; that done, they took a bunch of little sticks prepared for that purpose, continuing still their devotion, and at the end of every song and oration they laid down a stick betwixt the divisions of corn. Till night, neither he nor they did either eat or drink, and then they feasted merrily with the best provisions they could make. Three days they used this ceremony, the meaning whereof they told him was to know if he intended them well or no. The circle of meal signified their country, the circles of corn the bounds of the sea, and the sticks his country. They imagined the world to be flat and round, like a trencher, and they in the midst. After this they brought him a bag of gunpowder, which they carefully preserved till the next spring to plant as they did their corn because they would be acquainted with the nature of that seed. Opitchapam, the King's brother, invited him to his house, where, with as many platters of bread, fowl, and wild beasts, as did environ him, he bid him welcome; but not any of them would eat a bit with him, but put up all the remainder in baskets. At his return to Opechancanough's, all the King's women and their children flocked about him for their parts, as a due by custom, to be merry with such fragments.

But his waking mind in hideous dreams did oft see wondrous shapes,
Of bodies strange, and huge in growth, and of stupendous makes.

At last they brought him to Meronocomoco, where was Powhatan, their emperor. Here more than two hundred of those grim courtiers stood wondering at him, as he had been a monster, till Powhatan and his train had put themselves in their greatest braveries. Before a fire upon a seat like a bedstead, he sat covered with a great robe made of raccoon skins, and all the tails hanging by. On either hand did sit a young wench of 16 or 18 years and along on each side the house two rows of men, and behind them as many women, with all their heads and shoulders painted red; many of their heads bedecked with the white down of birds; but every one with something, and a great chain of white beads about their necks. At his entrance before the King, all the people gave a great shout. The Queen of Appomattoc was appointed to bring him water to wash his hands, and another brought him a bunch of feathers, instead of a towel, to dry them. Having feasted him after their best barbarous manner they could, a long consultation was held, but the conclusion was, two great stones were brought before Powhatan. Then as many as could, laid hands on him, dragged him to them, and thereon laid his head and being ready with their clubs to beat out his brains, Pocahontas, the King's dearest daughter, when no entreaty could prevail, got his head in her arms and laid her own upon his to save him from death. Whereat the emperor was contented he should live to make him hatchets, and her bells, beads, and copper; for they thought him as well of all occupations as themselves. For the King himself will make his own robes, shoes, bows, arrows, pots; plant, hunt, or do anything so well as the rest.

> They say he bore a pleasant show,
> But sure his heart was sad.
> For who can pleasant be, and rest,
> That lives in fear and dread:
> And having life suspected, doth
> It still suspected lead.

Two days after, Powhatan having disguised himself in the most fearfulest manner he could, caused Captain Smith to be brought forth to a great house in the woods and there upon a mat by the fire to be left alone. Not long after, from behind a mat that divided the house, was made the most dolefulest noise he ever heard; then Powhatan, more like a devil than a man, with some two hundred more as black as himself, came unto him and told him now they were friends, and presently he should go to Jamestown to send him two great guns and a grindstone, for which he would give him the country of Capahowosic and forever esteem him as his son Nantaquoud. So to Jamestown with 12 guides Powhatan sent him. That night they quartered in the woods, he still expecting (as he had done all this long time of his imprisonment) every hour to be put to one death or other, for all their feasting. But almighty God (by His divine providence) had mollified the hearts of those stern barbarians with compassion. The next morning betimes they came to the fort, where Smith having used the savages with what kindness he could, he showed Rawhunt, Powhatan's trusty servant two demi-culverings and a millstone to carry Powhatan; they found them somewhat too heavy, but when they did see him discharge them, being loaded with stones, among the boughs of a great tree loaded with icicles, the ice and branches came so tumbling down that the poor savages ran away half dead with fear. But at last we regained some conference with them and gave them such toys and sent to Powhatan, his women and children such presents, as gave them in general full content. Now in Jamestown they were all in combustion, the strongest preparing once more to run away with the pinnace; which with the hazzard of his life, with saker falcon and musket shot, Smith forced now the third time to stay or sink. Some no better than they should be, had plotted with the president the next day to put him to death by the Levitical law for the lives of Robinson and Emry, pretending the fault was his that had led them to their ends; but he quickly took such order with such lawyers, that he laid them by the heels till he sent some of them prisoners for England. Now ever once in four or five days, Pocahontas with her attendants brought him so much provision that saved many of their lives that else for all this had starved with hunger.

Thus from numb death our good God sent relief,
The sweet assuager of all other grief.

ANONYMOUS

Although the official account of the colonizing of Plymouth Plantation is William Bradford's *History of Plymouth Plantation, Mourt's Relation* (1606-1646) provides a fuller account than Bradford's work of the earliest encounters between Indians and Pilgrims. *Mourt's Relation*, as the anonymous *A Relation or Journal of the Beginning and Proceedings of the English Plantation Settled at Plymouth in New England* has come to be known, also has the advantage of having been written contemporaneously with the events themselves, in contrast to Bradford's *History*, begun in 1630 and completed in 1651. Although the author is unknown, the book is believed to have been compiled by one George Morton of London and based on information sent from the colony by William Bradford and Edward Winslow.

The passage here excerpted is an account of the first significant contact between the Plymouth colonists and the Indians in 1621, from March 16 to March 23. Some limited contact between the Plymouth colonists and the Indians had taken place in the preceding December during an exploratory expedition along the coast. The colonists had repeatedly sighted the Indians or recent traces of the Indians; they had explored an empty Indian village and had even conducted their first Indian fight. But the colonists had never actually come face to face with an Indian until Samoset "boldly" walked into the settlement on March 16. The earlier events build up some suspense for Samoset's appearance and illustrate the suspicion, distrust, and fear of the "savages" with which the colonists arrived in the New World. Although the colonists, after the appearance of Samoset, took care to participate in the ceremonial formalities of Indian greeting and hospitality, the tone of the passage is that such ceremonies are frivolous activities which, although necessary, detract from the conduct of the main business of the colony.

21

From A Journall, 1622

Friday, the 16th, a fair warm day towards. This morning we determined to conclude of the military orders, which we had begun to consider of before but were interrupted by the savages, as we mentioned formerly. And whilst we were busied hereabout, we were interrupted again, for there presented himself a savage, which caused an alarm. He very boldly came all alone and along the houses straight to the rendezvous, where we intercepted him, not suffering him to go in, as undoubtedly he would, out of his boldness. He saluted us in English and bade us welcome, for he had learned some broken English among the Englishmen that came to fish at Monchiggon and knew by name the most of the captains, commanders, and masters that usually come. He was a man free in speech, so far as he could express his mind, and of a seemly carriage. We questioned him of many things; he was the first savage we could meet withal. He said he was not of these parts, but of Morattiggon, and one of the sagamores or lords thereof, and had been eight months in these parts, it lying hence a day's sail with a great wind and five days by land. He discoursed of the whole country and of every province, and of their sagamores and their number of men and strength. The wind beginning to rise a little, we cast a horseman's coat about him, for he was stark naked, only a leather about his waist, with a fringe about a span long, or little more; he had a bow and two arrows, the one headed and the other unheaded. He was a tall straight man, the hair of his head black, long behind, only short before, none on his face at all. He asked some beer, but we gave him strong water and biscuit and butter and cheese and pudding and a piece of mallard, all which he liked well, and had been acquainted with such amongst the English. He told us the place where we now live is called Patuxet and that about four years ago all the inhabitants died of an extra-ordinary plague and there is neither man, woman, nor child remaining, as indeed we have found none, so as there is none to hinder our possession, or to lay claim unto it. All the afternoon we spent in communication with him; we would gladly have been rid of him at night, but he was not willing to go this night. Then we thought to carry him on shipboard, wherewith he was well content and went into the shallop, but the wind was high and the water scant that it could not return back. We lodged him that night at

A Relation or Journal of the Beginning and Proceedings of the English Plantation settled at Plimoth in New England (London, 1622), pp. 32–39.

Stephen Hopkin's house and watched him. The next day he went away back to the Massasoits, from whence he said he came, who are our next bordering neighbors. They are sixty strong, as he saith. The Nausets are as near southeast of them and are a hundred strong, and those were they of whom our people were encountered, as we before related. They are much incensed and provoked against the English and about eight months ago slew three Englishmen, and two more hardly escaped by flight to Monchiggon; they were Sir Ferdinando Gorge his men, as this savage told us, as he did likewise of the *huggery*, that is, fight, that our discoverers had with the Nausets, and of our tools that were taken out of the woods, which we willed him should be brought again, otherwise, we would right ourselves. These people are ill affected towards the English, by reason of one Hunt, a master of a ship, who deceived the people, and got them under color of trucking with them, twenty out of this very place where we inhabit, and seven men from the Nausets, and carried them away, and sold them for slaves like a wretched man (for twenty pound a man) that cares not what mischief he doth for his profit.

Saturday in the morning we dismissed the savage and gave him a knife, a bracelet, and a ring; he promised within a night or two to come again and to bring with him some of the Massasoits, our neighbors, with such beavers skins as they had to truck with us.

Saturday and Sunday, reasonable fair days. On this day came again the savage and brought with him five other tall proper men; they had every man a deer's skin on him, and the principal of them had a wild cat's skin, or such like on the one arm. They had most of them long hosen up to their groins, close made; and above their groins to their waist another leather. They were altogether like the Irish trousers. They are of complexion like our English gypsies, no hair or very little on their faces, on their heads long hair to their shoulders, only cut before, some trussed up before with a feather, broad-wise like a fan, another a fox-tail hanging out. These left (according to our charge given him before) their bows and arrows a quarter of a mile from our town. We gave them entertainment as we thought was fitting them; they did eat liberally of our English victuals. They made semblance unto us of friendship and amity; they sang and danced after their manner, like antics. They brought with them in a thing like a bow-case (which the principal of them had about his waist) a little of their corn pounded to powder, which, put to a little water, they eat. He had a little tobacco in a bag, but none of them drank but when he listed. Some of them had their faces painted black, from the forehead to the chin, four or five fingers broad; others after other fashions, as they liked. They brought three or four skins, but we would not truck with them at all that day, but wished them to bring more, and we would truck for all, which they promised within a night or two, and would leave these behind them, though we were not willing they should. And they brought us all our tools again which were taken in the woods in our men's absence. So because of the day we dismissed them so soon as we could. But Samoset, our first acquaintance, either was sick or feigned himself so, and would not go with them, and stayed with us till Wednesday morning. Then we sent him to them to know the reason they came not according to their words, and we gave him a hat, a pair of stockings and shoes, a shirt, and a piece of cloth to tie about his waist.

The Sabbath day, when we sent them from us, we gave every one of them some trifles, especially the principal of them. We carried them along with our arms to the place where they left their bows and arrows; whereat they were amazed, and two of them began to slink away, but that the other called them. When they took their arrows, we bade them farewell, and they were glad, and so with many thanks given us they departed, with promise they would come again.

Monday and Tuesday proved fair days. We digged our grounds and sowed our garden seeds.

Wednesday, a fine warm day. We sent away Samoset.

That day we had again a meeting to conclude of laws and orders for ourselves and to confirm those military orders that were formerly propounded and twice broken off by the savages' coming; but so we were again the third time, for after we had been an hour together on the top of the hill over against us two or three savages presented themselves, that made semblance of daring us, as we thought. So Captain Standish with another, with their muskets went over to them, with two of the master's mates that follow them without arms, having two muskets with them. They whetted and rubbed their arrows and strings and made show of defiance, but when our men drew near them, they ran away; thus were we again interrupted by them. This day with much ado we got our carpenter that had been long sick of the scurvy to fit our shallop, to fetch all from aboard.

Thursday, the 22nd of March, was a very fair warm day. About noon we met again about our public business, but we had scarce been an hour together, but Samoset came again, and Squanto, the only native of Patuxet, where we now inhabit, who was one of the twenty captives that by Hunt were carried away, and had been in England and dwelt in Cornhill with Master John Slanie, a merchant, and could speak a little English, with three others; and they brought with them some few skins to truck, and some red herrings newly taken and dried, but not salted, and signified unto us that their great sagamore Massasoit was hard by with Quadequina his brother and all their men. They could not well express in English what they would, but after an hour the king came to the top of a hill over against us and had in his train sixty men that we could well behold them and they us. We were not willing to send our governor to them, and they unwilling to come to us; so Squanto went again unto him, who brought word that we should send one to parley with him, which we did, which was Edward Winslow, to know his mind and to signify the mind and will of our governor, which was to have trading and peace with him. We sent to the king a pair of knives and a copper chain with a jewel at it. To Quadequina we sent likewise a knife and a jewel to hang in his ear, and withal a pot of strong water, a good quantity of biscuit, and some butter, which were all willingly accepted. Our messenger made a speech unto him, that King James saluted him with words of love and peace, and did accept of him as his friend and ally, and that our governor desired to see him and to truck with him, and to confirm a peace with him, as his next neighbor. He liked well of the speech and heard it attentively, though the interpreters did not well express it. After he had eaten and drunk himself and given the rest to his company, he looked upon our messenger's sword and armor which he had on, with intimation of his desire to buy it; but on the other side, our messenger showed his unwillingness to part with it. In the end he left him in the custody of Quadequina, his brother, and came over the brook, and some twenty men following him, leaving all their bows and arrows behind them. We kept six or seven as hostages for our messenger; Captain Standish and Master Williamson met the king at the brook with half a dozen musketeers. They saluted him and he them, so one going over, the one on the one side and the other on the other, conducted him to a house then in building, where we placed a green rug and three or four cushions. Then instantly came our governor with drum and trumpet after him and some few musketeers. After salutations, our governor kissing his hand, the king kissed him, and so they sat down. The governor called for some strong water, and drunk to him, and he drunk a great draught that made him sweat all the while after; he called for a little fresh meat, which the king did eat willingly and did give his followers. Then they treated of peace, which was:

1. That neither he nor any of his should injure or do hurt to any of our people.
2. And if any of his did hurt to any of ours, he should send the offender, that we might punish him.
3. That if any of our tools were taken away when our people were at work, he should cause them to be restored, and if ours did any harm to any of of his, we would do the like to them.
4. If any did unjustly war against him, we would aid him; if any did war against us, he should aid us.
5. He should send to his neighbor confederates to certify them of this, that they might not wrong us, but might be likewise comprised in the

conditions of peace.

6. That when their men came to us, they should leave their bows and arrows behind them, as we should do our pieces when we came to them.

Lastly, that doing thus, King James would esteem of him as his friend and ally; all which the king seemed to like well, and it was applauded of his followers. All the while he sat by the governor he trembled for fear. In his person he is a very lusty man, in his best years, an able body, grave of countenance, and spare of speech; in his attire little or nothing differing from the rest of his followers, only in a great chain of white bone beads about his neck, and at it behind his neck hangs a little bag of tobacco, which he drank and gave us to drink. His face was painted with a sad red, like murrey, and oiled both head and face, that he looked greasily. All his followers likewise were in their faces, in part or in whole, painted, some black, some red, some yellow, and some white, some with crosses, and other antic works; some had skins on them, and some naked, all strong, tall, all men in appearance.

So after all was done, the governor conducted him to the brook, and there they embraced each other and he departed. We diligently keeping our hostages, we expected our messenger's coming, but anon, word was brought us that Quadequina was coming, and our messenger was stayed till his return, who presently came and a troop with him. So likewise we entertained him, and conveyed him to the place prepared. He was very fearful of our pieces and made signs of dislike that they should be carried away, whereupon commandment was given they should be laid away. He was a very proper tall young man, of a very modest and seemly countenance, and he did kindly like of our entertainment, so we conveyed him likewise as we did the king, but divers of their people stayed still. When he was returned, then they dismissed our messenger. Two of his people would have stayed all night, but we would not suffer it. One thing I forgot, the king had in his bosom, hanging in a string, a great long knife; he marvelled much at our trumpet, and some of his men would sound it as well as they could. Samoset and Squanto, they stayed all night with us, and the king and all his men lay all night in the woods, not above half an English mile from us, and all their wives and women with them. They said that within eight or nine days they would come and set corn on the other side of the brook and dwell there all summer, which is hard by us. That night we kept good watch, but there was no appearance of danger. The next morning divers of their people came over to us, hoping to get some victuals as we imagined; some of them told us the king would have some of us come see him. Captain Standish and Isaac Allerton went venturously, who were welcomed of him after their manner: he gave them three or four ground-nuts, and some tobacco. We cannot yet conceive but that he is willing to have peace with us, for they have seen our people sometimes alone two or three in the woods at work and fowling, when as they offered them no harm as they might easily have done, and especially because he hath a potent adversary, the Narragansets, that are at war with him, against whom he thinks we may be some strength to him, for our pieces are terrible unto them. This morning they stayed till ten or eleven of the clock, and our governor bid them send the king's kettle, and filled it full of peas, which pleased them well, and so they went their way.

Friday was a very fair day. Samoset and Squanto still remained with us. Squanto went at noon to fish for eels; at night he came home with as many as he could well lift in one hand, which our people were glad of. They were fat and sweet; he trod them out with his feet and so caught them with his hands without any other instrument.

This day we proceeded on with our common business, from which we had been so often hindered by the savages' coming, and concluding both of military orders and of some laws and orders as we thought behooveful for our present estate and condition, and did likewise choose our governor for this year, which was Master John Carver, a man well approved amongst us.

THOMAS MORTON

(1590–1647)

Perhaps the most infamous settler of early New England, Thomas Morton repeatedly incurred the wrath of the Plymouth and Massachusetts Bay colonists. In 1625 he settled between Boston and Plymouth at the present site of Quincy, Massachusetts, then called Merrymount. Merrymount soon came into trading competition with the Plymouth colony and Morton made himself unpopular with the Pilgrims by trading guns to the Indians and by his supposedly licentious behavior. In 1628 Miles Standish led an attack on Merrymount, captured Morton and sent him under arrest to England. Morton twice returned to New England and was twice more arrested. In 1643 he was released and allowed to spend his last two years of life in Maine.

In keeping with his unorthodox life, Morton's view of the Indians, as revealed in *The New English Canaan,* is in sharp contrast with the Puritan view of the Indians as a savage incarnation of the devil. The passage excerpted here, chapter 20, reveals a sympathy for the Indian, an attempt not only to understand his ways but to credit some of his ways above those of the Englishmen. Most likely Morton's views had a pragmatic rather than philosophic basis, but his views are the closest any New England writer comes to a "noble savage" perspective prior to 1800.

From **New English Canaan,** *1637*

THAT THE SAVAGES LIVE A CONTENTED LIFE

A gentleman and a traveller that had been in the parts of New England for a time, when he returned again, in his discourse of the country, wondered (as he said) that the natives of the land lived so poorly in so rich a country, like to our beggars in England. Surely that gentleman had not time or leisure while he was there truly to inform himself of the state of that country and the happy life the savages would lead were they once brought to Christianity.

I must confess they want the use and benefit of navigation (which is the very sinews of a flourishing Commonwealth), yet are they supplied with all manner of needful things for the maintenance of life and livelihood. Food and raiment are the chief of all that we make true use of; and of these they find no want, but have, and may have, them in a most plentiful manner.

If our beggars of England should, with so much ease as they, furnish themselves with food at all seasons, there would not be so many starved in the streets, neither would so many gaols be stuffed, or gallows furnished with poor wretches, as I have seen them.

But they of this sort of our own nation, that are fit to go to this Canaan, are not able to transport themselves, and most of them unwilling to go from the good ale tap, which is the very lodestone of the land by which our English beggars steer their course; it is the Northpole to which the flower-de-luce of their compass points; the more is the pity that the commonalty of our land are of such leaden capacities as to neglect so brave a country, that doth so plentifully feed many lusty and a brave, able men, women, and children that have not the means that a civilized nation hath to purchase food and raiment; which that country with a little industry will yield a man in a very comfortable measure, without overmuch carking.

I cannot deny but a civilized nation has the preeminence of an uncivilized, by means of those instruments that are found to be common among civil people, and the uncivil want the use of, to make themselves masters of those ornaments that make such a glorious show, that will give a man

Thomas Morton, *The New English Canaan,* in *Publications of the Prince Society,* XIV (Boston, 1883), pp. 175–78.

occasion to cry, *sic transit gloria Mundi.*

Now since it is but food and raiment that men that live need (though not all alike), why should not the natives of New England be said to live richly, having no want of either? Clothes are the badge of sin, and the more variety of fashions is but the greater abuse of the creature. The beasts of the forest there do serve to furnish them at any time when they please; fish and flesh they have in great abundance, which they both roast and boil.

They are indeed not served in dishes of plate with variety of sauces to procure appetite; that needs not there. The rarity of the air begot by the medicinable quality of the sweet herbs of the country, always procures good stomachs to the inhabitants.

I must needs commend them in this particular, that, though they buy many commodities of our nation, yet they keep but few, and those of special use.

They love not to be encumbered with many utensils, and although every proprietor knows his own, yet all things (so long as they will last) are used in common amongst them: a biscuit cake given to one, that one breaks it equally into so many parts as there be persons in his company and distributes it. Plato's commonwealth is so much practised by these people.

According to human reason, guided only by the light of nature, these people lead the more happy and freer life, being void of care, which torments the minds of so many Christians. They are not delighted in baubles, but in useful things.

Their natural drink is of the crystal fountain, and this they take up in their hands, by joining them close together. They take up a great quantity at a time and drink at the wrists. It was the sight of such a feat, which made Diogenes hurl away his dish, and like one that would have this principal confirmed, *Natura paucis contentat,* used a dish no more.

I have observed that they will not be troubled with superfluous commodities. Such things as they find they are taught by necessity to make use of, they will make choice of, and seek to purchase with industry. So that, in respect that their life is so void of care, and they are so loving also that they make use of those things they enjoy (the wife only excepted) as common goods, and are therein so compassionate that, rather than one should starve through want, they would starve all. Thus do they pass away the time merrily, not regarding our pomp (which they see daily before their faces), but are better content with their own, which some men esteem so meanly of.

They may be rather accompted to live richly, wanting nothing that is needful; and to be commended for leading a contented life, the younger being ruled by the Elder, and the Elder ruled by the Powahs, and the Powahs are ruled by the devil, and then you may imagine what good rule is like to be amongst them.

DAVID PIETERZEN DeVRIES
(1592c.–1655)

Born in Rochelle, France, in 1592 or 1593, David DeVries lived most of his life in Holland. In the period from 1618 to 1630, DeVries made six voyages, the last three of which were to America. DeVries settled in New Amsterdam and was a patroon in the Dutch colony during William Kieft's administration. The present excerpt describes the notorious Dutch massacre Kieft directed on the Indians of New York.

DeVries's journals were not translated into English until 1841, and unfortunately DeVries's description of Kieft's massacre was unknown to Washington Irving. Had Irving known of it, his Indian sympathies would undoubtedly have led him to use it in his characterization of Kieft in *Knickerbocker's History of New York.*

From *Voyages from Holland to America, 1632-1644*

The 24th of February, sitting at a table with the Governor, he began to state his intentions, that he had a mind to *wipe the mouths* of the savages; that he had been dining at the house of Jan Claesen Damen, where Maryn Adriaensen and Jan Claesen Damen, together with Jacob Planck, had presented a petition to him to begin this work. I answered him that they were not wise to request this; that such work could not be done without the approbation of the Twelve Men; that it could not take place without my assent, who was one of the Twelve Men; that moreover I was the first

David Pieterzen DeVries, *Voyages from Holland to America, A. D. 1632-1644.* Trans. by Henry C. Murphy (New York, 1853), pp. 114-117. Reprinted in *Historic Chronicles of New Amsterdam, Colonial New York and Long Island.* First Series, ed. Cornell Jaray (Port Washington, N. Y., 1968).

patroon, and no one else hitherto had risked there so many thousands, and also his person, as I was the first to come from Holland or Zeeland to plant a colony; and that he should consider what profit he could derive from this business, as he well knew that on account of trifling with the Indians we had lost our colony in the South River at Swanendael, in the Hoere-kil, with thirty-two men, who were murdered in the year 1630; and that in the year 1640, the cause of my people being murdered on Staten Island was a difficulty which he had brought on with the Raritaen Indians, where his soldiers had for some trifling thing killed some savages, and brought the brother of the chief a prisoner to the Mannates, who was ransomed there, as I have before more particularly related. But it appeared that my speaking was of no avail. He had, with his co-murderers, determined to commit the murder, deeming it a Roman deed, and to do it without warning the inhabitants in the open lands that each one might take care of himself against the retaliation of the savages, for he could not kill all the Indians. When I had expressed all these things in full, sitting at the table, and the meal was over, he told me he wished me to go to the large hall, which he had been lately adding to his house. Coming to it, there stood all his soldiers ready to cross the river to Pavonia to commit the murder. Then spoke I again to Governor Willem Kieft: "Let this work alone; you wish to break the mouths of the Indians, but you will also murder our own nation, for there are none of the settlers in the open country who are aware of it. My own dwelling, my people, cattle, corn, and tobacco will be lost." He answered me, assuring me that there would be no danger; that some soldiers should go to my house to protect it. But that was not done. So was this business begun between the 25th and 26th of February in the year 1643. I remained that night at the Governor's, sitting up. I went and sat by the kitchen fire, when about midnight I heard a great shrieking, and I ran to the ramparts of the fort, and looked over to Pavonia. Saw nothing but firing, and heard the shrieks of the savages murdered in their sleep. I returned again to the house by the fire. Having sat there awhile, there came an Indian with his squaw, whom I knew well, and who lived about an hour's walk from my house, and told me that they two had fled in a small skiff, which they had taken from the shore at Pavonia; that the Indians from Fort Orange had surprised them; and that they had come to conceal themselves in the fort. I told them that they must go away immediately; that this was no time for them to come to the fort to conceal themselves; that they who had killed their people at Pavonia were not Indians, but the Swannekens, as they call the Dutch, had done it. They then asked me how they should get out of the fort. I took them to the door, and there was no sentry there, and so they betook themselves to the woods. When it was day the soldiers returned to the fort, having massacred or murdered eighty Indians, and considering they had done a deed

33

of Roman valor, in murdering so many in their sleep; where infants were torn from their mother's breasts, and hacked to pieces in the presence of the parents, and the pieces thrown into the fire and in the water, and other sucklings, being bound to small boards, were cut, stuck, and pierced, and miserably massacred in a manner to move a heart of stone. Some were thrown into the river, and when the fathers and mothers endeavored to save them, the soldiers would not let them come on land but made both parents and children drown—children from five to six years of age, and also some old and decrepit persons. Those who fled from this onslaught, and concealed themselves in the neighboring sedge, and when it was morning, came out to beg a piece of bread, and to be permitted to warm themselves, were murdered in cold blood and tossed into the fire or the water. Some came to our people in the country with their hands, some with their legs cut off, and some holding their entrails in their arms, and others had such horrible cuts and gashes, that worse than they were could never happen. And these poor simple creatures, as also many of our own people, did not know any better than that they had been attacked by a party of other Indians—the Maquas. After this exploit, the soldiers were rewarded for their services, and Director Kieft thanked them by taking them by the hand and congratulating them. At another place, on the same night, on Corler's Hook near Corler's plantation, forty Indians were in the same manner attacked in their sleep, and massacred there in the same manner. Did the Duke of Alva in the Netherlands ever do anything more cruel? This is indeed a disgrace to our nation, who have so generous a governor in our Fatherland as the Prince of Orange, who has always endeavored in his wars to spill as little blood as possible. As soon as the savages understood that the Swannekens had so treated them, all the men whom they could surprise on the farm-lands, they killed; but we have never heard that they have ever permitted women or children to be killed. They burned all the houses, farms, barns, grain, haystacks, and destroyed everything they could get hold of. So there was an open destructive war begun. They also burnt my farm, cattle, corn, barn, tobacco-house, and all the tobacco. My people saved themselves in the house where I alone lived, which was made with embrasures, through which they defended themselves. Whilst my people were in alarm the savage whom I had aided to escape from the fort in the night came there, and told the other Indians that I was a good chief, that I had helped him out of the fort, and that the killing of the Indians took place contrary to my wish. Then they all cried out together to my people that they would not shoot them; that if they had not destroyed my cattle they would not do it, nor burn my house; that they would let my little brewery stand, though they wished to get the copper kettle, in order to make darts for their arrows; but hearing now that it had been done contrary to my wish, they all went away, and left my house unbesieged. When now the Indians had destroyed so many farms and men in revenge for their people, I went to Governor Willem Kieft, and asked him if it was not as I had said it would be, that he would only effect the spilling of Christian blood. Who would now compensate us for our losses? But he gave me no answer. He said he wondered that no Indians came to the fort. I told him that I did not wonder at it; "why should the Indians come here where you have so treated them?"

BENJAMIN TOMPSON

(1642-1714)

Benjamin Tompson, claimed with some exaggeration by his biographer and editor to be the first native-born American poet, was born the son of a minister in Quincy, Massachusetts, former site of Morton's Merrymount settlement. He graduated from Harvard in 1662, and in 1667 he became master of the Boston Latin School, where Cotton Mather was his pupil. Tompson's major poetic contribution was *New-England's Crisis; or A Brief Narrative, of New-Englands Lamentable Estate at Present . . .* , published in Boston in 1676, the supplement to which, along with a few additional poems, was published the same year in London as *New-Englands Tears for Her Present Miseries.*

The chief virtue of the excerpt from *New-Englands Crisis* here printed is to show the nadir of relations between white man and red in New England, which had been achieved a mere fifty-five years after the appearance of Samoset to trade with the Plymouth colonists. Written at the height of intensity of King Philip's War, *New-Englands Crisis* makes no pretense toward accommodation or understanding of the Indian's plight. Although Tompson includes a speech by Philip (11. 19–42) citing the grievances of the Indians, Tompson's pitiful attempt to duplicate Pidgin English makes a mockery of Indian oratory; after a brief mention of English land hunger, the principal motivations Tompson attributes to Philip are lechery and greed. Tompson's view of the Indian is even less palatable than his pupil Cotton Mather's, for it is unaccompanied by any religious justification and exaggerated by his rhetorical excesses.

From *New-England's Crisis, 1676*

In seventy-five the critic of our years
Commenc'd our war with Philip and his peers.
Whither the sun in Leo had inspir'd
A feav'rish heat, and pagan spirits fir'd?
Whither some Romish agent hatched the plot?
Or whither they themselves? appeareth not.
Whither our infant thrivings did invite?
Or whither to our land's pretended right?
Is hard to say; but Indian spirits need
No grounds but lust to make a Christian bleed.

And here methinks I see this greasy lout
With all his pagan slaves coil'd round about,
Assuming all the majesty his throne
Of rotten stump, or of the rugged stone
Could yield; casting some bacon-rind-like looks,
Enough to fright a student from his books,
Thus treat his peers, and next to them his Commons,
Kennel'd together all without a summons.
"My friends, our fathers were not half so wise
As we ourselves who see with younger eyes.
They sell our land to English man who teach
Our nation all so fast to pray and preach:
Of all our country they enjoy the best,
And quickly they intend to have the rest.
This no wunnegin, so big matchit law,
Which our old fathers' fathers never saw.
These English make and we must keep them too,
Which is too hard for them or us to do,
We drink we so big whipped, but English they
Go sneep, no more, or else a little pay.
Me meddle squaw me hang'd, our fathers kept
What squaws they would whither they waked or slept.

Benjamin Tompson, *New-Englands Crisis* (Boston, 1676), pp. 10–13.

Now if you'll fight I'll get you English coats,
And wine to drink out of their captains' throats.
The richest merchants' houses shall be ours,
We'll lie no more on mats or dwell in bowers
We'll have their silken wives, take they our squaws,
They shall be whipped by virtue of our laws.
If ere we strike 'tis now before they swell
To greater swarms then we know how to quell.
This my resolve, let neighboring sachems know,
And every one that hath club, gun or bow."
This was assented to, and for a close
He stroked his smutty beard and cursed his foes.
This counsel lightning-like their tribes invade,
And something like a muster's quickly made,
A ragged regiment, a naked swarm,
Whom hopes of booty doth with courage arm,
Set forth with bloody hearts, the first they meet
Of men or beasts they butcher at their feet.
They round our skirts, they pare, they fleece, they kill,
And to our bordering towns do what they will.
Poor hovels (better far than Caesar's court
In the experience of the meaner sort)
Receive from them their doom next execution,
By flames reduc'd to horror and confusion:
Here might be seen the smoking funeral piles
Of wildred towns pitched distant many miles,
Here might be seen the infant from the breast
Snatched by a pagan hand to lasting rest:
The mother Rachel-like shrieks out "my child!"
She wrings her hands and raves as she were wild.
The brutish wolves suppress her anxious moan
By cruelties more deadly of her own.
Will she or nill the chastest turtle must
Taste of the pangs of their unbridled lust.
From farms to farms, from towns to towns they
      post,
They strip, they bind, they ravish, flea and roast.
The beasts which want their master's crib to know,
Over the ashes of their shelters low.
What the inexorable flames do spare
More cruel heathen lug away for fare.

These tidings ebbing from the outward parts
Makes tradesmen cast aside their wanted arts
And study arms: the craving merchants plot
Not to augment but keep what they have got.
And every soul which hath but common sense
Thinks it the time to make a just defense.

MARY ROWLANDSON

(1635c.–1678c.)

Mary Rowlandson's narrative of her captivity by the Indians for eleven weeks and five days remains a classic example of the genre. Unlike John Smith and other early explorers who published accounts of their captivity, Mary Rowlandson was captured in the midst of a war, out of a palisaded settlement in Lancaster, Massachusetts; she was suddenly wrenched from a life of relative ease and security into the perils of the wilderness. The narrative is dramatized both by the immediacy of her fear and by her peculiarly Puritan perspective: all the events of this world are but an allegory of God's struggle to teach man and raise him to heavenly bliss. Mary Rowlandson is, in her own words, one of the "sheep torn by wolves."

Mary Rowlandson's narrative gains strength also through her personality. Without attempting to apologize for the Indians, it is evident that Mary Rowlandson was unprepared for the rigors of a nomadic life in the midst of a New England winter during which the Indians were clearly starving. Yet she adapted remarkably well to her circumstances, too well some might say. She found a useful role for herself by knitting garments which she bartered with the Indians for food. By the Eighteenth Remove (the narrative is divided into twenty removes), Mary Rowlandson had no compunctions about taking meat from the hands of even an English child. This development of Mary Rowlandson's personality in the course of the narrative is impossible to convey in an excerpt and is not even attempted here. In the interests of continuity the selection here presented consists of the introduction and nearly all the first three removes. This section is, of course, also the most dramatic.

From *A Narrative of the Captivity and Restoration of Mrs. Mary Rowlandson, 1682*

On the tenth of February, 1675, came the Indians with great numbers upon Lancaster. Their first coming was about sun-rising; hearing the noise of some guns, we looked out; several houses were burning, and the smoke ascending to heaven. There were five persons taken in one house, the father, and the mother and a sucking child they knocked on the head; the other two they took and carried away alive. There were two others who, being out of their garrison upon some occasion, were set upon; one was knocked on the head, the other escaped. Another there was who running along was shot and wounded and fell down; he begged of them his life, promising them money (as they told me) but they would not hearken to him but knocked him in head and stripped him naked and split open his bowels. Another, seeing many of the Indians about his barn, ventured and went out, but was quickly shot down. There were three others belonging to the same garrison who were killed; the Indians, getting up upon the roof of the barn, had advantage to shoot down upon them over their fortification. Thus these murderous wretches went on, burning and destroying before them.

At length they came and beset our own house, and quickly it was the dolefulest day that ever mine eyes saw. The house stood upon the edge of a hill; some of the Indians got behind the hill, others into the barn, and others behind anything that could shelter them; from all which places they shot against the house, so that the bullets seemed to fly like hail; and quickly they wounded one man among us, then another, and then a third. About two hours (according to my observation, in that amazing time) they had been about the house before they prevailed to fire it (which they did with flax and hemp, which they brought out of the barn, and there being no defense about the house, only two flankers at two opposite corners and one of them not finished) they fired it once and one ventured out and quenched it, but they quickly fired it again, and that took. Now is the dreadful hour come, that I have often heard of (in time of war, as it was the case of others) but now mine eyes see it. Some in our house were fighting for their lives, others wallowing in their blood, the house on fire over our heads, and the bloody heathen ready to knock us on the head if we stirred

Narratives of the Indian Wars, 1675-1699, ed. Charles H. Lincoln (New York, 1913), pp. 118–28.

out. Now might we hear mothers and children crying out for themselves and one another, Lord, What shall we do? Then I took my children (and one of my sisters, hers) to go forth and leave the house; but as soon as we came to the door and appeared, the Indians shot so thick that the bullets rattled against the house, as if one had taken an handful of stones and threw them, so that we were fain to give back. We had six stout dogs belonging to our garrison, but none of them would stir, though another time, if any Indian had come to the door, they were ready to fly upon him and tear him down. The Lord hereby would make us the more to acknowledge his hand and to see that our help is always in him. But out we must go, the fire increasing and coming along behind us, roaring, and the Indians gaping before us with their guns, spears and hatchets to devour us. No sooner were we out of the house, but my brother-in-law (being before wounded, in defending the house, in or near the throat) fell down dead, whereat the Indians scornfully shouted and hallowed and were presently upon him, stripping off his clothes. The bullets flying thick, one went through my side, and the same (as would seem) through the bowels and hand of my dear child in my arms. One of my elder sister's children, named William, had then his leg broken, which, the Indians perceiving, they knocked him on head. Thus were we butchered by those merciless heathen, standing amazed, with the blood running down to our heels. My eldest sister being yet in the house, and seeing those woeful sights, the infidels hauling mothers one way, and children another, and some wallowing in their blood; and her elder son telling her that her son William was dead, and myself was wounded, she said, And, Lord, let me die with them; which was no sooner said, but she was struck with a bullet and fell down dead over the threshold. I hope she is reaping the fruit of her good labors, being faithful to the service of God in her place. In her younger years she lay under much trouble upon spiritual accounts, till it pleased God to make that precious Scripture take hold of her heart, 2 Cor. 12. 9. *And he said unto me, my Grace is sufficient for thee.* More than twenty years after I have heard her tell how sweet and comfortable that place was to her. But to return: the Indians laid hold of us, pulling me one way and the children another, and said, Come, go along with us; I told them they would kill me. They answered, if I were willing to go along with them, they would not hurt me.

Oh, the doleful sight that now was to behold at this house! *Come, behold the works of the Lord, what dissolations he has made in the Earth.* Of thirty-seven persons who were in this one house, none escaped either present death or a bitter captivity, save only one, who might say as he, Job 1.15, *And I only am escaped alone to tell the news.* There were twelve killed, some shot, some stabbed with their spears, some knocked down with their hatchets. When we are in prosperity, oh, the little that we think of such dreadful sights, and to see our dear friends, and relations lie bleeding out their heart-blood upon the ground. There was one who was chopped into the head with a hatchet, and stripped naked, and yet was crawling up and down. It is a solemn sight to see so many Christians lying in their blood, some here, and some there, like a company of sheep torn by wolves, all of them stripped naked by a company of hell-hounds, roaring, singing, ranting and insulting, as if they would have torn our very hearts out; yet the Lord by his almighty power preserved a number of us from death, for there were twenty-four of us taken alive and carried captive.

I had often before this said that if the Indians should come, I should choose rather to be killed by them than taken alive, but when it came to the trial my mind changed; their glittering weapons so daunted my spirit, that I chose rather to go along with those (as I may say) ravenous beasts, than that moment to end my days; and that I may the better declare what happened to me during that grievous captivity, I shall particularly speak of the several removes we had up and down the wilderness.

The first Remove.

Now away we must go with those barbarous creatures, with our bodies wounded and bleeding, and our hearts no less than our bodies. About a mile we went that night, up upon a hill within sight of the town where they intended to lodge. There was hard by a vacant house (deserted by the English before, for fear of the Indians). I asked them whither I might not lodge in the house that night to which they answered, What, will you love English men still? this was the dolefulest night that ever my eyes saw. Oh, the roaring and singing and dancing and yelling of those black creatures in the night, which made the place a lively resemblance of hell. And as miserable was the waste that was there made of horses, cattle, sheep, swine, calves, lambs, roasting pigs, and fowl (which they had plundered in the town) some roasting, some lying and burning, and some boiling to feed our merciless enemies, who were joyful enough though we were disconsolate. To add to the dolefulness of the former day, and the dismalness of the present night, my thoughts ran upon my losses and sad bereaved condition. All was gone, my husband gone (at least separated from me, he being in the Bay; and to add to my grief, the Indians told me they would kill him as he came homeward), my children gone, my relations and friends gone, our house and home and all our comforts within door, and without, all was gone (except my life), and I knew not but the next moment that might go too. There remained nothing to me but one poor wounded babe, and it seemed at present worse than death that it was in such a pitiful condition, bespeaking compassion, and I had no refreshing for it, nor suitable things to revive it. Little do many think what is the savageness and brutishness of this barbarous enemy, ay, even those that seem to profess more than others among them, when the English have fallen into their hands.

Those seven that were killed at Lancaster the summer before upon a Sabbath day, and the one that was afterward killed upon a week day, were slain and mangled in a barbarous manner, by one-ey'd John, and Marlborough's Praying Indians, which Capt. Mosely brought to Boston, as the Indians told me.

The second Remove.

But now, the next morning, I must turn my back upon the town, and travel with them into the vast and desolate wilderness, I knew not whither. It is not my tongue, or pen can express the sorrows of my heart, and bitterness of my spirit, that I had at this departure: but God was with me, in a wonderful manner, carrying me along and bearing up my spirit that it did not quite fail. One of the Indians carried my poor wounded babe upon a horse; it went moaning all along, I shall die, I shall die. I went on foot after it, with sorrow that cannot be expressed. At length I took it off the horse and carried it in my arms till my strength failed, and I fell down with it. Then they set me upon a horse with my wounded child in my lap, and there being no furniture upon the horseback, as we were going down a steep hill, we both fell over the horse's head, at which they like unhumane creatures laughed and rejoiced to see it, though I thought we should there have ended our days, as overcome with so many difficulties. But the Lord renewed my strength still, and carried me along that I might see more of his power; yea, so much that I could never have thought of, had I not experienced it.

After this it quickly began to snow, and when night came on, they stopped, and now down I must sit in the snow, by a little fire, and a few boughs behind me, with my sick child in my lap; and calling much for water, being now (through the wound) fallen into a violent fever. My own wound also growing so stiff that I could scarce sit down or rise up; yet so it must be, that I must sit all this cold winter night upon the cold snowy ground, with my sick child in my arms, looking that every hour would be the last of its life; and having no Christian friend near me, either to comfort or help me. Oh, I may see the wonderful power of God, that my spirit did not utterly sink under my affliction; still the Lord upheld me with his gracious and merciful Spirit, and we were both alive to see the light of the next morning.

The third Remove.

The morning being come, they prepared to go on their way. One of the Indians got up upon a horse, and they set me up behind him, with my poor sick babe in my lap. A very wearisome and tedious day I had of it; what with my own wound, and my child's being so exceeding sick, and in a lamentable condition with her wound. It may be easily judged what a poor feeble condition we were in, there being not the least crumb of refreshing that came within either of our mouths, from Wednesday night to Saturday night, except only a little cold water. This day in the afternoon, about an hour by sun, we came to the place where they intended, *viz.,* an Indian town, called Wenimesset, north of Quabaug. When we were come, oh, the number of pagans (now merciless enemies) that there came about me, that I may say as David, Psal. 27.13, *I had fainted, unless I had believed,* etc. The next day was the Sabbath. I then remembered how careless I had been of God's holy time, how many Sabbaths I had lost and misspent, and how evilly I had walked in God's sight; which lay so close unto my spirit, that it was easy for me to see how righteous it was with God to cut off the thread of my life and cast me out of his presence forever. Yet the Lord still showed mercy to me and upheld me; and as he wounded me with one hand, so he healed me with the other. This day there came to me one Robert Pepper (a man belonging to Roxbury) who was taken in Captain Beers's fight, and had been now a considerable time with the Indians; and up with them almost as far as Albany, to see King Philip, as he told me, and was now very lately come into these parts. Hearing, I say, that I was in this Indian town, he obtained leave to come and see me. He told me, he himself was wounded in the leg at Captain Beers's fight and was not able some time to go; but as they carried him, and as he took oaken leaves and laid to his wound, and through the blessing of God he was able to travel again. Then I took oaken leaves and laid to my side, and with the blessing of God it cured me also; yet before the cure was wrought, I may say, as it is in Psal. 38. 5, 6. *My wounds stink and are corrupt, I am troubled, I am bowed down greatly, I go mourning all the day long.* I sat much alone with a poor wounded child in my lap, which moaned night and day, having nothing to revive the body or cheer the spirits of her, but instead of that, sometimes one Indian would come and tell me one hour, that your master will knock your child in the head, and then a second, and then a third, your master will quickly knock your child in the head.

This was the comfort I had from them, miserable comforters are ye all, as he said. Thus nine days I sat upon my knees, with my babe in my lap, till my flesh was raw again; my child being even ready to depart this sorrowful world, they bade me carry it out to another wigwam (I suppose because they would not be troubled with such spectacles), whither I went with a very heavy heart, and down I sat with the picture of death in my lap. About two hours in the night, my sweet babe like a lamb departed this life, on Feb. 18, 1675, it being about six years, and five months old. It was nine days from the first wounding, in this miserable condition, without any refreshing of one nature or other, except a little cold water. I cannot but take notice how at another time I could not bear to be in the room where any dead person was, but now the case is changed; I must and could lie down by my dead babe, side by side all the night after. I have thought since of the wonderful goodness of God to me, in preserving me in the use of my reason and senses, in that distressed time, that I did not use wicked and violent means to end my own miserable life. In the morning, when they understood that my child was dead they sent for me home to my master's wigwam (by my master in this writing, must be understood Quanopin, who was a Sagamore, and married King Philip's wife's sister; not that he first took me, but I was sold to him by another Narrhaganset Indian, who took me when first I came out of the garrison). I went to take up my dead child in my arms to carry it with me, but they bid me let it alone: there was no resisting, but go I must and leave it. When I had been at my master's wigwam, I took the first opportunity I could get, to go look after my dead child. When I came I asked them what they had done with it. Then they told me it was upon the hill. Then they went and showed me where it was, where I saw the ground was newly digged and there they told me they had buried it. There I left that child in the wilderness, and must commit it, and myself also in this wilderness-condition, to him who is above all. God having taken away this dear child, I went to see my daughter Mary, who was at this same Indian town, at a wigwam not very far off, though we had little liberty or opportunity to see one another. She was about ten years old and taken from the door at first by a Praying Indian and afterward sold for a gun. When I came in sight, she would fall a-weeping, at which they were provoked and would not let me come near her, but bade me be gone, which was a heart-cutting word to me. I had one child dead, another in the wilderness, I knew not where, the third they would not let me come near to: *Me* (as he said) *have ye bereaved of my children, Joseph is not, and Simeon is not, and ye will take Benjamin also, all these things are against me.* I could not sit still in this condition, but kept walking from one place to another. And as I was going along, my heart was even overwhelmed with the thoughts of my condition, and that I should have children, and a nation which I knew not ruled over them. Whereupon I earnestly entreated the Lord that he would consider my low estate, and show me a token for good, and if it were his blessed will, some sign and hope of some relief. And indeed quickly the Lord answered, in some measure, my poor prayers; for as I was going up and down mourning and lamenting my condition, my son came to me and asked me how I did. I had not seen him before, since the destruction of the town, and I knew not where he was till I was informed by himself that he was amongst a smaller parcel of Indians, whose place was about six miles off; with tears in his eyes, he asked me whether his sister Sarah was dead and told me he had seen his sister Mary, and prayed me, that I would not be troubled in reference to himself. The occasion of his coming to see me at this time was this: there was, as I said, about six miles from us, a small plantation of Indians, where it seems he had been during his captivity: and at this time, there were some forces of the Indians gathered out of our company, and some also from them (among whom was my son's master) to go to assault and burn Medfield. In this time of the absence of his master, his dame brought him to see me. I took this to be some gracious answer to my earnest and unfeigned desire. The next day, *viz.* to this, the Indians returned from Medfield, all the company, for those that belonged to the other small company, came through the town that now we were at. But before they came to us, Oh! the outrageous roaring and whooping that there was. They began their din about a mile before they came to us. By their noise and whooping they signified how many they had destroyed (which was at that time twenty-three.) Those that were with us at home were gathered together as soon as they heard the whooping, and every time that the other went over their number, these at home gave a shout, that the very earth rung again. And thus they continued till those that had been upon the expedition were come up to the Sagamore's wigwam; and then, Oh, the hideous insulting and triumphing that there was over some Englishmen's scalps that they had taken (as their manner is) and brought with them. I cannot but take notice of the wonderful mercy of God to me in those afflictions, in sending me a Bible. One of the Indians that came from the Medfield fight, had brought some plunder, came to me, and asked me, if I would have a Bible, he had got one in his basket. I was glad of it, and asked him, whether he thought the Indians would let me read. He answered yes. So I took the Bible, and in that melancholy time, it came into my mind to read first the 28 Chap. of Deut., which I did, and when I had read it, my dark heart wrought on this manner: that there was no mercy for me, that the blessings were gone, and the curses come in their room, and that I had lost my opportunity. But the Lord helped me still to go on reading till I came to Chap. 30, the seven first verses, where I found, there was mercy promised again, if we would return to him by repentance; and though we were scattered from one end of the earth to the other, yet the Lord would gather us together, and turn all those curses upon our enemies. I do not desire to live to forget this scripture, and what comfort it was to me.

Now the Indians began to talk of removing from this place, some one way, and some another. There were now besides myself nine English captives in this place (all of them children, except one woman). I got an opportunity to go and take my leave of them; they being to go one way, and I another,

I asked them whether they were earnest with God for deliverance. They told me, they did as they were able, and it was some comfort to me that the Lord stirred up children to look to him. The woman, *viz.,* Goodwife Joslin, told me she should never see me again, and that she could find in her heart to run away; I wished her not to run away by any means, for we were near thirty miles from any English town, and she very big with child, and had but one week to reckon; and another child in her arms, two years old, and bad rivers there were to go over, and we were feeble, with our poor and coarse entertainment. I had my Bible with me, I pulled it out, and asked her whether she would read; we opened the Bible and lighted on Psal. 27, in which Psalm we especially took notice of that, *ver. ult., Wait on the Lord, be of good courage, and he shall strengthen thine heart, wait I say on the Lord.*

WILLIAM PENN

(1644–1718)

William Penn is the first of a number of Quaker writers represented here for their uniformly temperate and humane view of the Indians. Penn, born into a wealthy family, displayed an early interest in the Puritan movements prevalent in his day in England. In the late 1660s, he rejected the military and courtly influences of his father and joined with the Quakers. He published a number of religious tracts and, for a time, was imprisoned in the Tower of London. Unlike most Quakers, Penn became an active participant in English politics; he helped to draft the New Jersey charter, which guaranteed such rights as free speech, trial by jury, religious freedom, an elected assembly, and treaties with the Indians. In 1681, Penn collected, as payment for a debt owed his father by Charles II, a tract of land now known as Pennsylvania. It was here that his policies of dealing fairly with the Indians were carried out in fact. Although earlier colonists recognized the value of dealing in a conciliatory way with the Indians, no other individual was able to present his views so forcibly nor carry them out so successfully as William Penn. Perhaps his success was due to the amount of control he maintained over all aspects of his colony in the early years.

The discussion of the Indians here printed is taken from a pamphlet published in London in 1683. We see Penn here attempting to manipulate the attitude of future colonists toward the Indian. His view of their customs is temperate and sympathetic. The passage ends with a plea for justice in all dealings of white men with red and a condemnation of those white men who have abused the Indian.

From **A Description of Pennsylvania,** *1683*

Thus much of the Country, next of the Natives or Aborigines.

XI. The natives I shall consider in their persons, language, manners, religion and government, with my sense of their original. For their persons, they are generally tall, straight, well-built, and of singular proportion; they tread strong and clever, and mostly walk with a lofty chin; of complexion black, but by design, as the gypsies in England. They grease themselves with bear's fat clarified, and, using no defense against sun or weather, their skins must needs be swarthy. Their eye is little and black, not unlike a straight-looked Jew. The thick lip and flat nose, so frequent with the East Indians and blacks, are not common to them; for I have seen as comely European-like faces among them of both, as on your side the sea; and truly an Italian complexion hath not much more of the white, and the noses of several of them have as much of the Roman.

XII. Their language is lofty, yet narrow, but like the Hebrew; in signification full, like short-hand in writing; one word serveth in the place of three, and the rest are supplied by the understanding of the hearer; imperfect in their tenses, wanting in their moods, participles, adverbs, conjunctions, interjections. I have made it my business to understand it, that I might not want an interpreter on any occasion. And I must say that I know not a language spoken in Europe that hath words of more sweetness or greatness in accent and emphasis than theirs. For instance, "Octorockon," "Rancocas," "Oricton," "Shakamacon," "Poquerim," all of which are names of places, and have grandeur in them. Of words of sweetness, "anna," is mother; "issimus," a brother; "netcap," friend; "usque oret," very good; "pane," bread; "metse," eat; "matta," no; "hatta," to have; "payo," to come; "Sepassen," "Passijon," the names of places; "Tamane," "Secane," "Menanse," "Secatereus," are the names of persons. If one ask them for anything they have not they will answer, "mattá ne hattá," which to translate is, not I have instead of I have not.

XIII. Of their customs and manners there is much to be said; I will begin with children. So soon as they are born, they wash them in water,

A Letter from William Penn, Proprietary and Governour of Pennsylvania in America, to the Committee of the Free Society of Traders.... (London, 1683), reprint by J. Coleman (London, 1881).

and while very young and in cold weather to choose they plunge them in the rivers to harden and embolden them. Having wrapped them in a clout, they lay them on a straight, thin board, a little more than the length and breadth of the child, and swaddle it fast upon the board to make it straight; wherefore all Indians have flat heads; and thus they carry them at their backs. The children will go very young, at nine months commonly; they wear only a small clout round their waist till they are big; if boys, they go fishing till ripe for the woods, which is about fifteen; then they hunt, and, after having given some proofs of their manhood by a good return of skins, they may marry, else it is a shame to think of a wife. The girls stay with their mothers and help to hoe the ground, plant corn, and carry burdens, and they do well to use them to that young, they must do when they are old; for the wives are the true servants of the husbands; otherwise the men are very affectionate to them.

XIV. When the young women are fit for marriage, they wear something upon their heads for an advertisement, but so as their faces are hardly to be seen but when they please. The age they marry at, if women, is about thirteen and fourteen; if men, seventeen and eighteen; they are rarely older.

XV. Their houses are mats or barks of trees set on poles in the fashion of an English barn, but out of the power of the winds, for they are hardly higher than a man; they lie on reeds or grass. In travel they lodge in the woods about a great fire, with the mantle of duffels they wear by day wrapped about them and a few boughs stuck round them.

XVI. Their diet is maize or Indian corn, divers ways prepared; sometimes roasted in the ashes, sometimes beaten and boiled with water, which they call "homine"; they also make cakes, not unpleasant to eat. They have likewise several sorts of beans and peas that are good nourishment, and the woods and rivers are their larder.

XVII. If a European comes to see them or calls for lodging at their house or "wigwam," they give him the best place, and first cut. If they come to visit us, they salute us with an "itah," which is as much as to say, good be to you, and set them down, which is mostly on the ground, close to their heels, their legs upright; it may be they speak not a word, but observe all passages. If you give them anything to eat or drink, well, for they will not ask; and be it little or much, if it be with kindness, they are well pleased, else they go away sullen, but say nothing.

XVIII. They are great concealers of their own resentments, brought to it, I believe, by the revenge that hath been practised among them; in either of these they are not exceeded by the Italians. A tragical instance fell out since I came into the country. A king's daughter, thinking herself slighted by her husband in suffering another woman to lie down between them, rose up, went out, plucked a root out of the ground, and ate it, upon which she immediately died; and for which, last week, he made an offering to her kindred for atonement and liberty of marriage, as two others did to the kindred of their wives that died a natural death. For till widowers have done so they must not marry again. Some of the young women are said to take undue liberty before marriage, for a portion; but when married, chaste; when with child, they know their husbands no more till delivered; and during their month they touch no meat they eat but with a stick, lest they should defile it; nor do their husbands frequent them till that time be expired.

XIX. But in liberality they excel; nothing is too good for their friends. Give them a fine gun, coat, or other thing, it may pass twenty hands before it sticks; light of heart, strong affections, but soon spent, the most merry creatures that live, feast, and dance perpetually; they never have much, nor want much. Wealth circulateth like the blood, all parts partake; and though none shall want what another hath, yet exact observers of property. Some kings have sold, others presented me with several parcels of land; the pay or presents I made them were not hoarded by the particular owners, but the neighboring kings and their clans being present when the goods were brought out, the parties chiefly concerned consulted what and to whom they should give them. To every king then, by the hands of a person for that work appointed, is a proportion sent, so sorted and folded, and with that gravity that is admirable. Then that king subdivideth it in like manner among his dependents, they hardly leaving themselves an equal share with one of their subjects. And be it on such occasions, at festivals, or at their common meals, the kings distribute, and to themselves last. They care for little, because they want but little, and the reason is, a little contents them. In this they are sufficiently revenged on us; if they are ignorant of our pleasures, they are also free from our pains. They are not disquieted with bills of lading and exchange, nor perplexed with Chancery suits and Exchequer reckonings. We sweat and toil to live; their pleasure feeds them; I mean, their hunting, fishing, and fowling, and this table is spread everywhere. They eat twice a day, morning and evening; their seats and table are the ground. Since the Europeans came into these parts, they are grown great lovers of strong liquors, rum especially, and for it exchange the richest of their skins and furs. If they are heated with liquors, they are restless till they have enough to sleep; that is their cry, some more, and I will go to sleep; but when drunk, one of the most wretchedest spectacles in the world.

XX. In sickness, impatient to be cured, and for it give anything, especially for their children, to whom they are extremely natural; they drink at those times a teran or decoction of roots in spring water; and if they eat any flesh it must be of the female of any creature. If they die, they bury them with their apparel, be they man or woman, and the nearest of kin fling in

52

something precious with them as a token of their love: their mourning is blacking of their faces, which they continue for a year. They are choice of the graves of their dead; for lest they should be lost by time and fall to common use, they pick off the grass that grows upon them and heap up the fallen earth with great care and exactness.

XXI. These poor people are under a dark night in things relating to religion, to be sure, the tradition of it; yet they believe a God and immortality without the help of metaphysics; for they say, there is a great king that made them, who dwells in a glorious country to the southward of them, and that the souls of the good shall go thither where they shall live again. Their worship consists of two parts, sacrifice and cantico: their sacrifice is their first fruits; the first and fattest buck they kill goeth to the fire where he is all burnt, with a mournful ditty of him that performeth the ceremony, but with such marvelous fervency and labor of body that he will even sweat to a foam. The other part is their cantico, performed by round dances, sometimes words, sometimes songs, then shouts, two being in the middle that begin, and by singing and drumming on a board direct the chorus. Their postures in the dance are very antic, and differing, but all keep measure. This is done with equal earnestness and labor, but great appearance of joy. In the fall, when the corn cometh in, they begin to feast one another; there have been two great festivals already, to which all come that will. I was at one myself; their entertainment was a green seat by a spring, under some shady trees, and twenty bucks with hot cakes of new corn, both wheat and beans, which they make up in a square form in the leaves of the stem, and bake them in the ashes; and after that they fell to dance. But they that go must carry a small present in their money, it may be sixpence, which is made of the bone of a fish; the black is with them as gold, the white, silver; they call it all "wampum."

XXII. Their government is by kings, which they call "Sachema" and those by succession, but always of the mother's side. For instance, the children of him that is now king will not succeed, but his brother by the mother or the children of his sister, whose sons (and after them the children of her daughter) will reign; for no woman inherits; the reason they render for this way of descent is that their issue may not be spurious.

XXIII. Every king hath his council, and that consists of all the old and wise men of his nation, which perhaps is two hundred people. Nothing of moment is undertaken, be it war, peace, selling of land, or traffic, without advising with them, and which is more, with the young men too. It is admirable to consider how powerful the kings are, and yet how they move by the breath of their people. I have had occasion to be in council with them upon treaties for land, and to adjust the terms of trade. Their order is thus: the king sits in the middle of a half moon, and hath his council, the old and wise, on each hand; behind them, or at a little distance, sit the younger fry in the same figure. Having consulted and resolved their business, the king ordered one of them to speak to me; he stood up, came to me, and in the name of his king saluted me, then took me by the hand and told me that he was ordered by his king to speak to me, and that now it was not he but the king that spoke, because what he should say was the king's mind. He first prayed me to excuse them that they had not complied with me the last time; he feared there might be some fault in the interpreter, being neither Indian nor English; besides it was the Indian custom to deliberate and take up much time in council before they resolve; and that if the young people and owners of the land had been as ready as he, I had not met with so much delay. Having thus introduced his matter, he fell to the bounds of the land they had agreed to dispose of, and the price (which now is little and dear, that which would have bought twenty miles, not buying now two). During the time that this person spoke not a man of them was observed to whisper or smile; the old grave, the young reverend in their deportment; they do speak little, but fervently and with elegancy: I have never seen more natural sagacity, considering them without the help (I was going to say the spoil) of tradition; and he will deserve the name of wise that outwits them in any treaty about a thing they understand. When the purchase was agreed, great promises passed between us of kindness and good neighborhood, and that the Indians and English must live in love as long as the sun gave light. Which done, another made a speech to the Indians in the name of all the sachamakers or kings, first to tell them what was done; next, to charge and command them to love the Christians, and particularly live in peace with me and the people under my government; that many governors had been in the river, but that no governor had come himself to live and stay here before; and having now such a one that had treated them well, they should never do him or his any wrong. At every sentence of which they shouted and said, Amen, in their way.

XXIV. The justice they have is pecuniary. In case of any wrong or evil fact, be it murder itself, they atone by feasts and presents of their wampum, which is proportioned to the quality of the offence or person injured, or of the sex they are of: for in case they kill a woman they pay double, and the reason they render is that she breedeth children, which men cannot do. It is rare that they fall out, if sober; and if drunk, they forgive it, saying it was the drink and not the man that abused them.

XXV. We have agreed that in all differences between us six of each side shall end the matter: do not abuse them, but let them have justice, and you win them. The worst is that they are the worse for the Christians who have propagated their vices and yielded them tradition for ill, and not for good things. But as low an ebb as they are at, and as glorious as their condition looks, the Christians have not outlived their sight with all their pretensions to a higher manifestation: what good then might not a good people graft, where there is so distinct a knowledge left between good and evil? I beseech God to incline the hearts of all that come into these parts to outlive the knowledge of the natives by a fixed obedience to their greater knowledge of the will of God; for it were miserable indeed for us to fall under the just censure of the poor Indian conscience, while we make profession of things so far transcending.

COTTON MATHER
(1663-1728)

Use of Cotton Mather to determine a New England or Puritan view of the Indian must be made with great care. Cotton Mather has been variously assessed by historians and literary critics as arrogant, vain, prolific, influential, brilliant, old-fashioned, and a significant stylist. Any easy assessment of the man is impossible. Politically his views were Puritan and orthodox in an age which turned from orthodoxy. Yet it is likely that his views on the Indian were fairly representative of a colony plagued by Indian wars. Mather not only views the Indians as an instrument of the devil, but capitalized upon this interpretation for propoganda.

The first selection offered here is Mather's account of John Eliot's missionary work among the Indians; the selection was published in 1702 as part of Mather's *Magnalia Christi Americana*, a history of the wars of the early settlers and a series of biographies of their leaders. John Eliot, as the subject of Mather's biography, presented a problem to Mather. Mather, the castigator of the Indians as "formidable savages," "furious tawnies," and "raging dragons" in the captivity of Hannah Duston, must find a way to praise a man who devoted his life to improving the lot of the Indians. The result in the *Magnalia Christi Americana* is a framing of the work of Eliot less in terms of what he accomplished among the Indians than as what he accomplished for the side of righteousness in the eternal battle between God and the devil. Mather's highly rhetorical and elaborate style produces a sarcastic tone in his description of Eliot. After a lengthly description of the miserable condition of the Indians, Mather can conclude:

This was the miserable people which our Eliot propounded unto himself to teach and save! And he had a double work incumbent on him; he was to make men of them, ere he could hope to see them saints; they must be *civilized* ere they could be *Christianized;* he could not, as Gregory once of our nation, see anything *angelical* to bespeak his labors for their eternal welfare: all among them was *diabolical.* To think on raising a number of these hideous creatures unto the elevations of our holy religion, must argue more than common or little sentiments in the undertaker; but the faith of an Eliot could encounter it!

The second section contains examples of the captivity narrative as developed by Mather to its propagandistic form. All the captivities are part of Mather's *Decennium Luctuosum,* later incorporated into the *Magnalia Christi Americana* as the seventh chapter of Book VII. The first captivity is the well-known story of Hannah Duston, a subject treated in the nineteenth century by Thoreau and Hawthorne. It is followed by a series of four captivities which, being stories of gory deeds committed by savage Indians upon innocent women and children, are calculated to arouse hatred and contempt of the red man.

From **Magnalia Christi Americana,** *1702*

PART III
OR, ELIOT AS AN EVANGELIST.

The titles of a Christian and of a minister have rendered our Eliot considerable; but there is one memorable title more, by which he has been signalized unto us. An honorable person did once in print put the name of an evangelist upon him; whereupon, in a letter of his to that person, afterwards printed, his expressions were, "There is a redundancy where you put the title of Evangelist upon me; I beseech you suppress all such things; let us do and speak and carry all things with humility; it is the Lord who hath done what is done; and it is most becoming the spirit of Jesus Christ to lift up him, and lay our selves low; I wish that word could be obliterated." My reader sees what a caution Mr. Eliot long since entered against our giving him the title of an evangelist; but his death has now made it safe, and his life had long made it just, for us to acknowledge him with such a title. I know not whither that of an evangelist, or one separated for the employment of preaching the gospel in such places whereunto churches have hitherto been gathered, be not an office that should be continued in our days; but this I know, that our Eliot very notably did the service and business of such an officer.

Cambden could not reach the height of his conceit who bore in his shield a savage of America, with his hand pointing to the sun, and this motto:

Cotton Mather, *Magnalia Christi Americana,* vol. I (Hartford, 1852), pp. 556–62.

Mihi Accessu, Tibi Recessu. * Reader, prepare to behold this device illustrated!

The natives of the country now possessed by the New-Englanders had been forlorn and wretched heathen ever since their first herding here; and though we know not when or how those Indians first became inhabitants of this mighty continent, yet we may guess that probably the devil decoyed those miserable savages hither, in hopes that the gospel of the Lord Jesus Christ would never come here to destroy or disturb his absolute empire over them. But our Eliot was in such ill terms with the devil, as to alarm him with sounding the silver trumpets of Heaven in his territories, and make some noble and zealous attempts towards ousting him of ancient possessions here. There were, I think, twenty several nations (if I may call them so) of Indians upon that spot of ground which fell under the influence of our Three United Colonies; and our Eliot was willing to rescue as many of them as he could from that old usurping landlord of America, who is, "by the wrath of God, the prince of this world."

I cannot find that any besides the Holy Spirit of God first moved him to the blessed work of evangelizing these perishing Indians; it was that Holy Spirit which laid before his mind the idea of that which was on the seal of the Massachuset colony: a poor Indian having a label going from his mouth, with a *come over and help us.* It was the spirit of our Lord Jesus Christ, which enkindled in him a pity for the dark souls of these natives, whom the "god of this world had blinded," through all the bypast ages. He was none of those that make "the salvation of the heathen" an article of their creed; but (setting aside the unrevealed and extraordinary steps which the "Holy One of Israel" may take out of his usual paths) he thought men to be lost if our gospel be hidden from them; and he was of the same opinion with one of the ancients, who said, "Some have endeavored to prove Plato a Christian till they prove themselves little better than heathens." It is indeed a principle in the Turkish Alcoran, that "let a man's religion be what it will, he shall be saved, if he conscientiously live up to the rules of it": but our Eliot was no Mahometan. He could most heartily subscribe to that passage in the articles of the Church of England, "They are to be held accursed who presume to say, that every man shall be saved by the law or sect which he professeth, so that he be diligent to frame his life according to that law and light of nature; for Holy Scripture doth set out unto us only the name of Jesus Christ whereby men must be saved." And it astonished him to see many dissembling subscribers of those articles, while they have grown up to such a frenzy as to deny peremptorily all church state, and all salvation to all that are not under Diocesan Bishops,

---

*As I approach, thou recedest.

yet at the same time to grant that the heathen might be saved without the knowledge of the Lord Jesus Christ.

But when this charitable pity had once began to flame, there was a concurrence of many things to cast oil into it. All the good men in the country were glad of his engagement in such an undertaking; the ministers especially encouraged him, and those in the neighborhood kindly supplied his place, and performed his work in part for him at Roxbury, while he was abroad laboring among them that were without. Hereunto he was further awakened by those expressions in the royal charter, in the assurance and protection whereof this wilderness was first peopled; namely, "To win and incite the natives of that country to the knowledge and obedience of the only true God and Saviour of mankind, and the Christian faith, in our royal intention, and the adventurer's free profession is the principal end of the plantation." And the remarkable zeal of the Romish missionaries, "compassing sea and land, that they might make proselytes," made his devout soul think of it with a further disdain, that we should come any whit behind in our care to evangelize the Indians whom we dwelt among. Lastly, when he had well begun this evangelical business, the good God, in an answer to his prayers, mercifully stirred up a liberal contribution among the godly people in England for the promoting of it; by means whereof a considerable estate and income was at length entrusted in the hands of an honorable corporation, by whom it is to this day very carefully employed in the Christian service which it was designed for. And then, in short, inasmuch as our Lord Jesus had bestowed on us, our Eliot was gratefully and generously desirous to obtain for him "the heathen for an inheritance, and the utmost parts of the earth for a possession."

The exemplary charity of this excellent person in this important affair, will not be seen in its due lusters, unless we make some reflections upon several circumstances which he beheld these forlorn Indians in. Know, then, that these doleful creatures are the veriest ruins of mankind which are to be found anywhere upon the face of the earth. No such estates are to be expected among them, as have been the baits which the pretended converters in other countries have snapped at. One might see among them what a hard master the devil is to the most devoted of his vassals! These abject creatures live in a country full of mines; we have already made entrance upon our iron; and in the very surface of the ground among us, it is thought there lies copper enough to supply all this world; besides other mines hereafter to be exposed; but our shiftless Indians were never owners of so much as a knife till we come among them; their name for an English man was a "Knife-man"; stone was instead of metal for their tools; and for their coins, they have only little beads with holes in them to string them upon a bracelet, whereof some are white; and of these there go six for a penny; some are black or blue, and of these go three for a penny: this wampum, as they call it, is made of the shell-fish which lies upon the sea-coast continually.

They live in a country where we now have all the conveniences of human life: but as for them, their housing is nothing but a few mats tied about poles fastened in the earth, where a good fire is their bed-clothes in the coldest seasons; their clothing is but skin of a beast, covering their hind-parts, their fore-parts having but a little apron, where nature calls for secrecy; their diet has not a greater dainty than their *Nokehick*—that is, a spoonful of their parched meal, with a spoonful of water, which will strengthen them to travel a day together; except we should mention the flesh of deers, bears, moose, raccoons, and the like, which they have when they can catch them; as also a little fish, which, if they would preserve, it was by drying, not by salting; for they had not a grain of salt in the world, I think, till we bestowed it on them. Their physic is, excepting a few odd specifics, which some of them encounter certain cases with, nothing hardly but an hot-house or a "powaw"; their hot-house is a little cave, about eight foot over, where, after they have terribly heated it, a crew of them go sit and sweat and smoke for an hour together, and then immediately run into some very cold adjacent brook, without the least mischief to them; it is this way they recover themselves from some diseases, particularly from the French; but in most of their dangerous distempers, it is a "powaw" that must be sent for; that is, a priest, who has more familiarity with Satan than his neighbors; this conjurer comes and roars, and howls, and uses magical ceremonies over the sick man, and will be well paid for it when he has done; if this don't effect the cure, the "man's time is come, and there's an end."

They live in a country full of the best ship-timber under heaven: but never saw a ship till some came from Europe hither; and then they were scared out of their wits to see the "monster" come sailing in, and spitting fire with a mighty noise out of her floating side; they cross the water in canoes, made sometimes of trees, which they burn and hew, till they have hollowed them; and sometimes of barks, which they stitch into a light sort of a vessel, to be easily carried over land; if they overset, it is but a little paddling like a dog, and they are soon where they were.

Their way of living is infinitely barbarous: the men are most abominably slothful; making their poor squaws, or wives, to plant and dress, and barn and beat their corn, and build their wigwams for them: which perhaps may be the reason of their extraordinary ease in childbirth. In the mean time, their chief employment, when they'll condescend unto any, is that of hunting; wherein they'll go out some scores, if not hundreds of them in a company, driving all before them.

They continue in a place till they have burnt up all the wood thereabouts,

and then they pluck up stakes; to follow the wood, which they cannot
fetch home unto themselves; hence when they enquire about the English,
"Why come they hither?" they have themselves very learnedly determined
the case, "'Twas because we wanted firing." No arts are understood among
them, except just so far as to maintain their brutish conversation, which
is little more than is to be found among the very beavers upon our streams.

Their division of time is by "sleeps," and "moons," and "winters"; and,
by lodging abroad, they have somewhat observed the motions of the stars;
among which it has been surprising unto me to find that they have always
called "Charles's Wain" by the name of "Paukunnawaw," or "the Bear,"
which is the name whereby Europeans also have distinguished it. Moreover,
they have little, if any, traditions among them worthy of our notice; and
reading and writing is altogether unknown to them, though there is a rock
or two in the country that has unaccountable characters engraved upon it.
All the religion they have amounts unto thus much: they believe that there
are many gods, who made and own the several nations of the world; of
which a certain great God in the south-west regions of heaven bears the
greatest figure. They believe that every remarkable creature has a peculiar
god within it or about it: there is with them a Sun God, a Moon God, and
the like; and they cannot conceive but that the fire must be a kind of a god,
inasmuch as a spark of it will soon produce very strange effects. They
believe that when any good or ill happens to them, there is the favor or the
anger of a god expressed in it; and hence, as in a time of calamity, they
keep a dance, or a day of extravagant ridiculous devotions to their god; so
in a time of prosperity they likewise have a feast, wherein they also make
presents one unto another. Finally, they believe that their chief god
(Kautantowit) made a man and a woman of a stone; which, upon dislike,
he broke to pieces, and made another man and woman of a tree, which were
the fountains of mankind; and that we all have in us immortal souls, which,
if we were godly, shall go to a splendid entertainment with Kautantowit,
but otherwise must wander about in restless horror forever. But if you
say to them anything of a resurrection, they will reply upon you, "I shall
never believe it!" And when they have any weighty undertaking before
them, it is a usual thing for them to have their assemblies, wherein, after
the usage of some diabolical rites, a devil appears unto them, to inform
them and advise them about their circumstances; and sometimes there are
odd events of their making these applications to the devil. For instance, it
is particularly affirmed that the Indians, in their wars with us, finding a sore
inconvenience by our dogs, which would make a sad yelling if in the night
they scented the approaches of them, they sacrificed a dog to the devil;
after which no English dog would bark at an Indian for divers months
ensuing. This was the miserable people which our Eliot propounded unto

himself to teach and save! And he had a double work incumbent on him; he was to make men of them, ere he could hope to see them saints; they must be civilized ere they could be Christianized; he could not, as Gregory once of our nation, see anything angelical to bespeak his labors for their eternal welfare: all among them was diabolical. To think on raising a number of these hideous creatures unto the elevations of our holy religion, must argue more than common or little sentiments in the undertaker; but the faith of an Eliot could encounter it!

I confess that was one—I cannot call it so much guess as wish—wherein he was willing a little to indulge himself; and that was, "that our Indians are the posterity of the dispersed and rejected Israelites, concerning whom our God has promised, that they shall yet be saved by the deliverer coming to turn away ungodliness from them." He saw the Indians using many parables in their discourses; much given to anointing of their heads; much delighted in dancing, especially after victories; computing their times by nights and months; giving dowries for wives, and causing their women to "dwell by themselves," at certain seasons, for secret causes; and accustoming themselves to grievous mournings and yellings for the dead; all which were usual things among the Israelites. They have, too, a great unkindness for our swine; but I suppose that is because our hogs devour the clams which are a dainty with them. He also saw some learned men looking for the lost Israelites among the Indians in America, and counting that they had thorough-good reasons for doing so. And a few small arguments, or indeed but conjectures, meeting with a favorable disposition in the hearer, will carry some conviction with them; especially if a report of a *Menasseh ben Israel* be to back them. He saw likewise the judgments threatened unto the Israelites of old, strangely fulfilled upon our Indians; particularly that "Ye shall eat the flesh of your sons," which is done with exquisite cruelties upon the prisoners that they take from one another in their battles. Moreover, it is a prophesy in Deuteronomy xxviii. 68, "The Lord shall bring thee into Egypt again with ships, by the way whereof I spake unto thee, thou shalt see it no more again; and there shall ye be sold unto your enemies, and no man shall buy you." This did our Eliot imagine accomplished, when the captives taken by us in our late wars upon them, were sent to be sold in the coasts lying not very remote from Egypt on the Mediterranean sea, and scarce any chapmen would offer to take them off. Being upon such as these accounts not unwilling, if it were possible, to have the Indians found Israelites, they were, you may be sure, not a whit the less "beloved for their (supposed) father's sake"; and the fatigues of his travails went on the more cheerfully, or at least the more hopefully, because of such possibilities.

The first step which he judged necessary now to be taken by him, was to learn the Indian language; for he saw them so stupid and senseless, that they would never do so much as enquire after the religion of the strangers now come into their country, much less would they so far imitate us as to leave off their beastly way of living, that they might be partakers of any spiritual advantage by us: unless we could first address them in a language of their own. Behold, new difficulties to be surmounted by our indefatigable Eliot! He hires a native to teach him this exotic language, and, with a laborious care and skill, reduces it into a grammar, which afterwards he published. There is a letter or two of our alphabet, which the Indians never had in theirs; though there were enough of the dog in their temper, there can scarce be found an *R* in their language (any more than in the language of the Chinese or of the Greenlanders) save that the Indians to the northward, who have a peculiar dialect, pronounce an *R* where an *N* is pronounced by our Indians; but if their alphabet be short, I am sure the words composed of it are long enough to tire the patience of any scholar in the world; they are *Sesquipedalia Verba,* [interminable words] of which their *linguo* is composed; one would think they had been growing ever since Babel unto the dimensions to which they are now extended. For instance, if my reader will count how many letters there are in this one word, *Nummatchekodtantamooonganunnonash,* when he has done, for his reward, I'll tell him it signifies no more in English than "our lusts"; and if I were to translate "our loves," it must be nothing shorter than *Noowomantammooonkanunonnash.* Or, to give my reader a longer word than either of these, *Kummogkodonattoottummooetiteaongannunnonash* is in English "our question": but I pray, sir, count the letters! Nor do we find in all this language the least affinity to, or derivation from any European speech that we are acquainted with. I know not what thoughts it will produce in my reader, when I inform him that once, finding that the Demons in a possessed young woman understood the Latin, and Greek, and Hebrew languages, my curiosity led me to make trial of this Indian language, and the Demons did seem as if they did not understand it. This tedious language our Eliot (the anagram of whose name was *Toile)* quickly became a master of; he employed a pregnant and witty Indian, who also spoke English well, for his assistance in it; and compiling some discourses by his help, he would single out a word, a noun, a verb, and pursue it through all its variations: having finished his grammar, at the close he writes, "Prayers and pains through faith in Christ Jesus will do anything!" and being by his prayers and pains thus furnished, he set himself in the year 1646 to preach the gospel of our Lord Jesus Christ among these desolate outcasts.

From **Decennium Luctuosum,** *1699*

A NOTABLE EXPLOIT; WHEREIN *DUX FEMINA FACTI*

On March 15, 1697, the savages made a descent upon the skirts of
Haverhill, murdering and captivating about thirty-nine persons and burning
about half a dozen houses. In this broil, one Hannah Dustan, having lain
in about a week attended with her nurse, Mary Neff, a widow, a body of
terrible Indians drew near unto the house where she lay, with designs to
carry on their bloody devastations. Her husband hastened from his employments abroad unto the relief of his distressed family; and first bidding seven
of his eight children (which were from two to seventeen years of age) to
get away as fast as they could unto some garrison in the town, he went in to
inform his wife of the horrible distress come upon them. E'er she could
get up, the fierce Indians were got so near that, utterly despairing to do
her any service, he ran out after his children, resolving that on the horse
which he had with him, he would ride away with that which he should in
this extremity find his affections to pitch most upon, and leave the rest
unto the care of the divine providence. He overtook his children about
forty rod from his door; but then, such was the agony of his parental
affections that he found it impossible for him to distinguish any one of
them from the rest; wherefore he took up a courageous resolution to live
and die with them all. A party of Indians came up with him; and now,
though they fired at him and he fired at them, yet he manfully kept at the
rear of his little army of unarmed children while they marched off, with
the pace of a child of five years old; until, by the singular providence of
God, he arrived safe with them all unto a place of safety, about a mile or
two from his house. But his house must in the meantime have more dismal
tragedies acted at it. The nurse, trying to escape with the newborn infant,
fell into the hands of the formidable savages; and those furious tawnies
coming into the house bid poor Dustan to rise immediately. Full of
astonishment, she did so; and sitting down in the chimney with a heart
full of most fearful expectation, she saw the raging dragons rifle all that
they could carry away and set the house on fire. About nineteen or twenty
Indians now led these away, with about half a score other English captives;
but e'er they had gone many steps, they dashed out the brains of the infant

Cotton Mather, *Decennium Luctuosum*, in *Narratives of the Indian Wars, 1675-1699*,
ed. Charles H. Lincoln (New York, 1913), pp. 208-13, 163-66.

against a tree; and several of the other captives, as they began to tire in the sad journey, were soon sent unto their long home; the savages would presently bury their hatchets in their brains and leave their carcases on the ground for birds and beasts to feed upon. However, Dustan (with her nurse), notwithstanding her present condition, travelled that night about a dozen miles, and then kept up with their new masters in a long travel of a hundred and fifty miles, more or less, within a few days ensuing, without any sensible damage in their health from the hardships of their travel, their lodging, their diet, and their many other difficulties.

These two poor women were now in the hands of those whose tender mercies are cruelties; but the good God, who hath all hearts in his own hands, heard the sighs of these prisoners and gave them to find unexpected favor from the master who laid claim unto them. That Indian family consisted of twelve persons: two stout men, three women, and seven children; and for the shame of many an English family that has the character of prayerless upon it, I must now publish what these poor women assure me: 'Tis this: in obedience to the instructions which the French have given them, they would have prayers in their family no less than thrice every day; in the morning, at noon, and in the evening; nor would they ordinarily let their children eat or sleep without first saying their prayers. Indeed, these idolaters were like the rest of their whiter brethren, persecutors; and would not endure that these poor women would retire to their English prayers if they could hinder them. Nevertheless, the poor women had nothing but fervent prayers to make their lives comfortable, or tolerable; and by being daily sent out upon business they had opportunities together and asunder to do like another Hannah, in pouring out their souls before the Lord; nor did their praying friends among ourselves forbear to pour out supplications for them. Now, they could not observe it without some wonder that their Indian master sometimes, when he saw them dejected, would say unto them, "What need you trouble yourself? If your God will have you delivered you shall be so!" And it seems our God would have it so to be. This Indian family was now travelling with these two captive women (and an English youth, taken from Worcester a year and a half before), unto a rendezvous of savages, which they call a town, somewhere beyond Penacook; and they still told these poor women that when they came to this town, they must be stripped and scourged, and run the gauntlet through the whole army of Indians. They said, this was the fashion when the captives first came to a town; and they derided some of the faint-hearted English, which, they said, fainted and swooned away under the torments of this discipline. But on April 30, while they were yet, it may be, about an hundred and fifty miles from the Indian town, a little before break of day, when the whole crew was in a dead sleep (Reader, see if it prove not so!) one of these women took up a resolution, to imitate the action of Jael upon Sisera; and being where she had not her own life secured by any law unto her, she thought she was not forbidden by any law to take away the life of the murderers, by whom her child had been butchered. She heartened the nurse and the youth to assist her in the enterprise; and all furnishing themselves with hatchets for the purpose, they struck such home blows, upon the heads of their sleeping oppressors, that e'er they could any of them struggle into any effectual resistance, *at the feet* of these poor prisoners, *they bowed, they fell, they lay down: at their feet they bowed, they fell; where they bowed, there they fell down dead* [Judges v. 27]. Only one squaw escaped sorely wounded from them, in the dark; and one boy, whom they reserved asleep, intending to bring him away with them, suddenly waked, and skuttled away from this desolation. But cutting off the scalps of the ten wretches, they came off, and received fifty pounds from the General Assembly of the Province, as a recompense of their action; besides which they received many presents of congratulation from their more private friends; but none gave 'em a greater taste of bounty than Colonel Nicholson, the Governor of Maryland, who hearing of their action, sent 'em a very generous token of his favor.

. . . .

THE CONDITION OF THE CAPTIVES, THAT FROM TIME TO TIME FELL INTO THE HANDS OF THE INDIANS; WITH SOME VERY REMARKABLE ACCIDENTS

We have had some occasion, and shall have more, to mention captives falling into the hands of the Indians. We will here, without anything worthy to be called a digression, a little stand still, and with mournful hearts look upon the condition of the captives in those cruel hands. Their condition truly might be expressed in the terms of the ancient lamentations (thus by some translated), Lam. 4:3. *The daughter of my people is in the hands of the cruel, that are like the ostrich in the wilderness.* Truly, the dark places of New England, where the Indians had their unapproachable kennels, were habitations of cruelty; and no words can sufficiently describe the cruelty undergone by our captives in those habitations. The cold, and heat, and hunger, and weariness, and mockings, and scourgings, and insolencies endured by the captives, would enough deserve the name of cruelty; but there was this also added unto the rest, that they must ever now and then have their friends made a sacrifice of devils before their eyes, but be afraid of dropping a tear from those eyes, lest it should, upon that provocation, be next their own turn to be so barbarously sacrificed. Indeed, some few of the captives did very happily escape from their barbarous oppressors by a flight wisely managed; and many more of them were bought by the French, who treated them with a civility ever to be acknowledged, until care was taken to fetch 'em home. Nevertheless many scores of 'em died among the Indians; and what usage they had, may be gathered from the following relations, which I have obtained from credible witnesses.

Relation I

James Key, son to John Key of Quochecho, was a child of about five years of age, taken captive by the Indians at Salmon Falls; and that hellish fellow, Hope-Hood, once a servant of a Christian master in Boston, was become the master of this little Christian. This child, lamenting with tears the want of parents, his master threatened him with death, if he did not refrain his tears; but these threatenings could not extinguish the natural affections of a child. Wherefore upon his next lamentations, this monster stripped him stark naked, and lashed both his hands round a tree, and scourged him, so that from the crown of his head unto the sole of his foot, he was all over bloody and swollen; and when he was tired with laying on his blows on the forlorn infant, he would lay him on the ground, with taunts remembering him of his parents. In this misery the poor creature lay horribly roaring for divers days together, while his master, gratified with the music, lay contriving of new torments wherewith to martyr him. It was not long before the child had a sore eye, which his master said, proceeded from his weeping on the forbidden accounts: whereupon, laying hold on the head of the child with his left hand, with the thumb of his right he forced the ball of his eye quite out, therewithal telling him, that when he heard him cry again he would serve t'other so too, and leave him never an eye to weep withal. About nine or ten days after, this wretch had occasion to remove, with his family, about thirty miles further; and when they had gone about six miles of the thirty, the child being tired and faint, sat him down to rest, at which this horrid fellow, being provoked, he buried the blade of his hatchet, in the brains of the child, and then chopped the breathless body to pieces before the rest of the company and threw it into the river. But for the sake of these and other such truculent things, done by Hope-Hood, I am resolved, that in the course of our story, I will watch to see what becomes of that hideous Loup-Garous, if he come to his end, as I am apt to think he will, before the story.

Relation II

Mehetabel Goodwin, being a captive among the Indians, had with her a child about five months old; which through hunger and hardship, she being unable to nourish it, often made most grievous ejaculations. Her Indian master told her that if the child were not quiet, he would soon dispose of it; which caused her to use all possible means that his Netopship might not be offended; and sometimes carry it from the fire, out of his hearing, where she sat up to the waist in snow and frost for several hours until it was lulled asleep. She thus for several days preserved the life of her babe, until he saw cause to travel, with his own cubs, farther afield; and then, lest he should be retarded in his travel, he violently snatched the babe out of its mother's arms, and before her face knocked out its brains and stripped it of the few rags it had hitherto enjoyed, and ordered her the task to go wash the bloody clothes. Returning from this melancholy task, she found the infant hanging by the neck in a forked bough of a tree. She desired leave to lay it in the earth; but he said it was better as it was, for now the wild beasts would not come at it (I am sure, they had been at it!), and she might have the comfort of seeing it again if ever they came that way. The journey now before them was like to be very long, even as far as Canada, where his purpose was to make merchandise of his captive, and glad was the captive of such happy tidings. But the desperate length of the way and want of food and grief of mind wherewith she now encountred caused her within a few days to faint under her difficulties. When at length she sat down for some repose, with many prayers and tears unto God for the salvation of her soul, she found herself unable to rise, until she espied her furious executioner coming towards her with fire in his eyes, the devil in his heart, and his hatchet in his hand, ready to bestow a mercy-stroke of death upon her. But then this miserable creature got on her knees, and with weeping and wailing and all expressions of agony and entreaty, pre-vailed on him to spare her life a little, and she did not question but God would enable her to walk a little faster. The merciless tyrant was prevailed withal to spare her this time; nevertheless her former weakness quickly returning upon her, he was just going to murder her; but a couple of Indians, just at that instant coming in, suddenly called upon him to hold his hand; whereat such an horror surprised his guilty soul that he ran away. But hearing them call his name, he returned, and then permitted these his friends to ransom his prisoner from him. After this, being seated by a riverside, they heard several guns go off on the other side, which they con-cluded was from a party of Albany Indians, who were enemies unto these; whereupon this bold blade would needs go in a canoe to discover what they were. They fired upon him and shot through him and several of his friends before the discovery could be made unto satisfaction. But some days after this, divers of his friends gathered a party to revenge his death on their supposed enemies, with whom they joined battle and fought several hours, until their supposed enemies did really put 'em to the rout. Among the captives, which they left in their flight, one was this poor

Goodwin, who was overjoyed in seeing herself thus at liberty; but the joy did not last long, for these Indians were of the same sort with the other, and had been by their own friends, thus, through a strange mistake set upon. However, this crew proved more favorable to her than the former, and went away silently with their booty, being loath to have any noise made of their foul mistake. And yet, a few days after, such another mistake happened; for, meeting with another party of Indians, which they imagined in the English interests, they furiously engaged each other, and many were killed and wounded on either side; but they proved a party of the French Indians, who took this poor Goodwin and presented her to the French captain, by whom she was carried unto Canada, where she continued five years, and then was brought safe back into New England.

Relation III

Mary Plaisted, the wife of Mr. James Plaisted, was made a captive by the Indians about three weeks after her delivery of a male child. They then took her, with her infant, off her bed and forced her to travel in this her weakness the best part of a day, without any respect or pity. At night the cold ground in the open air was her lodging; and for many a day she had no nourishment, but a little water with a little bear's flesh: which rendered her so feeble that she, with her infant, were not far from totally starved. Upon her cries to God, there was at length some supply sent in by her master's taking a moose, the broth whereof recovered her. But she must now travel many days through woods and swamps and rocks and over mountains and frost and snow, until she could stir no farther. Sitting down to rest, she was not able to rise until her diabolical master helped her up; which when he did, he took her child from her and carried it unto a river, where, stripping it of the few rags it had, he took it by the heels and against a tree dashed out its brains, and then flung it into the river. So he returned unto the miserable mother, telling her she was now eased of her burden and must walk faster than she did before!

Relation IV

Mary Ferguson, taken captive by the Indians at Salmon Falls, declares that another maid of about fifteen or sixteen years of age, taken at the same time, had a great burden imposed on her. Being over-born with her burden, she burst out into tears, telling her Indian master that she could go no further. Whereupon he immediately took off her burden and, leading her aside into the bushes, he cut off her head and, scalping it, he ran about laughing and bragging what an act he had now done; and showing the scalp unto the rest, he told them they should all be served so if they were not patient.

In fine, when the children of the English captive cried at any time, so that they were not presently quieted, the manner of the Indians was to dash out their brains against a tree.

And very often, when the Indians were on or near the water, they took the small children and held 'em under water, till they had near drowned them, and then gave 'em unto their distressed mothers to quiet 'em.

And the Indians in their frolics would whip and beat the small children until they set 'em into grievous outcries, and then throw 'em to their amazed mothers for them to quiet 'em again as well as they could.

This was Indian captivity!

Reader, a modern traveller assures us that at the Villa Ludovisia, not far from Rome, there is to be seen the body of a petrified man; and that he himself saw by a piece of the man's leg, broken for satisfaction, both the bone and the stone crusted over it. All that I will say is, that if thou canst read these passages without relenting bowels, thou thyself art as really petrified as the man at Villa Ludovisia.

Nescio tu quibus es, Lector, Lecturus Ocellis;
Hoc Scio quod Siccis scribere non potui.

EBENEZER COOK

(fl. 1708)

The fact that little biographical data about Ebenezer Cook survived has worked to the poet's advantage; it enabled a major twentieth-century writer, John Barth, to make Ebenezer Cook the hero of his novel *The Sot-Weed Factor* and to construct a life for Ebenezer Cook far more exciting than could ever have been actually possible.

Although Ebenezer Cook's fame will probably rest more on Barth's literary efforts than his own, Ebenezer Cook's satiric description of a visit to Maryland is interesting in its own right. The passage excerpted here (11.252-319), a description of an Indian male fleetingly viewed by Cook while en route to the capital of Calvert County, displays a curious and unique point of view toward the Indian. Cook's cynicism would seem to prohibit the Indian from being seen as a noble savage; yet, in contrast to Cook's devastating depiction of the crude Maryland planter immediately preceding the appearance of the Indian, the Indian comes off rather well. Cook's view of the Indian remains theoretical, perhaps as a deliberate satiric poke at theorists on Indian character. The end of the section describing the Indian appropriately represents Cook's attitude: without stopping to observe the Indian longer, Cook debates with his travelling companion whether the Indian was formed by God or the devil. The academic argument, however much a parody, supersedes any human relationship with the Indians.

From **The Sot-Weed Factor,** *1705*

Steering our course in trot or pace,
We sail'd directly for a place,
In Maryland of high renown,
Known by the name of Battle-Town:
To view the crowds did there resort,
Which Justice made, and Law, their sport,
In their sagacious county court.
Scarce had we enter'd on the way,
Which through the woods and marshes lay,
But Indian strange did soon appear
In hot pursuit of wounded deer;
No mortal creature can express
His wild fantastic air and dress;
His painted skin, in colors dy'd,
His sable hair, in satchel ty'd,
Show'd savages not free from pride.
His tawny thighs and bosom bare,
Disdain'd a useless coat to wear,
Scorn'd summer's heat, and winter's air;
His manly shoulders, such as please
Widows and wives, were bath'd with grease
Of cub and bear, whose supple oil,
Prepar'd his limbs in heat and toil.
Thus naked pict in battle fought,
Or undisguis'd his mistress sought;
And knowing well his ware was good,
Refus'd to screen it with a hood:
His visage dun, and chin that ne'er
Did razor feel, nor scissors bear,
Or know the ornament of hair,
Look'd sternly grim; surpris'd with fear,
I spurr'd my horse as he drew near;
But roan who better knew than I,

Ebenezer Cook, *The Sot-Weed Factor,* in *The Maryland Muse* (Annapolis, 1731), p. 20.

The little cause I had to fly,
Seem'd by his solemn steps and pace,
Resolv'd I should the spector face,
Nor faster mov'd, though spurr'd and prick'd,
Than Balam's ass by prophet kick'd.
Kekicnitop, the heathen cry'd,
How is it Tom, by friend reply'd;
Judging from thence, the brute was civil,
I boldly fac'd the courteous devil,
And lugging out a dram of rum,
I have his tawny worship some,
Who in his language as I guess,
My guide informing me no less,
Implor'd the devil me to bless.
I thank'd him for his good intent,
And forward on my journey went,
Discoursing as along I rode,
Whether this race was fram'd of God,
Or whether some malignant power,
Had fram'd them in an evil hour,
And from his own infernal look,
Their dusky form and image took.
From hence we fell to argument
Whence peopl'd was this continent?
My friend suppos'd Tartarians wild,
Or Chinese, from their home exil'd,
Wandring through mountains hid with snow,
And rills that in the valleys flow,
Far to the south of Mexico,
Broke through the bars which nature cast,
And wide unbeaten regions past,
'Till near those streams the human deluge roll'd,
Which sparkling shin'd with glittering sands of gold,
And fetch'd Pisarro from th' Iberian shore,
To rob the Indians of their native store.

JOHN LAWSON

(d. 1711)

John Lawson's life seems more typical of the seventeenth century than the eighteenth. Like John Smith, Henrick Hudson, and William Bradford, Lawson arrived in this country to chart hitherto unexplored lands, the Carolinas and Georgia. After his first voyage, Lawson returned to London to see *A New Voyage to Carolina,* as the first edition in 1709 was titled, through the press. Like Smith's and Alsop's works, Lawson's book served as propaganda to lure new settlers to North Carolina, and Lawson himself returned to North Carolina as surveyor general to found a colony of Palatines.

The passage excerpted here is from a section of Lawson's book titled "Regulation of the Savages." To a modern reader, the title suggests a master-slave solution to the Indian problem, but Lawson's attitude toward the Indians is benign. He enumerates the virtues of the Indians and castigates the unjust dealings of whites with the Indians. Lawson was one of the first white men to recognize and respect the difference in Indian education and rearing of their children from that of whites, and he boldly defends inter-marriage as a means of solving cultural differences between the white and red races. In light of Lawson's progressive ideas, it is ironic that he was killed by Indians during his attempt to settle in North Carolina.

From A New Voyage to Carolina, 1709

Now there appears to be one thousand six hundred and twelve fighting men, of our neighboring Indians, and probably there are three-fifths of women and children, not including old men, which amounts to four thousand and thirty savages besides the five nations lately come. Now, as I before hinted, we will see what grounds there are to make these people serviceable to us, and better themselves thereby.

On a fair scheme, we must first allow these savages what really belongs to them, that is, what good qualities and natural endowments they possess, whereby they being in their proper colors, the event may be better guessed at and fathomed.

First, they are as apt to learn any handicraft, as any people that the world affords; I will except none, as is seen by their canoes and stauking heads, which they make of themselves; but to my purpose, the Indian slaves in South Carolina and elsewhere make my argument good.

Secondly, we have no disciplined men in Europe but what have, at one time or other been branded with mutinying and murmuring against their chiefs. These savages are never found guilty of that great crime in a soldier. I challenge all mankind to tell me of one instance of it; besides, they never prove traitors to their native country, but rather choose death than partake and side with the enemy.

They naturally possess the righteous man's gift; they are patient under all afflictions, and have a great many other natural virtues, which I have slightly touched throughout the account of these savages.

They are really better to us than we are to them; they always give us victuals at their quarters and take care we are armed against hunger and thirst. We do not so by them (generally speaking), but let them walk by our doors hungry and do not often relieve them. We look upon them with scorn and disdain, and think them little better than beasts in human shape, though if well examined, we shall find that, for all our religion and education, we possess more moral deformities and evils than these savages do, or are acquainted withal.

We reckon them slaves in comparison to us, and intruders, as oft as they enter our houses or hunt near our dwellings. But if we will admit reason to

Lawson's History of North Carolina, ed. Frances L. Harriss (Richmond, Va., 1937), pp. 255–59.

be our guide, she will inform as that these Indians are the freest people in the world, and, so far from being intruders upon us, that we have abandoned our own native soil to drive them out and possess theirs, neither have we any true balance in judging of these poor heathens, because we neither give allowance for their natural disposition, nor the sylvan education, and strange customs (uncouth to us) they lie under and have ever been trained up to; these are false measures for Christians to take, and indeed no man can be reckoned a moralist only, who will not make choice and use of better rules to walk and act by. We trade with them, it is true, but to what end? Not to show them the steps of virtue, and the golden rule, to do as we would be done by. No, we have furnished them with the vice of drunkenness, which is the open road to all others, and daily cheat them in everything we sell, and esteem it a gift of Christianity not to sell them so cheap as we do to the Christians, as we call ourselves. Pray, let me know where is there to be found one sacred command or precept of our master, that counsels us to such behavior? Besides, I believe it will not appear but that all the wars which we have had with the savages were occasioned by the unjust dealings of the Christians towards them. I can name more than a few, which my own inquiry has given me a right understanding of, and I am afraid the remainder (if they come to the test) will prove themselves birds of the same feather.

As we are in Christian duty bound, so we must act and behave ourselves to these savages, if we either intend to be serviceable in converting them to the knowledge of the Gospel, or discharge the duty which every man, within the pale of the Christian church, is bound to do. Upon this score, we ought to show a tenderness for these heathens under the weight of infidelity; let us cherish their good deeds, and, with mildness and clemency, make them sensible and forewarn them of their ill ones; let our dealings be just to them in every respect and show no ill example, whereby they may think we advise them to practise that which we will not be conformable to ourselves. Let them have cheap penniworths (without guile in our trading with them), and learn them the mysteries of our handicrafts, as well as our religion, otherwise we deal unjustly by them. But it is highly necessary to be brought in practice, which is, to give encouragement to the ordinary people, and those of a lower rank, that they might marry with these Indians, and come into plantations, and houses, where so many acres of land and some gratuity of money (out of a public stock) are given to the new-married couple; and that the Indians might have encouragement to send their children apprentices to proper masters, that would be kind to them and make them masters of a trade, whereby they would be drawn to live amongst us and become members of the same ecclesiastical and civil government we are under; then we should have great advantages to make daily conversions amongst them, when they saw that we were kind and just to them in all our dealings. Moreover, by the Indians marrying with the Christians, and coming into plantations with their English husbands, or wives, they would become Christians, and their idolatry would be quite forgotten, and in all probability, a better worship come in its stead; for were the Jews engrafted thus, and alienated from the worship and conversation of Jews, their abominations would vanish and be no more.

Thus we should be let into a better understanding of the Indian tongue by our new converts; and the whole body of these people would arrive to the knowledge of our religion and customs, and become as one people with us. By this method, also, we should have a true knowledge of all the Indian's skill in medicine and surgery; they would inform us of the situation of our rivers, lakes and tracts of land in the Lord's dominions, where, by their assistance, greater discoveries may be made than has been hitherto found out; and by their accompanying us in our expeditions, we might civilize a great many other nations of the savages and daily add to our strength in trade, and interest; so that we might be sufficiently enabled to conquer or maintain our ground against all the enemies to the crown of England in America, both Christian and savage.

What children we have of theirs to learn trades, etc., ought to be put into those hands that are men of the best lives and characters, and that are not only strict observers of their religion, but also of a mild, winning, and sweet disposition, that these Indian parents may often go and see how well their children are dealt with, which would much win them to our ways of living, mildness being a virtue the Indians are in love withal, for they do not practice beating and correcting their children as we do. A general complaint is, that it seems impossible to convert these people to Christianity, as, at first sight it does; and as for those in New Spain, they have the prayers of that church in Latin by rote, and know the external behavior at mass and sermons; yet scarce any of them are steady and abide with constancy in good works and the duties of the Christian church. We find that the Fuentes and several other of the noted Indian families about Mexico, and in other parts of New Spain, had given several large gifts to the altar, and out-wardly seemed fond of their new religion; yet those that were the greatest zealots outwards, on a strict inquiry, were found guilty of idolatry and witchcraft; and this seems to proceed from their cohabiting, which, as I have noted before, gives opportunities of cabals to recall their ancient pristine infidelity and superstitions. They never argue against our religion, but with all imaginable indifference own, that it is most proper for us that have been brought up in it.

In my opinion, it is better for Christians of a mean fortune to marry with the civilized Indians than to suffer the hardships of four or five years' servitude, in which they meet with sickness and seasonings amidst a crowd of other afflictions, which the tyranny of a bad master lays upon such poor souls, all which those acquainted with our tobacco plantations are not strangers to.

This seems to be a more reasonable method of converting the Indians than to set up our Christian banner in a field of blood, as the Spaniards have done in New Spain, and baptize one hundred with the sword for one at the font. Whilst we make way for a Christian colony through a field of blood and defraud, and make away with those that one day may be wanted in this world, and in the next appear against us, we make way for a more potent Christian enemy to invade us hereafter, of which we may repent, when too late.

ROBERT ROGERS

(1731–1795)

Robert Rogers' career as soldier in the French and Indian wars and defender of western territories hardly prepares us to find him writing the first of the Indian dramas. Rogers' first contact with Indians occured at age fifteen as he helped defend against an attack by Indians near his home in New Hampshire. His life thereafter alternated between military appointments and economic disgraces. At the end of the French and Indian War, he commanded six hundred rangers and was well known for adopting Indian guerilla tactics. Later he defended Detroit against Pontiac's attack, but thereafter he was accused of illicitly trading with the Indians and went to England in disgrace. During this first stay in England, Rogers wrote his *Journals: A Concise Account of North America,* and *Ponteach.* In 1766 Rogers returned to America, where he commanded a Michigan fort and commissioned the expedition of Jonathan Carver, but again he faced disgrace, this time for suspicion of treason. After a six-year stay in England (1769–75), Rogers again returned to America and found himself in the midst of the Revolution. Despite his friendship with well-known patriotic colonists, Rogers was arrested as a spy by George Washington. Thereafter he escaped to the British and fought ardently for the Crown.

Ponteach represents the first idealization on the stage of an Indian hero and was later used as a source by Parkman for his depiction of Pontiac. Although Pontiac is the central character and the events of the play revolve about Pontiac's attempts to deal honestly and peacefully with the white men prior to the outbreak of war, the introduction of a love element in Act II usurps the central theme and seriously diminishes the effectiveness of the play from a literary point of view. Nonetheless, there are several scenes worthy of selection which illustrate Rogers' attempt to expose the white man's cheating and dishonest ways. In Act I, scene 1, Rogers depicts two Indian traders, one experienced and one newly arrived on the frontier. The former tutors the latter in the ways of cheating the Indians. The second scene rather crudely attempts to trace the motivations behind the white man's violence toward the Indian to his own frustrations in making a living by hunting. In another scene (IV, 4) Pontiac restrains his Indians, victorious in battle, from slaying the wife and children of a captured family. The scene selected here (I, 4) depicts Pontiac's conference with the English governors prior to the war. Pontiac's dignity and honest efforts at peace-making are contrasted to the cheating and distainful attitude of the white men.

From *Ponteach; or The Savages of America, 1766*

SCENE 4. AN APARTMENT IN THE FORT.
ENTER GOVERNORS *SHARP, GRIPE,* AND *CATCHUM.*

Sharp.
Here are we met to represent our king,
And by his royal bounties to conciliate
These Indians' minds to friendship, peace, and love.
But he that would an honest living get
In times so hard and difficult as these,
Must mind that good old rule, take care of one.

Gripe.
Ay, Christian charity begins at home;
I think it's in the Bible, I know I've read it.

Catchum.
I join with Paul, that he's an infidel
Who does not for himself and friends provide.

Sharp.
Yes, Paul in fact was no bad politician,
And understood himself as well as most.
All good and wise men certainly take care
To help themselves and families the first;
Thus dictates nature, instinct, and religion,
Whose easy precepts ought to be obey'd.

Ponteach; or, The Savages of America: A Tragedy by Robert Rogers (Chicago, 1914).

Gripe.
But how does this affect our present purpose?
We've heard the doctrine; what's the application?

Sharp,
We are intrusted with these Indian presents.
A thousand pound was granted by the king,
To satisfy them of his royal goodness,
His constant disposition to their welfare,
And reconcile their savage minds to peace.
Five hundred's gone; you know our late division,
Our great expense, *et cetera,* no matter:
The other half was laid out for these goods,
To be distributed as we think proper;
And whether half (I only put the question)
Of these said goods, won't answer every end,
And bring about as long a lasting peace
As though the whole were lavishly bestow'd?

Catchum.
I'm clear upon 't they will, if we affirm
That half's the whole was sent them by the king.

Gripe.
There is no doubt but that one third would answer,
For they, poor souls! are ign'rant of the worth
Of single things, nor know they how to add
Or calculate, and cast the whole amount.

Sharp.
Why, want of learning is a great misfortune.
How thankful should we be that we have schools,
And better taught and bred than these poor heathen.

Catchum.
Yes, only these two simple easy rules,
Addition and subtraction, are great helps,
And must contribute to our happiness.

Sharp.
'Tis these I mean to put in practice now;
Subtraction from these royal presents makes
Addition to our gains without a fraction.
But let us overhaul and take the best,
Things may be given that won't do to sell.
                    [They overhaul the goods, etc.]

Catchum.
Lay these aside; they'll fetch a noble price.

Gripe.
And these are very saleable, I think.

Sharp.
The Indians will be very fond of these.
Is there the half, think you?

Gripe.
It's thereabouts.

Catchum.
This bag of wampum may be added yet.

Sharp.
Here, lads, convey these goods to our apartment.

Servant.
The Indians, sir, are waiting at the gate.

Gripe.
Conduct them in when you've disposed of these.

Catchum.
This should have been new-drawn before they enter'd.
                         [Pulling out an inventory of the whole goods.]

Gripe.
What matters that? They cannot read, you know,
And you can read to them in gen'ral terms.

                 Enter *Ponteach*, with several of his chieftains.

Sharp.
Welcome, my brothers, we are glad to meet you,
And hope that you will not repent our coming.

Ponteach.
We're glad to see our brothers here the English.
If honourable peace be your desire,
We'd always have the hatchet buried deep,
While sun and moon, rivers and lakes endure,
And trees and herbs within our country grow.
But then you must not cheat and wrong the Indians,
Or treat us with reproach, contempt, and scorn;
Else we will raise the hatchet to the sky,

And let it never touch the earth again,
Sharpen its edge, and keep it bright as silver,
Or stain it red with murder and with blood.
Mind what I say, I do not tell you lies.

Sharp.

We hope you have no reason to complain
That Englishmen conduct to you amiss;
We're griev'd if they have given you offence,
And fain would heal the wound while it is fresh,
Lest it should spread, grow painful, and severe.

Ponteach.

Your men make Indians drunk, and then they cheat 'em.
Your officers, your colonels, and your captains
Are proud, morose, ill-natur'd, churlish men,
Treat us with disrespect, contempt, and scorn.
I tell you plainly this will never do,
We never thus were treated by the French,
Them we thought bad enough, but think you worse.

Sharp.

There's good and bad, you know, in every nation;
There's some good Indians, some are the reverse,
Whom you can't govern, and restrain from ill;
So there's some Englishmen that will be bad.
You must not mind the conduct of a few,
Nor judge the rest by what you see of them.

Ponteach.

If you've some good, why don't you send them here?
These every one are rogues, and knaves, and fools,
And think no more of Indians than of dogs.
Your king had better send his good men hither,
And keep his bad ones in some other country;
Then you would find that Indians would do well,
Be peaceable, and honest in their trade;
We'd love you, treat you, as our friends and brothers,
And raise the hatchet only in your cause.

Sharp.

Our king is very anxious for your welfare,
And greatly wishes for your love and friendship;
He would not have the hatchet ever raised,
But buried deep, stamp'd down and cover'd o'er,

As with a mountain that can never move:
For this he sent us to your distant country,
Bid us deliver you these friendly belts,
     [Holding out belts of wampum.]
All cover'd over with his love and kindness.
He like a father loves you as his children;
And like a brother wishes you all good;
We'll let him know the wounds that you complain of,
And he'll be speedy to apply the cure,
And clear the path to friendship, peace, and trade.

Ponteach.
Your king, I hear's a good and upright man,
True to his word, and friendly in his heart;
Not proud and insolent, morose and sour,
Like these his petty officers and servants:
I want to see your king, and let him know
What must be done to keep the hatchet dull,
And how the path of friendship, peace, and trade
May be kept clean and solid as a rock.

Sharp.
Our king is distant over the great lake,
But we can quickly send him your requests;
To which he'll listen with attentive ear,
And act as though you told him with your tongue.

Ponteach.
Let him know then his people here are rogues,
And cheat and wrong and use the Indians ill.
Tell him to send good officers, and call
These proud ill-natur'd fellows from my country,
And keep his hunters from my hunting ground.
He must do this, and do it quickly too,
Or he will find the path between us bloody.

Sharp.
Of this we will acquaint our gracious king,
And hope you and your chiefs will now confirm
A solid peace as if our king was present;
We're his ambassadors, and represent him,
And bring these tokens of his royal friendship
To you, your captains, chiefs, and valiant men.
Read, Mr. Catchum, you've the inventory.

"PONTEACH"

Catchum.
The British king, of his great bounty, sends
To Ponteach, king upon the lakes, and his chiefs,
Two hundred, no [*Aside*] a number of fine blankets,
Six hundred [*Aside*] yes, and several dozen hatchets,
Twenty thousand [*Aside*] and a bag of wampum,
A parcel too of pans, and knives, and kettles.

Sharp.
This rich and royal bounty you'll accept,
And as you please distribute to your chiefs,
And let them know they come from England's king,
As tokens to them of his love and favor.
We've taken this long journey at great charge,
To see and hold with you this friendly talk;
We hope your minds are all disposed to peace,
And that you like our sovereign's bounty well.

1st Chief.
We think it very small, we heard of more.
Most of our chiefs and warriors are not here,
They all expect to share a part with us.

2nd Chief.
These won't reach round to more than half our tribes,
Few of our chiefs will have a single token
Of your king's bounty, that you speak so much of.

3rd Chief.
And those who haven't will be dissatisfied,
Think themselves slighted, think your king is stingy,
Or else that you his governors are rogues,
And keep your master's bounty for yourselves.

4th Chief.
We hear such tricks are sometimes play'd with Indians.
King Astenaco, the great southern chief,
Who's been in England, and has seen your king,
Told me that he was generous, kind, and true,
But that his officers were rogues and knaves,
And cheated Indians out of what he gave.

Gripe.
The devil's in 't, I fear that we're detected. [*Aside.*]

Ponteach.

Indians a'n't fools, if white men think us so;
We see, we hear, we think as well as you;
We know the[re] 're lies, and mischiefs in the world;
We don't know whom to trust, nor when to fear;
Men are uncertain, changing as the wind,
Inconstant as the waters of the lakes,
Some smooth and fair, and pleasant as the sun,
Some rough and boist'rous, like the winter storm;
Some are insidious as the subtle snake,
Some innocent, and harmless as the dove;
Some like the tiger, raging, cruel, fierce,
Some like the lamb, humble, submissive, mild,
And scarcely one is every day the same;
But I call no man bad, till such he's found,
Then I condemn and cast him from my sight;
And no more trust him as a friend and brother.
I hope to find you honest men and true.

Sharp.

Indeed you may depend upon our honors,
We're faithful servants of the best of kings;
We scorn an imposition on your ignorance,
Abhor the arts of falsehood and deceit.
These are the presents our great monarch sent,
He's of a bounteous, noble, princely mind
And had he known the numbers of your chiefs,
Each would have largely shar'd his royal goodness;
But these are rich and worthy your acceptance,
Few kings on earth can such as these bestow,
For goodness, beauty, excellence, and worth.

Ponteach.

The presents from your sovereign I accept,
His friendly belts to us shall be preserved,
And in return convey you those to him.   [*Belts and furs.*]
Which let him know our mind, and what we wish,
That we dislike his crusty officers,
And wish the path of peace was made more plain,
The calumet I do not choose to smoke,
Till I see further, and my other chiefs
Have been consulted. Tell your king from me,
That first or last a rogue will be detected,

That I have warriors, am myself a king,
And will be honor'd and obey'd as such;
Tell him my subjects shall not be oppress'd,
But I will seek redress and take revenge;
Tell your king this; I have no more to say.

Sharp.
To our great king your gifts we will convey,
And let him know the talk we've had with you;
We're griev'd we cannot smoke the pipe of peace,
And part with stronger proofs of love and friendship;
Meantime we hope you'll so consider matters,
As still to keep the hatchet dull and buried,
And open wide the shining path of peace,
That you and we may walk without a blunder.

[*Exeunt Indians.*]

Gripe.
Th' appear not fully satisfied, I think.

Catchum.
I do not like old Ponteach's talk and air,
He seems suspicious, and inclin'd to war.

Sharp.
They're always jealous, bloody, and revengeful,
You see that they distrust our word and honor;
No wonder then if they suspect the traders,
And often charge them with downright injustice.

Gripe.
True, when even we that come to make them presents,
Cannot escape their fears and jealousies.

Catchum.
Well, we have this, at least, to comfort us;
Their good opinion is no commendation,
Nor their foul slanders any stain to honor.
I think we've done whatever men could do
To reconcile their savage minds to peace.
If they're displeas'd, our honor is acquitted,
And we have not been wanting in our duty
To them, our king, our country, and our friends.

Gripe.
But what returns are these they've left behind?
These belts are valuable, and neatly wrought.

Catchum.
This pack of furs is very weighty too;
The skins are pick'd, and of the choicest kind.

Sharp.
By jove, they're worth more money than their presents.

Gripe.
Indeed they are; the king will be no loser.

Sharp.
The king! who ever sent such trumpery to him?

Catchum.
What would the king of England do with wampum?
Or beaver skins, d'ye think? He's not a hatter!

Gripe.
Then it's a perquisite belongs to us?

Sharp.
Yes, they're become our lawful goods and chattels,
By all the rules and laws of Indian treaties.
The king would scorn to take a gift from Indians,
And think us madmen, should we send them to him.

Catchum.
I understand we make a fair division,
And have no words nor fraud among ourselves.

Sharp.
We throw the whole into one common stock,
And go copartners in the loss and gain.
Thus most who handle money for the crown
Find means to make the better half their own;
And, to your better judgments with submission,
The self neglecter's a poor politician.
These gifts, you see will all expences pay;
Heav'n send an Indian treaty every day;
We dearly love to serve our king this way.

JOHN WOOLMAN

(1720–1772)

Although he received little formal schooling, John Woolman was one of the most literate Quaker spokesmen, particularly on the subject of the American Indian. Born on a New Jersey farm, later proprietor of a tailor shop in Mount Holly, New Jersey, Woolman's life bore the external marks to match his philosophical and stylistic simplicity. At the age of twenty-three, Woolman was admitted to the Quaker ministry, an occupation to which he devoted progressively more of his time and energy as he matured. In 1758 he persuaded Friends at the Philadelphia Yearly Meeting to pass a resolution to free their own slaves. In 1763, Woolman made a ministerial visit to the Wehaloosing Indians on the Pennsylvania frontier at a time when fighting lingered on from the French and Indian wars. The description of that visit as recorded in Woolman's *Journal* constitutes the present selection.

Is it accurate to call Woolman's visit a missionary effort? Compared to the Jesuit or Puritan attempts to convert the Indians to Christianity, Woolman is no missionary, for the Indians he visited were already Christian. There was no overt attempt to preach to the Indians nor to convert them to Quakerism. Woolman could have set himself up as a rival to the Moravian minister in the village, but instead Woolman attended the Moravian meetings. Woolman's mission was an attempt at Christian communion with the Indians, a concept which can be interpreted only within the context of Quaker belief in "that of God in every man." That of God within Woolman, what Quakers call "the inner light," directed Woolman to seek out these Indians, despite the hardships involved in the journey. Woolman set forth without a particular goal or objective, except to open himself to communion with the Indians, hoping that "that of God within them" might provide him some instruction.

*From **The Journal**, 1774*

We lodged at Bethlehem . . . . and at this place we met with an Indian trader lately come from Wyoming. In conversation with him, I perceived that many white people often sell rum to the Indians, which I believe is a great evil. In the first place, they are thereby deprived of the use of reason, and, their spirits being violently agitated, quarrels often arise which end in mischief, and the bitterness and resentment occasioned hereby are frequently of long continuance. Again, their skins and furs, gotten through much fatigue and hard travels in hunting, with which they intended to buy clothing, they often sell at a low rate for more rum, when they become intoxicated; and afterward, when they suffer for want of the necessaries of life, are angry with those who, for the sake of gain, took advantage of their weakness. Their chiefs have often complained of this in their treaties with the English. Where cunning people pass counterfeits and impose on others that which is good for nothing, it is considered as wickedness; but for the sake of gain to sell that which we know does people harm, and which often works their ruin, manifests a hardened and corrupt heart, and is an evil which demands the care of all true lovers of virtue to suppress. While my mind this evening was thus employed, I also remembered that the people on the frontiers, among whom this evil is too common, are often poor; and that they venture to the outside of a colony in order to live more independently of the wealthy, who often set high rents on their land. I was renewedly confirmed in a belief, that if all our inhabitants lived according to sound wisdom, laboring to promote universal love and righteousness, and ceased from every inordinate desire after wealth, and from all customs which are tinctured with luxury, the way would be easy for our inhabitants, though they might be much more numerous than at present, to live comfortably on honest employments, without the temptation they are so often under of being drawn into schemes to make settlements on lands which have not been purchased of the Indians, or of applying to that wicked practice of selling rum to them.

. . . .

Twelfth of sixth month being the first of the week and a rainy day, we continued in our tent, and I was led to think on the nature of the exercise

The Journal of John Woolman, intro. by John G. Whittier (Boston, 1871), pp. 188–89, 192–95, 199–204.

which hath attended me. Love was the first motion, and thence a concern arose to spend some time with the Indians, that I might feel and understand their life and the spirit they live in, if haply I might receive some instruction from them, or they might be in any degree helped forward by my following the leadings of truth among them; and as it pleased the Lord to make way for my going at a time when the troubles of war were increasing, and when, by reason of much wet weather, travelling was more difficult than usual at that season, I looked upon it as a more favorable opportunity to season my mind, and to bring me into a nearer sympathy with them. As mine eye was to the great Father of Mercies, humbly desiring to learn his will concerning me, I was made quiet and content.

. . . .

Thirteenth of sixth month.—The sun appearing, we set forward, and as I rode over the barren hills my meditations were on the alterations in the circumstances of the natives of this land since the coming in of the English. The lands near the sea are conveniently situated for fishing; the lands near the rivers, where the tides flow, and some above, are in many places fertile, and not mountainous, while the changing of the tides makes passing up and down easy with any kind of traffic. The natives have in some places, for trifling considerations, sold their inheritance so favorably situated, and in other places have been driven back by superior force; their way of clothing themselves is also altered from what it was, and they being far removed from us have to pass over mountains, swamps, and barren deserts, so that travelling is very troublesome in bringing their skins and furs to trade with us. By the extension of English settlements, and partly by the increase of English hunters, the wild beasts on which the natives chiefly depend for subsistence are not so plentiful as they were, and people too often, for the sake of gain, induce them to waste their skins and furs in purchasing a liquor which tends to the ruin of them and their families.

My own will and desires were now very much broken, and my heart was with much earnestness turned to the Lord, to whom alone I looked for help in the dangers before me. I had a prospect of the English along the coast for upwards of nine hundred miles, where I travelled, and their favorable situation and the difficulties attending the natives as well as the negroes in many places were open before me. A weighty and heavenly care came over my mind, and love filled my heart towards all mankind, in which I felt a strong engagement that we might be obedient to the Lord while in tender mercy he is yet calling to us, and that we might so attend to pure universal righteousness as to give no just cause of offence to the gentiles, who do not profess Christianity, whether they be the blacks from Africa, or the native inhabitants of this continent. Here I was led into a close and laborious inquiry whether I, as an individual, kept clear from all things which tended to stir up or were connected with wars, either in this land or in Africa; my heart was deeply concerned that in future I might in all things keep steadily to the pure truth, and live and walk in the plainness and simplicity of a sincere follower of Christ. In this lonely journey I did greatly bewail the spreading of a wrong spirit, believing that the prosperous, convenient situation of the English would require a constant attention in us to Divine love and wisdom, in order to their being guided and supported in a way answerable to the will of that good, gracious, and Almighty Being, who hath an equal regard to all mankind. And here luxury and covetousness, with the numerous oppressions and other evils attending them, appeared very afflicting to me, and I felt in that which is immutable that the seeds of great calamity and desolation are sown and growing fast on this continent. Nor have I words sufficient to set forth the longing I then felt, that we who are placed along the coast, and have tasted the love and goodness of God, might arise in the strength thereof, and like faithful messengers labor to check the growth of these seeds, that they may not ripen to the ruin of our posterity.

. . . .

Parting from Job Chilaway on the 17th, we went on and reached Wehaloosing about the middle of the afternoon. The first Indian that we saw was a woman of a modest countenance, with a Bible, who spake first to our guide, and then with an harmonious voice expressed her gladness at seeing us, having before heard of our coming. By the direction of our guide we sat down on a log while he went to the town to tell the people we were come.

My companion and I, sitting thus together in a deep inward stillness, the poor woman came and sat near us; and, great awfulness coming over us, we rejoiced in a sense of God's love manifested to our poor souls. After a while we heard a conch-shell blow several times, and then came John Curtis and another Indian man, who kindly invited us into a house near the town, where we found about sixty people sitting in silence. After sitting with them a short time I stood up, and in some tenderness of spirit acquainted them, in a few short sentences, with the nature of my visit, and that a concern for their good had made me willing to come thus far to see them; which some of them understanding interpreted to the others, and there appeared gladness among them. I then showed them my certificate, which was explained to them; and the Moravian who overtook us on the way, being now here, bade me welcome. But the Indians knowing that this Moravian and I were of different religious societies, and as some of their people had encouraged him to come and stay awhile with them, they were, I believe, concerned that there might be no jarring or discord in their meetings; and having, I suppose, conferred together, they acquainted me that the people, at my request, would at any time come together and hold meetings. They also told me that they expected the Moravian would speak in their settled meetings, which are commonly held in the morning and near evening. So finding liberty in my heart to speak to the Moravian, I told him of the care I felt on my mind for the good of these people, and my belief that no ill effects would follow if I sometimes spake in their meetings when love engaged me thereto, without calling them together at times when they did not meet of course. He expressed his good-will towards my speaking at any time all that I found in my heart to say.

. . . .

Before our first meeting this morning, I was led to meditate on the manifold difficulties of these Indians who, by the permission of the Six Nations, dwell in these parts. A near sympathy with them was raised in me, and, my heart being enlarged in the love of Christ, I thought that the affectionate care of a good man for his only brother in affliction does not exceed what I then felt for that people. I came to this place through much trouble; and though through the mercies of God I believed that if I died in the journey it would be well with me, yet the thoughts of falling into the hands of Indian warriors were, in times of weakness, afflicting to me; and being of a tender constitution of body, the thoughts of captivity among them were also grievous; supposing that as they were strong and hardy they might demand service of me beyond what I could well bear. But the Lord alone was my keeper, and I believed that if I went into captivity it would be for some good end. Thus, from time to time, by mind was centred in resignation, in which I always found quietness. And this day, though I had the same dangerous wilderness between me and home, I was inwardly joyful that the Lord had strengthened me to come on this visit, and had manifested a fatherly care over me in my poor lowly condition, when, in mine own eyes, I appeared inferior to many among the Indians. . . .

. . . .

I was at two meetings on the 20th, and silent in them. The following morning, in meeting, my heart was enlarged in pure love among them, and in short plain sentences I expressed several things that rested upon me, which one of the interpreters gave the people pretty readily. The meeting ended in supplication, and I had cause humbly to acknowledge the loving-kindness of the Lord towards us; and then I believed that a door remained open for the faithful disciples of Jesus Christ to labor among these people. And now, feeling my mind at liberty to return, I took my leave of them in general at the conclusion of what I said in meeting, and we then prepared to go homeward. But some of their most active men told us that when we were ready to move the people would choose to come and shake hands with us. Those who usually came to meeting did so; and from a secret draught in my mind I went among some who did not usually go to meeting, and took my leave of them also. The Moravian and his Indian interpreter appeared respectful to us at parting.

MICHEL GUILLAUME
JEAN de CRÈVECOEUR
(1735–1813)

Crèvecoeur, born in Caen, France, arrived in the New World in 1754 as
a member of Montcalm's army in New France. Later, he explored New
York and Pennsylvania and, in 1769, married and settled on a farm in
Orange County, New York. Until the Revolution, Crèvecoeur combined
the lives of farmer and writer: he wrote *Letters from an American Farmer*
and *Sketches of Eighteenth-Century America* during this period, although
they were not published until later. The Revolution forced Crèvecoeur, a
loyalist, to flee to France. He returned to New York City in 1783 as the
French Consul, a post he retained until 1790. The remainder of Crèvecoeur's
life was spent in France.

At the end of *Letters from an American Farmer,* a passage from which
is selected here, Crèvecoeur's persona, like Crèvecoeur himself, is faced with
the turmoil of the Revolution. Unable to maintain a neutral position between rebels and Tories, the farmer finds himself and his family in constant
danger of attack. Their fears of the Hessian soldiers echo the fears of Indian
attack heard earlier among the Pilgrims. The farmer, valuing his connections
to civilized society, regretfully flees the turmoil of the Revolution to find
safety in an Indian village. He writes out of an attitude of despair and
desperation; his stance is expedient, and he is fully aware of the dangers of
exposing his children to Indian society. The farmer equates cultivation
with civilization and virtue; in contrast, the forest is a dangerous place
which fosters "a strange sort of lawless profligacy." Yet the farmer
distinguishes in an earlier comparison of frontiersman to Indian (Letter III)
between the effects of the forest on white man and red, the dangers for the
former being stronger:

. . . our bad people are those who are half cultivators and half hunters; and
the worst of them are those who have degenerated altogether into the
hunting state. As old ploughmen and new men of the woods, as Europeans
and new-made Indians, they contract the vices of both; they adopt the
moroseness and ferocity of a native, without his mildness or even his
industry at home.

From *Letters from an American Farmer, 1782*

Self-preservation is above all political precepts and rules, and even
superior to the dearest opinions of our minds; a reasonable accommodation
of ourselves to the various exigencies of the time in which we live is the
most irresistible precept. To this great evil I must seek some sort of remedy
adapted to remove or to palliate it; situated as I am, what steps should I
take that will neither injure nor insult any of the parties, and at the same
time save my family from that certain destruction which awaits it if I
remain here much longer. Could I insure them bread, safety, and subsistence,
not the bread of idleness, but that earned by proper labor as heretofore;
could this be accomplished by the sacrifice of my life, I would willingly
give it up. I attest before heaven, that it is only for these I would wish to
live and to toil: for these whom I have brought into this miserable existence.

I resemble, methinks, one of the stones of a ruined arch, still retaining
that pristine form that anciently fitted the place I occupied, but the center
is tumbled down; I can be nothing until I am replaced, either in the former
circle or in some stronger one. I see one on a smaller scale, and at a considerable distance, but it is within my power to reach it: and since I have
ceased to consider myself as a member of the ancient state now convulsed,
I willingly descend into an inferior one. I will revert into a state approaching
nearer to that of nature, unencumbered either with voluminous laws or
contradictory codes, often galling the very necks of those whom they
protect; and at the same time sufficiently remote from the brutality of
unconnected savage nature.

Do you, my friend, perceive the path I have found out? It is that which
leads to the tenants of the great——village of——, where, far removed
from the accursed neighborhood of Europeans, its inhabitants live with
more ease, decency, and peace than you imagine: where, though governed
by no laws, yet find in uncontaminated simple manners all that laws can
afford. Their system is sufficiently complete to answer all the primary
wants of man, and to constitute him a social being, such as he ought to be
in the great forest of nature. There it is that I have resolved at any rate to
transport myself and family: an eccentric thought, you may say, thus to
cut asunder all former connections, and to form new ones with a people

J. Hector St. John Crèvecoeur, *Letters from an American Farmer,* ed. W. P. Trent
(New York, 1904), pp. 299–309.

whom nature has stamped with such different characteristics! But as the happiness of my family is the only object of my wishes, I care very little where we be, or where we go, provided that we are safe, and all united together. Our new calamities being shared equally by all, will become lighter; our mutual affection for each other will in this great transmutation become the strongest link of our new society, will afford us every joy we can receive on a foreign soil, and preserve us in unity, as the gravity and coherency of matter prevents the world from dissolution. Blame me not, it would be cruel in you, it would beside be entirely useless; for when you receive this we shall be on the wing.

When we think all hopes are gone, must we, like poor pusillanimous wretches, despair and die? No; I perceive before me a few resources, though through many dangers, which I will explain to you hereafter. It is not, believe me, a disappointed ambition which leads me to take this step; it is the bitterness of my situation, it is the impossibility of knowing what better measure to adopt. My education fitted me for nothing more than the most simple occupations of life; I am but a feller of trees, a cultivator of land, the most honorable title an American can have. I have no exploits, no discoveries, no inventions to boast of; I have cleared about 370 acres of land, some for the plough, some for the scythe; and this has occupied many years of my life. I have never possessed, or wish to possess anything more than what could be earned or produced by the united industry of my family. I wanted nothing more than to live at home independent and tranquil, and to teach my children how to provide the means of a future ample subsistence, founded on labor like that of their father. This is the career of life I have pursued, and that which I had marked out for them and for which they seemed to be so well calculated by their inclinations, and by their constitutions. But now these pleasing expectations are gone; we must abandon the accumulated industry of nineteen years; we must fly we hardly know whither, through the most impervious paths, and become members of a new and strange community.

Oh, virtue! is this all the reward thou hast to confer on thy votaries? Either thou art only a chimera, or thou art a timid useless being; soon affrighted, when ambition, thy great adversary, dictates, when war re-echoes the dreadful sounds, and poor helpless individuals are mowed down by its cruel reapers like useless grass. I have at all times generously relieved what few distressed people I have met with; I have encouraged the industrious; my house has always been opened to travellers; I have not lost a month in illness since I have been a man; I have caused upwards of an hundred and twenty families to remove hither. Many of them I have led by the hand in the days of their first trial; distant as I am from any places of worship or school of education, I have been the pastor of my family, and the teacher

of many of my neighbors. I have learnt them as well as I could, the gratitude they owe to God, the father of harvests; and their duties to man: I
have been as useful a subject; ever obedient to the laws, ever vigilant to see
them respected and observed. My wife hath faithfully followed the same
line within her province; no woman was ever a better economist, or spun
or wove better linen; yet we must perish, perish like wild beasts, included
within a ring of fire!

Yes, I will cheerfully embrace that resource, it is an holy inspiration: by
night and by day, it presents itself to my mind: I have carefully revolved
the scheme; I have considered in all its future effects and tendencies, the
new mode of living we must pursue, without salt, without spices, without
linen and with little other clothing; the art of hunting, we must acquire, the
new manners we must adopt, the new language we must speak; the dangers
attending the education of my children we must endure. These changes
may appear more terrific at a distance perhaps than when grown familiar
by practice: what is it to us, whether we eat well made pastry, or pounded
àlagrichés; well roasted beef, or smoked venison; cabbages, or squashes?
Whether we wear neat home-spun, or good beaver; whether we sleep on
feather-beds, or on bear-skins? The difference is not worth attending to.
The difficulty of the language, fear of some great intoxication among the
Indians; finally, the apprehension lest my younger children should be caught
by that singular charm, so dangerous at their tender years; are the only considerations that startle me. By what power does it come to pass, that
children who have been adopted when young among these people, can never
be prevailed on to re-adopt European manners? Many an anxious parent I
have seen last war, who at the return of the peace, went to the Indian
villages where they knew their children had been carried in captivity; when
to their inexpressible sorrow, they found them so perfectly Indianized, that
many knew them no longer, and those whose more advanced ages permitted
them to recollect their fathers and mothers, absolutely refused to follow
them, and ran to their adopted parents for protection against the effusions
of love their unhappy real parents lavished on them! Incredible as this may
appear, I have heard it asserted in a thousand instances, among persons of
credit.

In the village of ——, where I purpose to go, there lived, about fifteen
years ago, an Englishman and a Swede, whose history would appear moving,
had I time to relate it. They were grown to the age of men when they were
taken; they happily escaped the great punishment of war captives, and were
obliged to marry the squaws who had saved their lives by adoption. By the
force of habit, they became at last thoroughly naturalized to this wild
course of life. While I was there, their friends sent them a considerable sum
of money to ransom themselves with. The Indians, their old masters, gave

them their choice, and without requiring any consideration, told them, that they had been long as free as themselves. They chose to remain; and the reasons they gave me would greatly surprise you: the most perfect freedom, the ease of living, the absence of those cares and corroding solicitudes which so often prevail with us; the peculiar goodness of the soil they cultivated, for they did not trust altogether to hunting; all these, and many more motives, which I have forgot, made them prefer that life, of which we entertain such dreadful opinions.

It cannot be, therefore, so bad as we generally conceive it to be; there must be in their social bond something singularly captivating, and far superior to anything to be boasted of among us; for thousands of Europeans are Indians, and we have no examples of even one of those aborigines having from choice become Europeans! There must be something more congenial to our native dispositions, than the fictitious society in which we live; or else why should children, and even grown persons, become in a short time so invincibly attached to it? There must be something very bewitching in their manners, something very indelible and marked by the very hands of nature. For, take a young Indian lad, give him the best education you possibly can, load him with your bounty, with presents, nay with riches; yet he will secretly long for his native woods, which you would imagine he must have long since forgot; and on the first opportunity he can possibly find, you will see him voluntarily leave behind him all you have given him, and return with inexpressible joy to lie on the mats of his fathers.

Mr.——, some years ago, received from a good old Indian, who died in his house, a young lad, of nine years of age, his grandson. He kindly educated him with his children, and bestowed on him the same care and attention in respect to the memory of his venerable grandfather, who was a worthy man. He intended to give him a genteel trade, but in the spring season when all the family went to the woods to make their maple sugar, he suddenly disappeared; and it was not until seventeen months after that his benefactor heard he had reached the village of Bald Eagle, where he still dwelt.

Let us say what we will of them, of their inferior organs, of their want of bread, etc., they are as stout and well made as the Europeans. Without temples, without priests, without kings, and without laws, they are in many instances superior to us; and the proofs of what I advance are that they live without care, sleep without inquietude, take life as it comes, bearing all its asperities with unparalleled patience, and die without any kind of apprehension for what they have done, or for what they expect to meet with hereafter. What system of philosophy can give us so many necessary qualifications for happiness? They most certainly are much more closely connected with nature than we are; they are her immediate children, the inhabitants of the woods are her undefiled offspring: those of the plains are her degenerated breed, far, very far removed from her primitive laws, from her original design.

It is therefore resolved on. I will either die in the attempt or succeed; better perish all together in one fatal hour, than to suffer what we daily endure. I do not expect to enjoy in the village of—— an uninterrupted happiness; it cannot be our lot, let us live where we will; I am not founding my future prosperity on golden dreams. Place mankind where you will, they must always have adverse circumstances to struggle with; from nature, accidents, constitution; from seasons, from that great combination of mischances which perpetually lead us to new diseases, to poverty, etc. Who knows but I may meet in this new situation, some accident from whence may spring up new sources of unexpected prosperity? Who can be presumptuous enough to predict all the good? Who can foresee all the evils which strew the paths of our lives? But after all, I cannot but recollect what sacrifice I am going to make, what amputation I am going to suffer, what transition I am going to experience.

BENJAMIN FRANKLIN
(1706–1790)

During his long and varied career, Benjamin Franklin several times had occasion to involve himself in Indian matters. Franklin's early interest in the Indians is evidenced by the thirteen Indian treaties published by his press. As a representative to the Assembly from Philadelphia, Franklin helped negotiate with the Ohio Indians the Treaty at Carlisle in 1753. During the French and Indian War, Franklin led three hundred volunteers in a defense of the Pennsylvania frontier and construction of a fort at Gnadenhütten. Later, when a peaceful settlement of Indians was attacked by the Paxton Boys, Franklin wrote a highly rhetorical condemnation of the massacre, "A Narrative of the Late Massacres in Lancaster County, 1764." In all these political activities of Franklin there is a certain consistency, for Franklin believed in the wisdom of Penn's policies toward the Indians and maintained that union among the colonies was imperative to defend against the French and Indian alliance.

Franklin did not formulate on paper his philosophical ideas concerning the Indians until late in life. The essay here printed is the best general statement by Franklin of his attitude toward the Indians. That attitude seems to have been deeply influenced by the Quakers, for Franklin, like Woolman and Penn and Bartram, sought to understand the Indian ways and, by comparison of these ways with those of the white man, to show the fallacy of whites in thinking their own ways superior. The "Remarks" represent as well the first major attack on the term "savage," hitherto used unthinkingly by even those white writers sympathetic to the Indians.

Remarks Concerning the Savages of North America, 1784

Savages we call them, because their manners differ from ours, which we think the perfection of civility; they think the same of theirs.

Perhaps, if we could examine the manners of different nations with impartiality, we should find no people so rude, as to be without any rules of politeness; nor any so polite, as not to have some remains of rudeness.

The Indian men, when young, are hunters and warriors; when old, counsellors; for all their government is by counsel of the sages; there is no force, there are no prisons, no officers to compel obedience, or inflict punishment. Hence they generally study oratory, the best speaker having the most influence. The Indian women till the ground, dress the food, nurse and bring up the children, and preserve and hand down to posterity the memory of public transactions. These employments of men and women are accounted natural and honorable. Having few artificial wants, they have abundance of leisure for improvement by conversation. Our laborious manner of life, compared with theirs, they esteem slavish and base; and the learning on which we value ourselves they regard as frivolous and useless. An instance of this occurred at the Treaty of Lancaster, in Pennsylvania, *anno* 1744, between the Government of Virginia and the Six Nations. After the principal business was settled, the commissioners from Virginia acquainted the Indians by a speech that there was at Williamsburg a College, with a fund for educating Indian youth; and that if the Six Nations would send down half a dozen of their young lads to that college, the government would take care that they should be well provided for and instructed in all the learning of the white people. It is one of the Indian rules of politeness not to answer a public proposition the same day that it is made; they think it would be treating it as a light matter and that they show it respect by taking time to consider it, as a matter important. They therefore deferred their answer till the day following; when their speaker began by expressing their deep sense of the kindness of the Virginia government in making

The Writings of Benjamin Franklin, vol. 10, ed. Albert Henry Smyth (New York, 1906), pp. 97–105.

them that offer; "for we know," says he, "that you highly esteem the
kind of learning taught in those colleges, and that the maintenance of
our young men, while with you, would be very expensive to you. We
are convinced, therefore, that you mean to do us good by your proposal;
and we thank you heartily. But you, who are wise, must know that
different nations have different conceptions of things; and you will
therefore not take it amiss, if our ideas of this kind of education happen
not to be the same with yours. We have had some experience of it;
several of our young people were formerly brought up at the colleges of
the northern provinces; they were instructed in all your sciences; but,
when they came back to us, they were bad runners, ignorant of every
means of living in the woods, unable to bear either cold or hunger, knew
neither how to build a cabin, take a deer, or kill an enemy, spoke our
language imperfectly, were therefore neither fit for hunters, warriors,
nor counsellors; they were totally good for nothing. We are however not
the less obliged by your kind offer, though we decline accepting it; and,
to show our grateful sense of it, if the gentlemen of Virginia will send
us a dozen of their sons, we will take great care of their education,
instruct them in all we know, and make *Men* of them."

Having frequent occasions to hold public councils, they have acquired
great order and decency in conducting them. The old men sit in the
foremost ranks, the warriors in the next, and the women and children
in the hindmost. The business of the women is to take exact notice of
what passes, imprint it in thier memories (for they have no writing), and
communicate it to their children. They are the records of the council,
and they preserve traditions of the stipulations in treaties 100 years back;
which, when we compare with our writings, we always find exact. He
that would speak, rises. The rest observe a profound silence. When he
has finished and sits down, they leave him five or six minutes to recollect,
that, if he has omitted anything he intended to say, or has anything to
add, he may rise again and deliver it. To interrupt another, even in
common conversation, is reckoned highly indecent. How different this
is from the conduct of a polite British House of Commons, where scarce
a day passes without some confusion, that makes the speaker hoarse in
calling *to Order;* and how different from the mode of conversation in
many polite companies of Europe, where, if you do not deliver your
sentence with great rapidity, you are cut off in the middle of it by the
impatient loquacity of those you converse with, and never suffered to
finish it!

The politeness of these savages in conversation is indeed carried to
excess, since it does not permit them to contradict or deny the truth of
what is asserted in their presence. By this means they indeed avoid

disputes; but then it becomes difficult to know their minds, or what impression you make upon them. The missionaries who have attempted to convert them to Christianity, all complain of this as one of the great difficulties of their mission. The Indians hear with patience the truths of the gospel explained to them, and give their usual tokens of assent and approbation; you would think they were convinced. No such matter. It is mere civility.

A Swedish minister, having assembled the chiefs of the Susquehanah Indians, made a sermon to them, acquainting them with the principal historical facts on which our religion is founded; such as the fall of our first parents by eating an apple, the coming of Christ to repair the mischief, his miracles and suffering, etc. When he had finished, an Indian orator stood up to thank him. "What you have told us," says he, "is all very good. It is indeed bad to eat apples. It is better to make them all into cider. We are much obliged by your kindness in coming so far, to tell us these things which you have heard from your mothers. In return, I will tell you some of those we have heard from ours. In the beginning, our fathers had only the flesh of animals to subsist on; and if their hunting was unsuccessful, they were starving. Two of our young hunters, having killed a deer, made a fire in the woods to broil some part of it. When they were about to satisfy their hunger, they beheld a beautiful young woman descend from the clouds, and seat herself on that hill, which you see yonder among the blue mountains. They said to each other, it is a spirit that has smelt our broiling venison, and wishes to eat of it; let us offer some to her. They presented her with the tongue; she was pleased with the taste of it, and said, 'Your kindness shall be rewarded; come to this place after thirteen moons, and you shall find something that will be of great benefit in nourishing you and your children to the latest generations.' They did so, and, to their surprise, found plants they had never seen before; but which, from that ancient time, have been constantly cultivated among us, to our great advantage. Where her right hand had touched the ground, they found maize; where her left hand had touched it, they found kidney-beans; and where her backside had sat on it, they found tobacco." The good missionary, disgusted with this idle tale, said, "What I delivered to you were sacred truths; but what you tell me is mere fable, fiction, and falsehood." The Indian, offended, replied, "My brother, it seems your friends have not done you justice in your education; they have not well instructed you in the rules of common civility. You saw that we, who understand and practise those rules, believed all your stories; why do you refuse to believe ours?"

When any of them come into our towns, our people are apt to crowd round them, gaze upon them, and incommode them, where they desire to be private; this they esteem great rudeness, and the effect of the want of instruction in the rules of civility and good manners. "We have," say they, "as much curiosity as you, and when you come into our towns, we wish for opportunities of looking at you; but for this purpose we hide ourselves behind bushes, where you are to pass, and never intrude ourselves into your company."

Their manner of entering one another's village has likewise its rules. It is reckoned uncivil in travelling strangers to enter a village abruptly, without giving notice of their approach. Therefore, as soon as they arrive within hearing, they stop and hollow, remaining there till invited to enter. Two old men usually come out to them, and lead them in. There is in every village a vacant dwelling, called *the Strangers' House.* Here they are placed, while the old men go round from hut to hut, acquainting the inhabitants, that strangers are arrived, who are probably hungry and weary; and every one sends them what he can spare of victuals, and skins to repose on. When the strangers are refreshed, pipes and tobacco are brought; and then, but not before, conversation begins, with inquiries who they are, whither bound, what news, etc.; and it usually ends with offers of service, if the strangers have occasion of guides, or any necessaries for continuing their journey; and nothing is exacted for the entertainment.

The same hospitality, esteemed among them as a principal virtue, is practised by private persons; of which Conrad Weiser, our interpreter, gave me the following instance. He had been naturalized among the Six Nations and spoke well the Mohock language. In going through the Indian country, to carry a message from our Governor to the Council at Onondaga, he called at the habitation of Canassatego, an old acquaintance, who embraced him, spread furs for him to sit on, placed before him some boiled beans and venison, and mixed some rum and water for his drink. When he was well refreshed, and had lit his pipe, Canassatego began to converse with him; asked how he had fared the many years since they had seen each other; whence he then came; what occasioned the journey, etc. Conrad answered all his questions; and when the discourse began to flag, the Indian, to continue it, said, "Conrad, you have lived long among the white people, and know something of their customs; I have been sometimes at Albany, and have observed, that once in seven days they shut up their shops, and assemble all in the great house; tell me what it is for? What do they do there?" "They meet there," says Conrad, "to hear and learn *good things.*" "I do not doubt," says the Indian, "that they tell you so; they have told me the same; but I doubt the truth of what they say, and I will tell you my reasons. I went lately to Albany to sell my skins and buy blankets, knives, powder, rum, etc. You know I used generally to deal with Hans Hanson; but I was a little inclined this time to try some other merchant. However, I called first upon Hans, and asked him what he would give for beaver. He said he could not give any more than four shillings a pound; 'but,' says he, 'I cannot talk on business now; this is the day when we meet together to learn *good things,* and I am going to the meeting.' So I thought to myself, 'Since we cannot do any business today, I may as well go to the meeting too,' and I went with him. There stood up a man in black, and began to talk to the people very angrily. I did not understand what he said; but, perceiving that he looked much at me and at Hanson, I imagined he was angry at seeing me there; so I went out, sat down near the house, struck fire, and lit my pipe, waiting till the meeting should break up. I thought too, that the man had mentioned something of beaver, and I suspected it might be the subject of their meeting. So, when they came out, I accosted my merchant. 'Well, Hans,' says I, 'I hope you have agreed to give more than four shillings a pound.' 'No,' says he, 'I cannot give so much; I cannot give more than three shillings and sixpence.' I then spoke to several other dealers, but they all sung the same song,—three and sixpence,—three and sixpence. This made it clear to me, that my suspicion was right; and, that whatever they pretended of meeting to learn *good things,* the real purpose was to consult how to cheat Indians in the price of beaver. Consider but a little, Conrad, and you must be of my opinion. If they met so often to learn *good things,* they would certainly have learnt some before this time. But they are still ignorant. You know our practice. If a white man, in travelling through our country, enters one of our cabins, we all treat him as I treat you; we dry him if he is wet, we warm him if he is cold, we give him meat and drink, that he may allay his thirst and hunger; and we spread soft furs for him to rest and sleep on; we demand nothing in return. But, if I go into a white man's house at Albany, and ask for victuals and drink, they say, 'Where is your money?' and if I have none, they say, 'Get out, you Indian dog.' You see they have not yet learned those little *good things,* that we need no meetings to be instructed in, because our mothers taught them to us when we were children; and therefore it is impossible their meetings should be, as they say, for any such purpose, or have any such effect; they are only to contrive *the cheating of Indians in the price of beaver.*"

NOTE.—It is remarkable that in all ages and countries hospitality has been allow'd as the virtue of those whom the civilized were pleas'd to call barbarians. The Greeks celebrated the Scythians for it. The Saracens possessed it eminently, and it is to this day the reigning virtue of the wild Arabs. St. Paul, too, in the relation of his voyage and shipwreck on the island of Melita says the barbarous people shewed us no little kindness; for they kindled a fire, and received us every one, because of the present rain, and because of the cold.—F.

THOMAS JEFFERSON
1743–1826)

Jefferson's respect for the American Indian, particularly his love of Indian oratory, had its roots in his contacts with Indians during his college days. In the spring of 1762 he met an Indian delegation of 165 Indians led by the Cherokee chief Ontasseté, better known as Outacity. Jefferson was much impressed at that time by Outacity's farewell speech, as he was later to be impressed by Logan's speech on the murder of his family during Cresap's War. The selection from *Notes on the State of Virginia* here reprinted includes Jefferson's account of Cresap's action and Logan's speech thereon, a section which later created political difficulties for Jefferson.

Jefferson's attitudes toward racial equality, cloaked in the language and methodology of scientific investigation, have undergone much scrutiny in recent years, particularly his comments on the Negro race. But unlike his attitude toward black men, Jefferson viewed red men as equal in mind and body to white men; in fact, Jefferson's attitude toward the Indians tended to idealize rather than denigrate. Despite his attempts at scientific detachment, Jefferson was heavily influenced by the ideas, current at the time, of the American landscape as paradise and the Indian as paradisal inhabitant or noble savage. Jefferson's comments on the Indians are thus appropriately read in conjunction with the selections from William Bartram, J. Hector St. John de Crèvecoeur, and Philip Freneau.

From *Notes on the State of Virginia*, *1784*

Hitherto I have considered this hypothesis [Buffon's assertion "that the domestic animals are subject to degeneration from the climate of America"] as applied to brute animals only, and not in its extension to the man of America, whether aboriginal or transplanted. It is the opinion of Mons. de Buffon that the former furnishes no exception to it:

Although the savage of the new world is about the same height as man in our world, this does not suffice for him to constitute an exception to the general fact that all living nature has become smaller on that continent. The savage is feeble, and has small organs of generation; he has neither hair nor beard, and no ardor whatever for his female; although swifter than the European because he is better accustomed to running, he is, on the other hand, less strong in body; he is also less sensitive, and yet more timid and cowardly; he has no vivacity, no activity of mind; the activity of his body is less an exercise, a voluntary motion, than a necessary action caused by want; relieve him of hunger and thirst, and you deprive him of the active principle of all his movements; he will rest stupidly upon his legs or lying down entire days. There is no need for seeking further the cause of the isolated mode of life of these savages and their repugnance for society: the most precious spark of the fire of nature has been refused to them; they lack ardor for their females, and consequently have no love for their fellow men: not knowing this strongest and most tender of all affections, their other feelings are also cold and languid; they love their parents and children but little; the most intimate of all ties, the family connection, binds them therefore but loosely together; between family and family there is no tie at all; hence they have no communion, no commonwealth, no state of society. Physical love constitutes their only morality; their heart is icy, their society cold, and their rule harsh. They look upon their wives only as servants for all work, or as beasts of burden, which they load without consideration with the burden of their hunting, and which they compel without mercy, without gratitude, to perform tasks which are often beyond their strength. They have only few children, and they take little care of them. Everywhere the original defect appears: they are indifferent because they have little sexual capacity, and this indifference to the other sex is the fundamental defect which weakens their nature, prevents its development, and—destroying the very germs of life—uproots society at the same time. Man is here no exception to the general rule. Nature, by refusing him the power of love, has treated him worse and lowered him deeper than any animal.

Thomas Jefferson, *Notes on the State of Virginia,* ed. William Peden (Chapel Hill, N. C., 1955), pp. 58–64.

An afflicting picture indeed, which, for the honor of human nature, I am glad to believe has no original. Of the Indian of South America I know nothing; for I would not honor with the appellation of knowledge, what I derive from the fables published of them. These I believe to be just as true as the fables of Aesop. This belief is founded on what I have seen of man, white, red, and black, and what has been written of him by authors, enlightened themselves, and writing amidst an enlightened people. The Indian of North America being more within our reach, I can speak of him somewhat from my own knowledge, but more from the information of others better acquainted with him, and on whose truth and judgment I can rely.

From these sources I am able to say, in contradiction to this representation, that he is neither more defective in ardor, nor more impotent with his female, than the white reduced to the same diet and exercise: that he is brave, when an enterprise depends on bravery; education with him making the point of honor consist in the destruction of an enemy by stratagem, and in the preservation of his own person free from injury; or perhaps this is nature; while it is education which teaches us to honor force more than finesse; that he will defend himself against an host of enemies, always choosing to be killed, rather than to surrender, though it be to the whites, who he knows will treat him well: that in other situations also he meets death with more deliberation, and endures tortures with a firmness unknown almost to religious enthusiasm with us: that he is affectionate to his children, careful of them, and indulgent in the extreme: that his affections comprehend his other connections, weakening, as with us, from circle to circle, as they recede from the center: that his friendships are strong and faithful to the uttermost extremity: that his sensibility is keen, even the warriors weeping most bitterly on the loss of their children, though in general they endeavor to appear superior to human events: that his vivacity and activity of mind is equal to ours in the same situation; hence his eagerness for hunting, and for games of chance.

The women are submitted to unjust drudgery. This I believe is the case with every barbarous people. With such, force is law. The stronger sex therefore imposes on the weaker. It is civilization alone which replaces women in the enjoyment of their natural equality. That first teaches us to subdue the selfish passions, and to respect those rights in others which we value in ourselves. Were we in equal barbarism, our females would be equal drudges. The man with them is less strong than with us, but their woman stronger than ours; and both for the same obvious reason; because our man and their woman is habituated to labor, and formed by it. With both races the sex which is indulged with ease is least athletic. An Indian man is small in the hand and wrist for the same reason for which a sailor is large and strong in the arms and shoulders, and a porter in the legs and thighs.

109

They raise fewer children than we do. The causes of this are to be found, not in a difference of nature, but of circumstance. The women very frequently attending the men in their parties of war and of hunting, child-bearing becomes extremely inconvenient to them. It is said, therefore, that they have learnt the practice of procuring abortion by the use of some vegetable; and that it even extends to prevent conception for a considerable time after. During these parties they are exposed to numerous hazards, to excessive exertions, to the greatest extremities of hunger. Even at their homes the nation depends for food, through a certain part of every year, on the gleanings of the forest: that is, they experience a famine once in every year. With all animals, if the female be badly fed, or not fed at all, her young perish: and if both male and female be reduced to like want, genera-tion becomes less active, less productive. To the obstacles then of want and hazard, which nature has opposed to the multiplication of wild animals, for the purpose of restraining their numbers within certain bounds, those of labor and of voluntary abortion are added with the Indian. No wonder then if they multiply less than we do. Where food is regularly supplied, a single farm will shew more of cattle, than a whole country of forests can of buffalos. The same Indian women, when married to white traders, who feed them and their children plentifully and regularly, who exempt them from excessive drudgery, who keep them stationary and unexposed to accident, produce and raise as many children as the white women. Instances are known, under these circumstances, of their rearing a dozen children. An inhuman practice once prevailed in this country of making slaves of the Indians. (This practice commenced with the Spaniards with the first dis-covery of America.) It is a fact well known with us, that the Indian women so enslaved produced and raised as numerous families as either the whites or blacks among whom they lived.

It has been said, that Indians have less hair than the whites, except on the head. But this is a fact of which fair proof can scarcely be had. With them it is disgraceful to be hairy on the body. They say it likens them to hogs. They therefore pluck the hair as fast as it appears. But the traders who marry their women, and prevail on them to discontinue this practice, say, that nature is the same with them as with the whites. Nor, if the fact be true, is the consequence necessary which has been drawn from it. Negroes have notoriously less hair than the whites; yet they are more ardent.

But if cold and moisture be the agents of nature for diminishing the races of animals, how comes she all at once to suspend their operation as to the physical man of the new world, whom the Count acknowledges to be "about the same size as the man of our hemisphere," and to let loose their influence on his moral faculties? How has this "combination of the elements and other physical causes, so contrary to the enlargement of animal nature in this new world, these obstacles to the developement [*sic*] and formation of great germs," been arrested and suspended, so as to permit the human body to acquire its just dimensions, and by what inconceivable process has their action been directed on his mind alone? To judge of the truth of this, to form a just estimate of their genius and mental powers, more facts are wanting, and great allowance to be made for those circumstances of their situation which call for a display of particular talents only. This done, we shall probably find that they are formed in mind as well as in body, on the same module with the "Homo sapiens Europaeus."

The principles of their society forbidding all compulsion, they are to be led to duty and to enterprise by personal influence and persuasion. Hence eloquence in council, bravery and address in war, become the foundations of all consequence with them. To these acquirements all their faculties are directed. Of their bravery and address in war we have multiplied proofs, because we have been the subjects on which they were exercised. Of their eminence in oratory we have fewer examples, because it is displayed chiefly in their own councils. Some, however, we have of very superior luster. I may challenge the whole orations of Demosthenes and Cicero, and of any more eminent orator, if Europe has furnished more eminent, to produce a single passage, superior to the speech of Logan, a Mingo chief, to Lord Dunmore, when governor of this state. And, as a testimony of their talents in this line, I beg leave to introduce it, first stating the incidents necessary for understanding it.

In the spring of the year 1774, a robbery was committed by some Indians on certain land-adventurers on the river Ohio. The whites in that quarter, according to their custom, undertook to punish this outrage in a summary way. Captain Michael Cresap, and a certain Daniel Great-house, leading on these parties, surprised, at different times, travelling and hunting parties of the Indians, having their women and children with them, and murdered many. Among these were unfortunately the family of Logan, a chief celebrated in peace and war, and long distinguished as the friend of the whites. This unworthy return provoked his vengeance. He accordingly signalized himself in the war which ensued. In the autumn of the same year a decisive battle was fought at the mouth of the Great Kanhaway, between the collected forces of the Shawanese, Mingoes, and Delawares, and a detachment of the Virginia militia. The Indians were defeated, and sued for peace. Logan, however, disdained to be seen among the suppliants. But, lest the sincerity of a treaty should be distrusted, from which so distinguished a chief absented himself, he sent by a messenger the following speech to be delivered to Lord Dunmore:

I appeal to any white man to say, if ever he entered Logan's cabin hungry, and he gave him not meat; if ever he came cold and naked, and he clothed him not. During the course of the last long and bloody war, Logan remained idle in his cabin, an advocate for peace. Such was my love for the whites, that my countrymen pointed as they passed, and said, "Logan is the friend of white men." I had even thought to have lived with you, but for the injuries of one man. Col. Cresap, the last spring, in cold blood, and unprovoked, murdered all the relations of Logan, not sparing even my women and children. There runs not a drop of my blood in the veins of any living creature. This called on me for revenge. I have sought it: I have killed many: I have fully glutted my vengeance. For my country, I rejoice at the beams of peace. But do not harbor a thought that mine is the joy of fear. Logan never felt fear. He will not turn on his heel to save his life. Who is there to mourn for Logan?—Not one.

Before we condemn the Indians of this continent as wanting genius, we must consider that letters have not yet been introduced among them. Were we to compare them in their present state with the Europeans north of the Alps, when the Roman arms and arts first crossed those mountains, the comparison would be unequal, because, at that time, those parts of Europe were swarming with numbers; because numbers produce emulation, and multiply the chances of improvement, and one improvement begets another. Yet I may safely ask, How many good poets, how many able mathematicians, how many great inventors in arts or sciences, had Europe north of the Alps then produced? And it was sixteen centuries after this before a Newton could be formed. I do not mean to deny, that there are varieties in the race of man, distinguished by their powers both of body and mind. I believe there are, as I see to be the case in the races of other animals. I only mean to suggest a doubt, whether the bulk and faculties of animals depend on the side of the Atlantic on which their food happens to grow, or which furnishes the elements of which they are compounded? Whether nature has enlisted herself as a Cis or Trans-Atlantic partisan? I am induced to suspect, there has been more eloquence than sound reasoning displayed in support of this theory; that it is one of those cases where the judgment has been seduced by a glowing pen: and whilst I render every tribute of honor and esteem to the celebrated zoologist, who has added, and is still adding, so many precious things to the treasures of science, I must doubt whether in this instance he has not cherished error also, by lending her for a moment his vivid imagination and bewitching language.

WILLIAM BARTRAM
(1739–1823)

The son of the first American botanist, a Philadelphia Quaker named John Bartram, William Bartram continued in his father's field, accompanying him on an exploration of the Saint John's River in 1765-1766. William Bartram's most important botanical venture was his exploration of Georgia, the Carolinas, and Florida, under the patronage of an English Quaker, Dr. John Fothergill. This latter trip produced his literary masterpiece, *The Travels* (1791), a selection from which is printed here, and *Observations on the Creek and Cherokee Indians* (written in 1789, but unpublished until 1853). Bartram's *Travels* was, as a description of natural landscapes, an important influence on English romantics, and it remains an important source of ethnological material on the southern Indian.

Bartram's love of nature influenced his view of the Indian, for he praises the Indian as a "natural" man. In the first passage selected here, Bartram attempts with difficulty to formulate a balanced view of the Indian; more often than not Bartram praises the Indian as fully as he praises the landscape itself. The second passage here excerpted, a Susannah at the Bath scene in which Bartram encounters and is tempted by a group of Indian maidens, is a good example of Bartram's more usual rhapsodic mode. Bartram's florid style contrasts sharply with the simple, plain style of John Woolman, as the following passage from early in *The Travels* will illustrate:

How happily situated is this retired spot of earth! What an elisium it is! where the wandering Seminole, the naked red warrior, roams at large, and after the vigorous chase retires from the scorching heat of the meridian sun. Here he reclines, and reposes under the odoriferous shades of Zanthoxilon, his verdant couch guarded by the Deity; Liberty, and the Muses, inspiring him with wisdom and valor, whilst the balmy zephyrs fan him to sleep.

113

From *The Travels, 1791*

Leaving the highway on our left hand, we ascended a sandy ridge, thinly planted by nature with stately pines and oaks, of the latter genus particularly q. sinuata, s. flammula, q. nigra, q. rubra. Passed by an Indian village situated on this high, airy sand ridge, consisting of four or five habitations; none of the people were at home, they were out at their hunting camps; we observed plenty of corn in their cribs. Following a hunting path eight or nine miles, through a vast pine forest and grassy savanna, well timbered, the ground covered with a charming carpet of various flowering plants, came to a large creek of excellent water, and here we found the encampment of the Indians, the inhabitants of the little town we had passed; we saw their women and children, the men being out hunting. The women presented themselves to our view as we came up, at the door of their tents, veiled in their mantle, modestly showing their faces when we saluted them. Towards the evening we fell into the old trading path, and before night came to camp at the Halfway Pond. Next morning, after collecting together the horses, some of which had strolled away at a great distance, we pursued our journey and in the evening arrived at the trading house on St. Juan's, from a successful and pleasant tour.

On my return to the store on St. Juan's the trading schooner was there, but as she was not to return to Georgia until the autumn, I found I had time to pursue my travels in Florida, and might at leisure plan my excursions to collect seeds and roots in boxes, etc.

At this time the talks (or messages between the Indians and white people) were perfectly peaceable and friendly, both with the Lower Creeks and the Nation or Upper Creeks; parties of Indians were coming in every day with their hunts: indeed, the Muscogulges or Upper Creeks very seldom disturb us. Bad talks from the Nation are always very serious affairs, and to the utmost degree alarming to the white inhabitants.

The Muscogulges are under a more strict government or regular civilization than the Indians in general. They lie near their potent and declared enemy, the Choctaws; their country having a vast frontier, naturally accessible and open to the incursions of their enemies on all sides, they find themselves under the necessity of associating in large, populous towns, and these towns as near together as convenient that they may be enabled to succor

William Bartram, *Travels Through North and South Carolina, Georgia, East and West Florida* (London, 1792), pp. 207–212, 352–356.

and defend one another in case of sudden invasion. This consequently occasions deer and bear to be scarce and difficult to procure, which obliges them to be vigilant and industrious; this naturally begets care and serious attention, which we may suppose in some degree forms their natural disposition and manners, and gives them that air of dignified gravity, so strikingly characteristic in their aged people, and that steadiness, just and cheerful reverence in the middle aged and youth, which sits so easy upon them, and appears so natural. For, however strange it may appear to us, the same moral duties which with us form the amiable, virtuous character, so difficult to maintain, there, without compulsion or visible restraint, operates like instinct, with a surprising harmony and natural ease, insomuch that it seems impossible for them to act out of the common highroad to virtue.

We will now take a view of the Lower Creeks or Seminoles, and the natural disposition which characterizes this people, when, from the striking contrast, the philosopher may approve or disapprove, as he may think proper, from the judgment and opinion given by different men.

The Seminoles are but a weak people, with respect to numbers. All of them, I suppose, would not be sufficient to people one of the towns in the Muscogulge, for instance, the Uches on the main branch of the Apalachucla river, which alone contains near two thousand inhabitants. Yet this handful of people possesses a vast territory, all East Florida and the greatest part of West Florida, which being naturally cut and divided into thousands of islets, knolls and eminences, by the innumerable rivers, lakes, swamps, vast savannas and ponds, form so many secure retreats and temporary dwelling places, that effectually guard them from their enemies; and being such a swampy, hommocky country, furnishes such a plenty and variety of supplies for the nourishment of varieties of animals, that I can venture to assert, that no part of the globe so abounds with wild game or creatures fit for the food of man.

Thus they enjoy a superabundance of the necessaries and conveniences of life, with the security of person and property, the two great concerns of mankind. The hides of deer, bears, tigers and wolves, together with honey, wax and other productions of the country, purchase their clothing, equipage and domestic utensils from the whites. They seem to be free from want or desires. No cruel enemy to dread; nothing to give them disquietude, but the gradual encroachments of the white people. Thus contented and undisturbed, they appear as blithe and free as the birds of the air, and like them as volatile and active, tuneful and vociferous. The visage, action and deportment of a Seminole form the most striking picture of happiness in this life; joy, contentment, love and friendship, without guile or affectation, seem inherent in them, or predominant in their vital principle, for it leaves them but with the last breath of life. It even seems imposing a constraint upon their ancient chiefs and senators, to maintain a necessary decorum and solemnity, in their public councils; not even the debility and decrepitude of extreme old age is sufficient to erase from their visages, this youthful, joyous simplicity; but like the grey eve of a serene and calm day, a gladdening, cheering blush remains on the Western horizon after the sun is set.

I doubt not but some of my countrymen who may read these accounts of the Indians, which I have endeavored to relate according to truth, at least as they appeared to me, will charge me with partiality or prejudice in their favor.

I will, however, now endeavor to exhibit their vices, immoralities and imperfections, from my own observations and knowledge, as well as accounts from the white traders, who reside amongst them.

The Indians make war against, kill and destroy their own species, and their motives spring from the same erroneous source as they do in all other nations of mankind; that is, the ambition of exhibiting to their fellows, a superior character of personal and national valor, and thereby immortalizing themselves, by transmitting their names with honor and lust to posterity; or revenge of their enemy, for public or personal insults; or lastly, to extend the borders and boundaries of their territories. But I cannot find upon the strictest inquiry that their bloody contests at this day are marked with deeper stains of inhumanity or savage cruelty than what may be observed amongst the most civilized nations: they do indeed scalp their slain enemy, but they do not kill the females or children of either sex: the most ancient traders, both in the Lower and Upper Creeks, assured me they never saw an instance of either burning or tormenting their male captives; though it is said they used to do it formerly. I saw in every town in the Nation and Seminoles that I visited, more or less male captives, some extremely aged, who were free and in as good circumstances as their masters; and all slaves have their freedom when they marry, which is permitted and encouraged, when they and their offspring are every way upon an equality with their conquerors. They are given to adultery and fornication, but I suppose in no greater excess than other nations of men. They punish the delinquents, male and female, equally alike, by taking off their ears. This is the punishment for adultery. Infamy and disgrace is supposed to be a sufficient punishment for fornication, in either sex.

They are fond of games and gambling, and amuse themselves like children in relating extravagant stories to cause surprise and mirth.

They wage eternal war against deer and bear, to procure food and clothing, and other necessaries and conveniences; which is indeed carried to an unreasonable and perhaps criminal excess, since the white people have dazzled their senses with foreign superfluities.

. . . .

After riding near two miles through Indian plantations of corn, which was well cultivated, kept clean of weeds and was well advanced, being near eighteen inches in height, and the beans planted at the corn-hills were above ground; we left the fields on our right, turning towards the mountains and ascending through a delightful green vale or lawn, which conducted us in amongst the pyramidal hills and crossing a brisk flowing creek, meandering through the meads which continued near two miles, dividing and branching in amongst the hills. We then mounted their steep ascents, rising gradually by ridges or steps one above another, frequently crossing narrow, fertile dales as we ascended; the air felt cool and animating, being charged with the fragrant breath of the mountain beauties, the blooming mountain cluster rose, blushing rhododendron and fair lily of the valley. Having now attained the summit of this very elevated ridge, we enjoyed a fine prospect indeed; the enchanting vale of Keowe, perhaps as celebrated for fertility, fruitfulness and beautiful prospects as the fields of Pharsalia or the vale of Temple; the town, the elevated peaks of the Jore mountains, a very distant prospect of the Jore village in a beautiful lawn, lifted up many thousand feet higher than our present situation, besides a view of many other villages and settlements on the sides of the mountains, at various distances and elevations; the silver rivulets gliding by them and snow white cataracts glimmering on the sides of the lofty hills; the bold promontories of the Jore mountain stepping into the Tanase river, whilst his foaming waters rushed between them.

After viewing this very entertaining scene we began to descend the mountain on the other side, which exhibited the same order of gradations of ridges and vales as on our ascent, and at length rested on a very expansive, fertile plain, amidst the towering hills, over which we rode a long time, through magnificent high forests, extensive green fields, meadows and lawns. Here had formerly been a very flourishing settlement, but the Indians deserted it in search of fresh planting land, which they soon found in a rich vale but a few miles' distance over a ridge of hills. Soon after entering on these charming, sequestered, prolific fields, we came to a fine little river, which crossing, and riding over fruitful strawberry beds and green lawns, on the sides of a circular ridge of hills in front of us, and going round the bases of this promontory, came to a fine meadow on an arm of the vale, through which meandered a brook, its humid vapors bedewing the fragrant strawberries which hung in heavy red clusters over the grassy verge. We crossed the rivulet, then rising a sloping, green, turfy ascent, alighted on the borders of a grand forest of stately trees, which we penetrated on foot a little distance to a horse-stamp, where was a large squadron of those useful creatures, belonging to my friend and companion, the trader, on the sight of whom they assembled together from all quarters; some at a distance saluted him with shrill neighings of gratitude, or came prancing up to lick the salt out of his hand, whilst the younger and more timorous came galloping onward, but coyly wheeled off, and fetching a circuit stood aloof; but as soon as their lord and master strewed the crystalline salty bait on the hard beaten ground, they all, old and young, docile and timorous, soon formed themselves in ranks and fell to licking up the delicious morsel.

It was a fine sight; more beautiful creatures I never saw; there were of them of all colors, sizes and dispositions. Every year as they become of age he sends off a troop of them down to Charleston, where they are sold to the highest bidder.

Having paid our attention to this useful part of the creation, who, if they are under our dominion, have consequently a right to our protection and favor, we returned to our trusty servants that were regaling themselves in the exuberant sweet pastures and strawberry fields in sight, and mounted again. Proceeding on our return to town, continued through part of this high forest skirting on the meadows; began to ascend the hills of a ridge which we were under the necessity of crossing, and having gained its summit, enjoyed a most enchanting view, a vast expanse of green meadows and strawberry fields; a meandering river gliding through, saluting in its various turnings the swelling, green, turfy knolls embellished with parterres of flowers and fruitful strawberry beds; flocks of turkeys strolling about them; herds of deer prancing in the meads or bounding over the hills; companies of young, innocent Cherokee virgins, some busy gathering the rich fragrant fruit, others having already filled their baskets, lay reclined under the shade of floriferous and fragrant native bowers of magnolia, azalea, philadelphus, perfumed calycanthus, sweet yellow jessamine and cerulian glycine frutescens, disclosing their beauties to the fluttering breeze, and bathing their limbs in the cool fleeting streams, whilst other parties, more gay and libertine, were yet collecting strawberries or wantonly chasing their companions, tantalizing them, staining their lips and cheeks with the rich fruit.

This sylvan scene of primitive innocence was enchanting, and perhaps too enticing for hearty young men long to continue idle spectators.

In fine, nature prevailing over reason, we wished at least to have a more active part in their delicious sports. Thus precipitately resolving, we cautiously made our approaches, yet undiscovered, almost to the joyous scene of action. Now, although we meant no other than an innocent frolic with this gay assembly of hamadryads, we shall leave it to the person of feeling and sensibility to form an idea to what lengths our passions might have hurried us, thus warmed and excited, had it not been for the vigilance and care of some envious matrons who lay in ambush, and espying us gave the alarm, time enough for the nymphs to rally and assemble together. We, however, pursued and gained ground on a group of them, who had incautiously strolled to a greater distance from their guardians, and finding their retreat now like to be cut off, took shelter under cover of a little grove, but on perceiving themselves to be discovered by us, kept their station, peeping through the bushes; when observing our approaches, they confidently discovered themselves and decently advanced to meet us, half unveiling their blooming faces, incarnated with the modest maiden blush, and with native innocence and cheerfulness, presented their little baskets, merrily telling us their fruit was ripe and sound.

We accepted a basket, sat down and regaled ourselves on the delicious fruit, encircled by the whole assembly of the innocently jocose sylvan nymphs; by this time the several parties under the conduct of the elder matrons, had disposed themselves in companies on the green, turfy banks.

My young companion, the trader, by concessions and suitable apologies for the bold intrusion, having compromised the matter with them, engaged them to bring their collections to his house at a stipulated price; we parted friendly.

And now taking leave of these Elysian fields, we again mounted the hills, which we crossed, and traversing obliquely their flowery beds, arrived in town in the cool of the evening.

PHILIP FRENEAU

(1752–1832)

A classmate of James Madison and Henry Brackenridge at Princeton, Freneau was deeply influenced by the revolutionary spirit which pervaded the class of 1771. Together with Brackenridge, he composed a commencement poem, "On the Rising Glory of America." After a period at sea, Freneau joined the revolution as a blockade runner and was captured by the British and held on their prison ship *Scorpion,* an experience which led to his violently anti-Tory poem *The British Prison-Ship* (1781). Following the war, Freneau became for a time a sea captain and entered one of his most productive poetic periods. He sought in his poetry distinctly American themes presented in a simple style, and it is to this period that "The Indian Burying Ground" belongs.

Freneau returned in 1791 to the essay form as editor of the Jeffersonian paper the *National Gazette.* His speech was direct and his satire sharp, prompting Washington to comment on "that rascal, Freneau." An example of Freneau's prose style follows "The Indian Burying Ground" and forms a fitting conclusion to the eighteenth-century views of the Indian. Freneau's essay takes the form of a dream vision in which a carved Indian figurehead speaks. Indian oratory becomes a vehicle for satire as the Indian reviews the treatment of his people by white men since the arrival of Columbus. The sense of regret which dominates the tone of the speech accentuates the message of this early example of the vanishing American theme.

Lines Occasioned by a Visit to An Old Indian Burying Ground, 1788

In spite of all the learn'd have said
I still my old opinion keep;
The posture that we give the dead
Points out the soul's eternal sleep.

Not so the ancients of these lands;—
The Indian, when from life releas'd,
Again is seated with his friends,
And shares again the joyous feast.

His imag'd birds, and painted bowl,
And ven'son, for a journey drest,
Bespeak the nature of the soul,
Activity, that wants no rest.

His bow for action ready bent,
And arrows, with a head of bone,
Can only mean that life is spent,
And not the finer essence gone.

Thou, stranger, that shalt come this way,
No fraud upon the dead commit,
Yet, mark the swelling turf, and say,
They do not lie, but here they sit.

Here, still a lofty rock remains,
On which the curious eye may trace
(Now wasted half by wearing rains)
The fancies of a ruder race.

Here, still an aged elm aspires,
Beneath whose far projecting shade
(And which the shepherd still admires)
The children of the forest play'd.

The Miscellaneous Works of Mr. Philip Freneau (Philadelphia, 1788), pp. 188–189.

There oft a restless Indian queen,
(Pale Marian with her braided hair)
And many a barbarous form is seen
To chide the man that lingers there.

By midnight moons, o'er moistening dews,
In vestments for the chace array'd,
The hunter still the deer pursues,
The hunter and the deer—a shade.

And long shall timorous Fancy see
The painted chief, and pointed spear,
And reason's self shall bow the knee
To shadows and delusions here.

From *The National Gazette, 1792*

All our curious dock-walkers must have taken notice of the fine Indian Head of the ship Delaware, *belonging to this port. Whether it was from a late attentive survey of that figure (which is a model of perfection in its kind) or from what other cause I know not, but upon my retiring to rest a few nights ago, I no sooner fell asleep than I imagined myself standing upon one of the wharves, with the carved Indian figure full in my front; when it instantly assumed the mien and attitude of an orator, and with a menacing frown uttered the following speech to a crowd that had collected upon this extraordinary occasion.*

I have every reason to believe, gentlemen, that I was placed here as the emblem of valor, activity, perseverance, industry and cunning. So far, therefore, have your countrymen testified in favor of an opinion, almost universally exploded, that the inhabitants of the western forests have some affinity with the human species. I wish they had gone a little farther, and in their general conduct towards our tribes in peace and war treated us as beings possessed of reason, and practicing some few of the inferior virtues. Alas, it is too evident from their actions that they place us upon a footing with the beasts of the wilderness, and consider an Indian and a buffalo as

National Gazette, Philadelphia, January 12, 1792.

alike entitled by nature to property or possession.

My heart bleeds within me when I reflect upon the wrongs of my countrymen, the insignificant rank they appear to hold in the scale of animated being, and their probable extirpation from the continent of America.

Nature is cruel in all her works. She successively destroys not only the individuals of a species, but at certain periods a whole class of a species; nay, even the species itself sometimes totally disappears. This cruel mother is nevertheless so merciful as, for the most part, to bring about such events imperceptibly and gradually. Why then would you anticipate her designs, and by every means in your power hurry us in a moment from this earth before nature has said, *There is an end to the children of the forest?*

Our habitations were once on the borders of the rivers of the ocean, and in the pleasant vicinity of its shores. The sails of Columbus, and Cabot, and Raleigh appeared. With grief we saw your superior skill, your surprising pre-eminence in art, your machines of death before which our arrows and darts were no more than the toys of children. In dread of your superior power, we retreated from the shore to the Allegheny; from the Allegheny to the Ohio; we have bid an everlasting adieu to the pleasant land of Kentucky; you have at length followed us over the Ohio—you meditate to drive us beyond the Mississippi—to the lake of the woods, to the frozen deserts of the north, and to the regions of darkness and desolation. But how unreasonable, how cruel are your designs. Compelling us to remove farther into the forests is the same to us as death and ruin. We must there fight for the possession of the soil before we can hunt in safety, as independent possessors; and as we retreat before you, remember that foes of our own color and kindred increase upon us, like swarms from the hollow tree: nations extremely tenacious of their hunting grounds, less enervated with your baneful liquors than ourselves, and consequently more warlike, more robust, and even gods, in comparison to the feeble tribes who yet exist between you and them.

You detest us for having the feelings of men; you despise, in us, the virtue of patriotism, so natural to all mankind and so extolled by yourselves. But what were your feelings when, only a few years ago, the great king on the other side of the water intruded upon your rights? You filled the world with your clamors—heaven and earth were called to witness that you were determined to defend those rights which had been bestowed upon you by the Great Man above, and for the preservation of which you prayed him to smile upon your warfare. He heard your prayers, and you were successful; the enemy retired with shame, and your warfare was crowned with an honorable peace.

You yourselves are now, in your turn, become the oppressors. Do not blame us then for possessing the same feelings with yourselves on the same occasion. Your desperation carried all before it, and why would not ours do the same, when we are obliged to act against you from the same motives?

Say not that you have purchased our territory. Was a keg of whiskey, some bundles of laced coats, or a few packages of blankets an equivalent for the extent of a kingdom? Or was a bargain with some drunken chiefs of one or two nations an obligation upon an hundred tribes?

How much do ye stand in your own light, ye free white men of America—How are you duped by the deep and designing! Not a single soldier need be sent to act offensively in the Indian country. Our commercial intercourse with you would effectually destroy us as fast as you could advance your frontier by cultivation and natural population. Your neighborhood is death to us. We cannot exist among you—but suffer us, we beseech you, to disappear gradually from this miserable stage of human existence, and not like a taper, by a sudden blast, be extinguished in a moment!

You have, at different times, been at much expense in sending among us religious missionaries to effect our conversion to your faith. I wish those gentlemen had been as assiduous in inculcating the practice of the moral and social virtues as they were busy in pestering us with mysteries.—They have, however, said enough upon the virtue of *temperance* to persuade us not to destroy ourselves with rum, brandy, or New-England whiskey during the remainder of the present century.—These good men have now quit us entirely, and given us up to the god of nature—you send armies in their room, not to convert, but to destroy us, to burn our towns and turn us out naked to the mercy of the elements; to shoot us down wherever they can see us, and propagate a principle as disgraceful to your pretended age of philosophy as it is repugnant to truth and reason, *that the rights of an Indian are not the rights of a man!*—

Being suddenly awaked by the yelpings of a spaniel that constantly sleeps at the foot of my bed, I lost the remainder of this extraordinary speech.

PART TWO

The Nineteenth Century

INTRODUCTION

Like the two centuries of active colonization that preceded it, the nineteenth century was marked by Indian-white conflict. It was the same story of inappeasable land hunger on the part of whites, yet troublesomely different, for it was the century in which the power and independence of all tribes were destroyed. In earlier years, although whole tribes of the eastern regions had been decimated, Indians were still a power to be faced in the western territories. After the Massacre at Wounded Knee, in 1890, this was no longer true.

The United States grew from a country of sixteen states, bordered by Kentucky and Tennessee, in 1800, to a continental nation in 1900; this expansion drove most Indians from their homelands and made their ways of life untenable. Two vivid images summarize the events of a century: the buffalo hides stacked high by the sides of raw railroad depots in the 1880s;[1] the appearance of Ishi, the last survivor of the Yana, in the butcher's corral in Oroville, California, in 1911.[2]

There were complex reasons, cultural, psychological, and economic, for this destruction of Indian cultures, but one immediate political cause was the defeat of the British in the Revolution and in the War of 1812. Once Indian leaders saw that it was impossible to dislodge the Europeans entirely, some shrewdly realized that a foreign administration would be less interested in the desires of colonial subjects than a home government, and more approachable on a nation-to-nation basis. One example was the Mohawk Joseph Brant, who set aside the ambitions of earlier leaders like Philip and Pontiac; he supported the English king, whose royal governor fathered Brant's sister's children. As the French were preferable to the English in the eighteenth century, so the English were preferable to the new Americans in the nineteenth.[3] How wise, if unlucky, a decision this was can be seen in the events that followed.

The new American government responded quickly to its expansionist constituency as well as to those who desired retaliation for Indian participation in the British cause. First the Indian trade was restricted to profiteering American citizens. Then, in 1830, the government passed the Removal Bill. This legislation provided for the forcible ejection of Indians from their home territories whenever those lands were desired by white citizens. Resettlement was accompanied by brutality and hardship, much of it caused by cheating on the part of suppliers. Best known among the Removal tragedies was that of the Cherokees, forced to march to Oklahoma from Georgia, where they had been farmers, businessmen, publishers of their own community newspaper. Other tribes also suffered dislocations of such magnitude; many of these stories remain to be told.[4]

Throughout the period in which the republic was pushing westward, new groups of Indians were met whose occupancy of the land was an obstacle to white settlement. Warlike or peaceable, sedentary or roving, they were victims of a policy which recognized no significant distinctions. Treaties were written, but the underlying tone of them, echoed by the rhetoric, was that of father to child. Just as a parent offers his child a bargain that sounds like an adult arrangement while it takes advantage of the child's naiveté, so the United States government "bought" homelands with hatchets, glass beads, pots and pans, and gunpowder. Again, like the parent who waives the whole agreement when it suits him, the government of the whites conveniently forgot that some treaties bound them for "as long as grass grows and water runs." Even so conscientious a president as Lincoln believed that arable land should not be left in the possession of those who did not farm it.

In a speech of March 27, 1863, Lincoln addressed a group of visiting Indians in a typical manner. First he showed them a globe and called on a scientist to describe the formation of the earth and point out other nations of the "pale-faced people." Beneath the layer of condescension one can discern a show of force. Lincoln staged an event intended to lower the morale of Indians who hoped for government support of treaty obligations. One wonders what the Indians made of the indulgent tone of Lincoln's concluding remarks:

It is the object of this Government to be on terms of peace with you, and with all our red brethren. We constantly endeavor to be so. We make treaties with you, and will try to observe them; and if our children should sometimes behave badly, and violate these treaties, it is against our wish.

You know it is not always possible for any father to have his children do precisely as he wishes them to do.

The charade of treaty-writing finally came to an end in the 1870s; during these years and those that followed, Crazy Horse, Chief Joseph, and Geronimo heroically tried to lead their people in resistance. While they enjoyed a few triumphs, like the defeat of Custer at the Battle of Little Big Horn, in 1876, the Plains Indians, like those of other tribes, found themselves weakened by disunity and demoralization. Starved and harried by the whites, they experienced a revival of the Messiah religion that had arisen intermittently among desperate tribes throughout the century. The whites' panicky response to what they called the Ghost Dance summed up not only "a century of dishonor,"[5] but a century of misunderstanding.

Most white Americans of the nineteenth century saw Indians as members of a doomed race. Occupied by the great facts of their time—the settlement of a moving frontier, the misery of Civil War, the growth of cities, increasing mechanization—they were supported by a secularized version of providential history. For them, the earth had been made fertile so that it might be cultivated; the western hemisphere discovered so that it might be peopled. Accepting the early tradition that the country was theirs by rights of discovery and conquest, they saw their displacement of the Indians as morally justified and inevitable. Even those who objected to brutal government practices rarely questioned the desirability of substituting "civilized" for "savage" nations. Exemplifying this sanguine view is Ralph Waldo Emerson's comment: "When the Indian trail gets widened, graded, and bridged to a good road, there is a benefactor, there is a missionary, a pacificator, a wealth-bringer, a maker of markets, a vent for industry."[6]

The inheritance, however diluted, of Puritan attitudes toward God, work, material acquisition, and land predisposed white Americans to harsh judgments of Indians. The Puritan was made in the image of a judging, jealous God; he and his descendants regarded Indian forms of worship as ignorant idolatry, dangerous and ridiculous. If Indian animism was not devil worship, it was gibberish. The persistence of the Puritan identification of "the savage" with the devil can be seen in Nathaniel Hawthorne's "Young Goodman Brown" and *The Scarlet Letter.*

Indians were children who would not work, who had not grasped the principle of harnessing nature to produce wealth. As respect for machinery grew with new developments—the telegraph, the sewing machine, the cotton gin—scorn for Indians was redoubled. Cotton Mather's contempt for the fools who did not use the wheel even after its uses were made plain to them, was amplified, one-hundred-fifty years later, in Horace Greeley's diatribe:

But the Indians are children. Their arts, wars, treaties, alliances, habitations, crafts, properties, commerce, comforts, all belong to the very lowest and rudest ages of human existence. Some few of the chiefs have a narrow and short-sighted shrewdness, and very rarely in their history, a really great man, like Pontiac or Tecumseh, has arisen among them; but this does not shake the general truth that they are utterly incompetent to cope in any way with the European or Caucasian race. Any band of schoolboys, from ten to fifteen years of age, are quite as capable of ruling their appetites, devising and upholding a public policy, constituting and conducting a state or community, as an average Indian tribe.[7]

Certainly the Indian understanding of the relation between man and nature was meaningless to most whites, whose Bible described the wilderness as a place of trial. The whites' ideal was a cultivated landscape, a land flowing with milk and honey. This preference is well expressed in the prologue to a popular Indian drama, *Metamora; or, The Last of the Wampanoags:*

> Now flies my hope-winged fancy o'er the gulf
> That lies between us and the after-time
> When this fine portion of the globe shall teem
> With civilized society; when arts
> And industry, and elegance shall reign
> As the shrill war-cry of the savage man
> Yields to the jocund shepherd's roundelay.[8]

In this materialistic view, nature becomes the commodity that man shapes to his own uses. Before the twentieth century there were very few white spokesmen for leaving lands uncultivated; even "improving" for recreational uses has been considered more desirable than leaving untouched wilderness. This view has remained a dominant one in the American philosophy of land use. It is only now that unimproved lands have nearly disappeared that ecology, the understanding of nature's hidden uses, has become a familiar science, and has provoked the reevaluation of Indian cultures.[9]

Of course, some whites did glory in the challenge of wild land: frontiersmen, traders, explorers. With few exceptions, however, they regarded nature as adversary, considering themselves necessary forerunners of permanent settlements. Daniel Boone, Davy Crockett, and the river and mountain men who have passed into legend lived lives of action rather than contemplation; many fled organized society not because of love of the wilds but because of hatred of civil restraints. Some of them, like Buffalo Bill, were caught in the painful position of being expert exterminators of the Indians whose way of life they adopted and respected.

Finally, the most important development of the Puritan inheritance in the nineteenth century was the growth of unrestrained chauvinism. The Puritans had an exaggerated sense of their significance in a God-centered universe. Many of them even came to accept the convenient heresy that their material prosperity was a sign of grace. Accepting a secular version of similar reasoning, nineteenth-century Americans proved the worth of their civilization by pointing to its successful exploitation of the continent's wealth. Prosperity encouraged them to express feelings of moral and intellectual superiority to others, emotions that cloaked a hidden sense of cultural inferiority to Europeans. Roy Harvey Pearce suggests that American whites resolved their uneasy psychological position by investing Indians with all the characteristics that were unacceptable to them in themselves. Summing these up in the single word "savagery," they hardened themselves to deal brutally with the Indian.[10] The old Puritan definition of a world divided between damned and saved persisted in the nineteenth-century dualism of defeated savagery, victorious civilization.

Despite these conditions for misunderstanding and contempt, another philosophic strain in nineteenth-century America was more congenial to Indian-white rapprochement. Not all whites who were influenced by the scientific discoveries of the enlightenment interpreted these gains in material terms; revelations of order, beauty, and symmetry in nature led some to deism. In turn, awareness of God-in-nature grew into appreciation of the wilds and disposed thinkers to favorable reception of the ideas of European romantics. One American, the naturalist William Bartram, who walked from Pennsylvania to Florida in the 1780s, reversed the usual pattern and exerted a significant influence on Coleridge and Wordsworth.

Thomas Jefferson, in his scientific study of the flora and fauna of the eastern United States, gave great impetus to lovers of wild nature. In his *Notes on the State of Virginia,* Jefferson drew attention to the natural beauties of the American landscape; the work of the painter John James Audubon is an example of how a combined scientific and artistic concern developed in the early nineteenth century.

In the 1830s and 40s, a new religious movement known as Transcendentalism turned its adherents away from churches and formal creeds and taught them to regard nature and themselves as expressions of divine spirit. Transcendentalism's chief spokesman, Emerson, explicitly challenged the view of nature as commodity, but he was a believer in progress and perfectibility. This optimism, combined with his firm planting in long-established New England, limited his commentary on the destruction of wilderness and its inhabitants. The Transcendentalists turned to the Orient for inspiration, not to the American West; only Thoreau, who admittedly felt more comfortable walking through his neighbor's woodlot, experienced and recorded

131

"the light that shone in the wilderness" for him.

Although writers and artists turned in increasing numbers to native themes, pride in American resources did not, in itself, promote a sympathetic understanding of Indian life. Too often those most open to such understanding remained in the cities and villages of the Northeast; on the frontier it was easier to see wilderness as threatening than as sublime. Moreover, so much artistic energy was absorbed in asserting equal competence with Europeans that little was left for investing in difficult subjects. Thus the art historian James Thomas Flexner comments, "One of the most surprising phenomena of American painting is how very little authentic and effective esthetic advantage was taken of the existence on this continent of those exotic peoples, the Indians."[11]

There were attempts to remedy this neglect among social scientists in the nineteenth century. Seeing good in nature, some saw good in the so-called natural man; they questioned the prevailing negative view of Indians. Along with missionaries, traders and explorers, a few practitioners of the new science of ethnology began to travel among Indian tribes. Among these were John Heckewelder, a Moravian missionary whose favorable view of the Delawares in *History, Manners and Customs of the Indian Nations who once Inhabited Pennsylvania and the Neighboring States* gave James Fenimore Cooper the material he needed; Henry Rowe Schoolcraft, whose *Algic Researches, comprising Inquiries respecting the Mental Characteristics of the North American Indians* provided material for Henry Wadsworth Longfellow; Lewis Henry Morgan, whose *League of the Iroquois* was one of the first major works of the new science of ethnology; Frank Hamilton Cushing, whose observation of the Zuñi helped inaugurate the Smithsonian Institute's Bureau of Ethnology. Toward the end of the century, other famous students of the Indian—Alfred Kroeber, George Bird Grinnell, Clark Wissler—continued this work; the magnificent photographs of Edward C. Curtis and the documentary paintings and commentary of George Catlin are other high points in a record of sympathetic views.

Two strong European influences must be noted here. Jean Jacques Rousseau's celebration of natural man gave renewed interest to a longstanding myth of the noble savage; François René de Chateaubriand helped to naturalize that myth on American soil with his novels *Atala* (1801) and *René* (1802). Criticizing high culture and centers of intellectual life, Rousseau and Chateaubriand suggested that goodness and strength would come from those who lived in harmony with beneficent nature. These European romantics were most admired by those who did their imagining far from the frontier. The most important American writer affected was James Fenimore Cooper, who superimposed the mythic noble savage on material gathered from Heckewelder. He produced figures of heroic proportion who embody severe criticism of the white-European development of the continent. Though Mark Twain and others have criticized him sharply, Cooper continues to satisfy a large audience.

In spite of Cooper's success, the idea of the noble savage was often ridiculed in nineteenth-century America; self-described realists saw no possibility of disinterested virtue or high-mindedness in the squalor of Indian life. A writer like Chateaubriand, whose sentimentality surfeits, could not be read by literalists. The significance of his work is in the writer's dream rather than in his representation of a "real" world; the work is to be interpreted as an imaginative statement about human possibilities. But during the nineteenth century, critics were turning away from appreciation of symbolic or allegorical modes, and praising more precise rendering of present surfaces; they, like American frontiersmen, had little patience for noble savages.

The mass audience, however, while it wanted to see itself mirrored in fiction and drama, had the same infinite appetite for sentiment exhibited today by soap-opera viewers. The Indian drama of the early nineteenth century and the popular dime novels after mid-century fulfilled this desire by exploiting the noble savage. In these works he is a sentimentalized figure who enables the reader to absorb and justify his displacement. One is led to speculate that the audience appeal of this figure, sensed by purveyors of popular culture, was caused by the submerged guilt of whites; they preferred magnanimous gestures of worthy Indians to "realistic" representations of genocide.

In addition to the influences of Puritan inheritance and European philosophy, family history intensified the bias of some American writers and helped them to create a private mythology in their depictions of Indians. Some were the children of immigrants who escaped insupportable conditions of life in Europe only to find Indians one more cruel menace in a land whose cultivation required endless toil. For some, the memory of massacre or captivity by Indians was kept alive in stories told by parents and grandparents.[12] For others, like Cooper and Mark Twain, growing up in rough but thoroughly "civilized" surroundings, isolated or degraded Indians could still provide evidence of an earlier occupation of familiar terrain.

Many turned to historical records in a Walter Scott-influenced century. As writers began to find the use of native materials rewarding, this record provided rich material already shaped by Puritans, priests, pioneer homemakers, statesmen, and farmers. These historical and autobiographical materials were valuable sources for imaginative writers who interpreted the present in terms of the past.[13]

Probably the richest sources, however, were contemporaneous accounts.

Imaginative writers are rarely those who open new passages through mountains, map land accessions, run a trading business. In the nineteenth century such activities were celebrated, talked over, written about. For example, the Lewis and Clark exploration of the Louisiana Purchase territory was an event of major proportion. Thomas Jefferson gave detailed instructions to Lewis and Clark on careful journal-keeping; as a result, we have eleven thick volumes of the journal of this expedition, and a two-volume redaction edited by Francis Biddle in 1814. This edition provided many suggestions to writers, among them Poe, whose landscapes of terror in the *Narrative of A. Gordon Pym* and the *Journal of Julius Rodman* exploit the tone as well as the details of journals of exploration.[14]

Some journeys, unlike Lewis's and Clark's, were undertaken for specifically literary purposes; Charles Fenno Hoffman, Washington Irving, Francis Parkman, Margaret Fuller and others all went west to record their impressions. They wanted to satisfy the great curiosity of nineteenth-century readers, to whom truth was much more interesting than fiction. Just as Herman Melville's reading list during the years in which he wrote *Moby Dick* included narratives of whaling captains, other nineteenth-century readers and writers fed their imaginations with real accounts of the vastness, wealth and beauty of uninhabited parts of the globe.

What, then, did white Americans make of the displacement of "savages," whose cultures were so imperfectly understood? In placing themselves in some relation to their society, testifying to their belonging and, at the same time, making their criticism, writers were led naturally to consider the role of whites in a "virgin land."[15] Some of them, reading their Shakespeare, had seen Montaigne's treatment of cannibal Indians transmuted to another literary purpose: Caliban, made to symbolize the irrational, brute part of humanity, to be harnessed, enslaved, lest disorder and animal passion destroy what is good and beautiful. They, too, composing their fables, found uses for the despised, feared, sometimes admired figures Indians were.

Indians, then, were part of both actual and imagined experience for many nineteenth-century Americans. For writers, a most important but too rarely invoked resource was Thoreau's sense of the historical situation: the establishment of a nation devoted to agriculture and progress and its inevitable effect on natives whose diverse cultures placed value not on work, production, and private ownership, but on communal religious and social life.

One must admit, with the art historian Flexner, that despite the overwhelming frequency of reference to the Indian in American literature, "little authentic esthetic advantage" has been taken. In drama, there have been only two or three memorable works; the others are interesting chiefly as sociological documents. In poetry, the achievement is equally spotty;

the long narratives, *Yamoyden, Hiawatha, Frontenac,* are exhumed as curiosities; the brief lyrics of Bryant are barely memorable; Whitman leaves a noteworthy few lines. Clearly fiction and prose narrative are richer fields. Brown, Cooper, Simms and Bird provide satisfying artistic experience, and writers of popular fiction provide an irresistible fund of documentation. But a neglected genre, nonfiction prose, offers the most distinguished writing; the varied works of Alexander Henry, Washington Irving, Henry Thoreau, Francis Parkman, Margaret Fuller, and Frank Cushing remain readable, vigorous, enlightening. Despite the needs satisfied by sentimentality, violence, distortion, some of these nineteenth-century images have a special integrity; Henry, Fuller, Thoreau, and Cushing bear witness to the fact that, in every time, there have been men and women who recognized that those of different races were as fully human as they themselves.

Nineteenth-century writers on the Indian can be divided simply into two categories: those who saw him as brutal or of inferior capacity to the whites, and those who saw him as noble, or as a being especially adapted to life in the natural world. Among the writers represented in this section, Barker, Irving, Cooper, Stone, Child, Thoreau, Whitman, Longfellow, and Jackson fall into the latter category; the former is represented by Brown, Simms, Parkman, Bird, Mark Twain. But stereotype-hunting is far less valuable than perceiving the uses of the Indian figure in the world of each work.

One important pattern does emerge. It will be noted that the favorite pose of literary Indians in the nineteenth century was the farewell stance: Hobomok vanishing into the forest, Tamenund murmuring over the grave of Uncas, Hiawatha departing with the setting sun, Metamora joining his wife and child in the "land of the happy" countless times every season for more than twenty years. Perhaps Melville's Indian harpooner Tashtego, who catches the sea-hawk's wing between his mallet and the Pequod's mast, is one of those vanishing Americans. Whitman, whose *Leaves of Grass* is a distillation of America in the nineteenth century, sums up this treatment of the Indian in a stanza from "The Sleepers." He tells of the beautiful red squaw who visited his mother once, but never came again. The Indian is used, then, again and again, in the nineteenth century, to represent undefined lost value.

This image, hinting at the guilty self-knowledge of whites, emerges more sharply in the twentieth century, when we begin to grasp the destructive nature of "civilization." A different kind of Indian, one who has faced extinction and understands his history, speaks to us in the twentieth-century works of Willa Cather, Frank Waters, Mari Sandoz, William Faulkner, Ken Kesey.

INTRODUCTION

NOTES

1. This image is exploited in fiction by Thomas Berger, in *Little Big Man,* New York, 1964. See chapter 22, "Bunco and Buffalo."
2. One of the most important recent works on the Indian is Theodora Kroeber's book *Ishi: In Two Worlds, A Biography of the Last Wild Indian in North America,* California, 1961.
3. The story of Brant is novelized by Charles Fenno Hoffman, in *Greyslaer: A Romance of the Mohawk,* New York, 1840.
4. An excellent short account of Indian-white hostilities can be found in William T. Hagan's history *American Indians,* Chicago, 1961.
5. This is the title of a famous indictment by Helen Hunt Jackson. For a further description of the book, see the headnote in this section for the author.
6. This remark comes from Emerson's essay "Civilization," first prepared as a lecture delivered in April, 1861. It was later revised and incorporated into *Society and Solitude: Twelve Chapters,* Boston, 1870.
7. Horace Greeley, *An Overland Journey, from New York to San Francisco in the Summer of 1859,* New York, 1860, p. 151.
8. John Augustus Stone's, *Metamora: or, The Last of the Wampanoags,* first produced in 1829, can be found in *America's Lost Plays,* volume 14, edited by Eugene R. Page, Princeton, 1941, pp. 1–40.
9. For an excellent discussion of the American attitude toward land use, see Roderick Nash, *Wilderness and the American Mind,* New Haven, 1967.
10. Roy Harvey Pearce, *The Savages of America: A Study of the Indian and the Idea of Civilization,* Baltimore, 1965.
11. James Thomas Flexner, *Nineteenth-Century American Painting,* New York, 1970.
12. A good example is the story told at the beginning of Ellen Glasgow's novel *Vein of Iron,* 1935.
13. See, for example, *A Spectre of Power,* by Mary Noailles Murfree, who wrote under the pseudonym of Charles Egbert Craddock.
14. Another interesting journal of travel is Josiah Gregg's *Commerce of the Prairies,* 1844.
15. See the important discussions of this idea by Albert Keiser, Henry Nash Smith, Roy Harvey Pearce and Edwin Fussell.

SUPPLEMENTARY READING

OTHER NINETEENTH-CENTURY VIEWS OF THE INDIANS:

Bandelier, Adolf. *The Delightmakers.* 1890. (fiction)

Beckwourth, James P. *The Life and Adventures of James P. Beckwourth.* 1856. (prose narrative)

Brougham, John. *Po-ca-hon-tas; or, The Gentle Savage.* 1855. (drama)

Custis, George Washington Parke. *Pocahontas; or, The Settlers of Virginia.* 1830. (drama)

INTRODUCTION

Davis, John. *The First Settlers of Virginia.* 1805. (fiction)

Eastburn, James, and Robert Sands. *Yamoyden: A Tale of the Wars of King Philip.* 1820. (narrative poetry)

French, James Strange. *Elkswatawa; or, The Prophet of the West.* 1836. (narrative poetry)

Gregg, Josiah. *Commerce of the Prairies.* 1844. (prose narrative)

Hoffman, Charles Fenno. *Greyslaer: A Romance of the Mohawk.* 1840. (fiction)

_____. *A Winter in the West: By a New Yorker.* 1835. (prose narrative)

Irving, John Treat. *Indian Sketches.* 1835. (prose narrative)

Judson, Edward Zane Carroll (pseud. Ned Buntline). *Stella DeLorme; or, The Comanche's Dream: A Wild and Fanciful Tale of Savage Chivalry.* 1860. (fiction)

Kelly, Fanny. *My Captivity Among the Sioux.* 1871. (prose narrative)

Miller, Joaquin. *Unwritten History: Life Amongst the Modocs,* 1873. (prose narrative)

Murfree, Mary Noailles (pseud. Charles Egbert Craddock). *A Spectre of Power.* 1903. (fiction)

Paulding, James Kirke. *Konigsmarke, the Long Finne: A Story of the New World.* 1823. (fiction)

_____. *The Dutchman's Fireside.* 1831. (fiction)

Simms, William Gilmore. *The Life of John Smith, the Founder of Virginia.* 1867. (biography)

Street, Alfred Billings. *Frontenac; or, The Atotarho of the Iroquois: A Metrical Romance.* 1849. (narrative poetry)

Thorpe, Thomas Bangs. *The Mysteries of the Backwoods; or, Sketches of the Southwest.* 1846. (fiction)

SCHOLARLY WORKS

Behen, Dorothy Forbis. *The Captivity Story in American Literature, 1577–1826.* Chicago, 1952.

Coan, Otis W. and Richard G. Lillard. *America in Fiction: An Annotated List of Novels that Interpret Aspects of Life in the U. S.* California, 1941.

Clough, Wilson O. *The Necessary Earth: Nature and Solitude in American Literature.* Texas, 1964.

Fairchild, Hoxie N. *The Noble Savage.* New York, 1928.

Fenton, William Nelson. *American Indian and White Relations to 1830: Needs and Opportunities for Study.* North Carolina, 1957.

Folsom, James K. *The American Western Novel.* Connecticut, 1966.

Fussell, Edwin. *Frontier: American Literature and the American West.* Princeton, 1965.

Hagan, William T. *American Indians.* Chicago, 1961.

Hallowell, A. Irving. "The Impact of the American Indian on American Culture." In *Folklore in Action,* edited by Horace P. Beck. Philadelphia, 1962.

Nash, Roderick. *Wilderness and the American Mind.* New Haven, 1967.

Sedgwick, William E. "The Materials for an American literature: a Critical Problem of the Early Nineteenth Century," *Harvard Studies and Notes in Philology and Literature,* XVII (1935), 141–162.

Wilkins, Thurman. *Cherokee Tragedy.* New York, 1970.

Zolla, Elémire. *The Writer and the Shaman: A Morphology of the American Indian.* New York, 1973.

CHARLES BROCKDEN BROWN

(1771–1810)

Trained as a lawyer in Philadelphia, Charles Brockden Brown was influenced by post-revolutionary nationalism to turn his gifts toward the creation of a native literature. In six novels written between 1798 and 1801, he brought the gothic conventions of English fiction to bear on American scenes; his novels and his magazine work earned him the title of "Father of American literature."

Wieland (1798), his best-known book, is a story of madness and murder narrated by a woman whose experience has been marked by mystery, terror and fear of sexual assault. The novel, in which ventriloquism plays an important role, is notable for its setting in Pennsylvania; its dramatization of man's precarious sanity is enhanced by Brown's use of a rocky and irregular landscape.

The following year Brown used American materials to greater advantage in *Edgar Huntly;* in this novel, terror is caused by Indian warfare directed against a small white settlement in the midst of a threatening wilderness. Ballasting his tale with precise local descriptions, Brown treats Indians as huge, faceless creatures responsible for murder and sexual assault; only one among them, a Delaware woman known as Old Deb, is individualized. She plots nightmares for the settlers while masked as a harmless relic of the past. Injuries to the Delawares are only briefly mentioned, for Brown uses Indians not realistically so much as symbolically, as embodiments of a dark power; they are associated, for this writer whose real subject was the nature of the human mind, with disorder, madness, murder and sexual abuse.

In the first passage that follows, Edgar has just emerged from a wilderness cavern into which he wandered in a somnambulistic trance; he encounters a group of Indians and is forced to kill one of them. In the second passage, Edgar describes Old Deb and her role in the dangers that beset him.

From **Edgar Huntley,** *1799*

Thus was I delivered from my prison, and restored to the enjoyment of the air and the light. Perhaps the chance was almost miraculous that led me to this opening. In any other direction, I might have involved myself in an inextricable maze and rendered my destruction sure; but what now remained to place me in absolute security? Beyond the fire I could see nothing; but, since the smoke rolled rapidly away, it was plain that on the opposite side the cavern was open to the air.

I went forward, but my eyes were fixed upon the fire; presently, in consequence of changing my station, I perceived several feet, and the skirts of blankets. I was somewhat startled at these appearances. The legs were naked, and scored into uncouth figures. The *moccasins* which lay beside them, and which were adorned in a grotesque manner, in addition to other incidents, immediately suggested the suspicion that they were Indians. No spectacle was more adapted than this to excite wonder and alarm. Had some mysterious power snatched me from the earth, and cast me, in a moment, into the heart of the wilderness? Was I still in the vicinity of my parental habitation, or was I thousands of miles distant?

Were these the permanent inhabitants of this region, or were they wanderers and robbers? While in the heart of the mountain, I had entertained a vague belief that I was still within the precincts of Norwalk. This opinion was shaken for a moment by the objects which I now beheld, but it insensibly returned; yet how was this opinion to be reconciled to appearances so strange and uncouth, and what measure did a due regard to my safety enjoin me to take?

I now gained a view of four brawny and terrific figures, stretched upon the ground. They lay parallel to each other, on their left sides; in consequence of which their faces were turned from me. Between each was an interval where lay a musket. Their right hands seemed placed upon the stocks of their guns, as if to seize them on the first moment of alarm.

The aperture through which these objects were seen was at the back of the cave, and some feet from the ground. It was merely large enough to suffer a human body to pass. It was involved in profound darkness, and

Charles Brockden Brown, *Edgar Huntly; or, Memoirs of a Sleep-Walker* (Philadelphia, 1799), vol 2, pp. 153–174 and 238–248.

there was no danger of being suspected or discovered as long as I maintained silence and kept out of view.

It was easily imagined that these guests would make but a short sojourn in this spot. There was reason to suppose that it was now night, and that, after a short repose, they would start up and resume their journey. It was my first design to remain shrouded in this covert till their departure, and I prepared to endure imprisonment and thirst somewhat longer.

Meanwhile my thoughts were busy in accounting for this spectacle. I need not tell thee that Norwalk is the termination of a sterile and narrow tract which begins in the Indian country. It forms a sort of rugged and rocky vein, and continues upwards of fifty miles. It is crossed in a few places by narrow and intricate paths, by which a communication is maintained between the farms and settlements on the opposite sides of the ridge.

During former Indian wars, this rude surface was sometimes traversed by the Red-men, and they made, by means of it, frequent and destructive inroads into the heart of the English settlements. During the last war, notwithstanding the progress of population, and the multiplied perils of such an expedition, a band of them had once penetrated into Norwalk, and lingered long enough to pillage and murder some of the neighboring inhabitants.

I have reason to remember that event. My father's house was placed on the verge of this solitude. Eight of these assassins assailed it at the dead of night. My parents and an infant child were murdered in their beds; the house was pillaged, and then burnt to the ground. Happily, myself and my two sisters were abroad upon a visit. The preceding day had been fixed for our return to our father's house; but a storm occurred, which made it dangerous to cross the river, and, by obliging us to defer our journey, rescued us from captivity or death.

Most men are haunted by some species of terror or antipathy, which they are, for the most part, able to trace to some incident which befell them in their early years. You will not be surprised that the fate of my parents, and the sight of the body of one of this savage band, who, in the pursuit that was made after them, was overtaken and killed, should produce lasting and terrific images in my fancy. I never looked upon or called up the image of a savage without shuddering.

I knew that, at this time, some hostilities had been committed on the frontier; that a long course of injuries and encroachments had lately exasperated the Indian tribes; that an implacable and exterminating war was generally expected. We imagined ourselves at an inaccessible distance from the danger, but I could not but remember that this persuasion was formerly as strong as at present, and that an expedition which had once succeeded might possibly be attempted again. Here was every token of enmity and bloodshed. Each prostrate figure was furnished with a rifled musket, and a leathern bag tied round his waist, which was, probably, stored with powder and ball.

From these reflections, the sense of my own danger was revived and enforced, but I likewise ruminated on the evils which might impend over others. I should, no doubt, be safe by remaining in this nook; but might not some means be pursued to warn others of their danger? Should they leave this spot without notice of their approach being given to the fearless and pacific tenants of the neighboring district, they might commit, in a few hours, the most horrid and irreparable devastation.

The alarm could only be diffused in one way. Could I not escape, unperceived, and without alarming the sleepers, from this cavern? The slumber of an Indian is broken by the slightest noise; but, if all noise be precluded, it is commonly profound. It was possible, I conceived, to leave my present post, to descend into the cave, and issue forth without the smallest signal. Their supine posture assured me that they were asleep. Sleep usually comes at their bidding, and, if perchance, they should be wakeful at an unseasonable moment, they always sit upon their haunches, and, leaning their elbows on their knees, consume the tedious hours in smoking. My peril would be great. Accidents which I could not foresee, and over which I had no command, might occur to awaken some one at the moment I was passing the fire. Should I pass in safety, I might issue forth into a wilderness, of which I had no knowledge, where I might wander till I perished with famine, or where my footsteps might be noted and pursued and overtaken by these implacable foes. These perils were enormous and imminent; but I likewise considered that I might be at no great distance from the habitations of men, and that my escape might rescue them from the most dreadful calamities. I determined to make this dangerous experiment without delay.

I came nearer to the aperture, and had, consequently, a larger view of this recess. To my unspeakable dismay, I now caught a glimpse of one seated at the fire. His back was turned towards me, so that I could distinctly survey his gigantic form and fantastic ornaments.

My project was frustrated. This one was probably commissioned to watch and to awaken his companions when a due portion of sleep had been taken. That he would not be unfaithful or remiss in the performance of the part assigned to him was easily predicted. To pass him without exciting his notice (and the entrance could not otherwise be reached) was impossible. Once more I shrunk back, and revolved with hopelessness and anguish the necessity to which I was reduced.

This interval of dreary foreboding did not last long. Some motion in him that was seated by the fire attracted my notice. I looked, and beheld him rise from his place and go forth from the cavern. This unexpected incident led my thoughts into a new channel. Could not some advantage be taken of his absence? Could not this opportunity be seized for making my escape? He had left his gun and hatchet on the ground. It was likely, therefore, that he had not gone far, and would speedily return. Might not these weapons be seized, and some provision be thus made against the danger of meeting him without, or of being pursued?

Before a resolution could be formed, a new sound saluted my ear. It was a deep groan, succeeded by sobs that seemed struggling for utterance but were vehemently counteracted by the sufferer. This low and bitter lamentation apparently proceeded from some one within the cave. It could not be from one of this swarthy band. It must, then, proceed from a captive, whom they had reserved for torment or servitude, and who had seized the opportunity afforded by the absence of him that watched to give vent to his despair.

I again thrust my head forward, and beheld, lying on the ground, apart from the rest, and bound hand and foot, a young girl. Her dress was the coarse russet garb of the country, and bespoke her to be some farmer's daughter. Her features denoted the last degree of fear and anguish, and she moved her limbs in such a manner as showed that the ligatures by which she was confined produced, by their tightness, the utmost degree of pain.

My wishes were now bent not only to preserve myself and to frustrate the future attempts of these savages, but likewise to relieve this miserable victim. This could only be done by escaping from the cavern and returning with seasonable aid. The sobs of the girl were likely to rouse the sleepers. My appearance before her would prompt her to testify her surprise by some exclamation or shriek. What could hence be predicted but that the band would start on their feet and level their unerring pieces at my head!

I know not why I was insensible to these dangers. My thirst was rendered by these delays intolerable. It took from me, in some degree, the power of deliberation. The murmurs which had drawn me hither continued still to be heard. Some torrent or cascade could not be far distant from the entrance of the cavern, and it seemed as if one draught of clear water was a luxury cheaply purchased by death itself. This, in addition to considerations more disinterested, and which I have already mentioned, impelled me forward.

The girl's cheek rested on the hard rock, and her eyes were dim with tears. As they were turned towards me, however, I hoped that my movements would be noticed by her gradually and without abruptness. This expectation was fulfilled. I had not advanced many steps before she discovered me. This moment was critical beyond all others in the course of my existence. My life was suspended, as it were, by a spider's thread. All rested on the effect which this discovery should make upon this feeble victim.

I was watchful of the first movement of her eye which should indicate a consciousness of my presence. I labored, by gestures and looks, to deter her from betraying her emotion. My attention was, at the same time, fixed upon the sleepers, and an anxious glance was cast towards the quarter whence the watchful savage might appear.

I stooped and seized the musket and hatchet. The space beyond the fire was, as I expected, open to the air. I issued forth with trembling steps. The sensations inspired by the dangers which environed me, added to my recent horrors, and the influence of the moon, which had now gained the zenith, and whose luster dazzled my long-benighted senses, cannot be adequately described.

For a minute, I was unable to distinguish objects. This confusion was speedily corrected, and I found myself on the verge of a steep. Craggy eminences arose on all sides. On the left hand was a space that offered some footing, and hither I turned. A torrent was below me, and this path appeared to lead to it. It quickly appeared in sight, and all foreign cares were, for a time, suspended.

This water fell from the upper regions of the hill, upon a flat projecture which was continued on either side, and on part of which I was now standing. The path was bounded on the left by an inaccessible wall, and on the right terminated at the distance of two or three feet from the wall in a precipice. The water was eight or ten paces distant, and no impediment seemed likely to rise between us. I rushed forward with speed.

My progress was quickly checked. Close to the falling water, seated on the edge, his back supported by the rock, and his legs hanging over the precipice, I now beheld the savage who left the cave before me. The noise of the cascade and the improbability of interruption, at least from this quarter, had made him inattentive to my motions.

I paused. Along this verge lay the only road by which I could reach the water, and by which I could escape. The passage was completely occupied by this antagonist. To advance towards him, or to remain where I was, would produce the same effect. I should, in either case, be detected. He was unarmed; but his outcries would instantly summon his companions to his aid. I could not hope to overpower him, and pass him in defiance of his opposition. But, if this were effected, pursuit would be instantly commenced. I was unacquainted with the way. The way was unquestionably difficult. My strength was nearly annihilated; I should be overtaken in a moment, or their deficiency in speed would be supplied by the accuracy of their aim. Their bullets, at least, would reach me.

There was one method of removing this impediment. The piece which I held in my hand was cocked. There could be no doubt that it was loaded. A precaution of this kind would never be omitted by a warrior of this hue. At a greater distance than this, I should not fear to reach the mark. Should I not discharge it, and, at the same moment, rush forward to secure the road which my adversary's death would open to me?

Perhaps you will conceive a purpose like this to have argued a sanguinary and murderous disposition. Let it be remembered, however, that I entertained no doubts about the hostile designs of these men. This was sufficiently indicated by their arms, their guise, and the captive who attended them. Let the fate of my parents be, likewise, remembered. I was not certain but that these very men were the assassins of my family, and were those who had reduced me and my sisters to the condition of orphans and dependants. No words can describe the torments of my thirst. Relief to these torments, and safety to my life, were within view. How could I hesitate?

Yet I did hesitate. My aversion to bloodshed was not to be subdued but by the direst necessity. I knew, indeed, that the discharge of a musket would only alarm the enemies who remained behind; but I had another and a better weapon in my grasp. I could rive the head of my adversary, and cast him headlong, without any noise which should be heard, into the cavern.

Still I was willing to withdraw, to re-enter the cave, and take shelter in the darksome recesses from which I had emerged. Here I might remain, unsuspected, till these detested guests should depart. The hazards attending my re-entrance were to be boldly encountered, and the torments of unsatisfied thirst were to be patiently endured, rather than imbrue my hands in the blood of my fellowmen. But this expedient would be ineffectual if my retreat should be observed by this savage. Of that I was bound to be incontestably assured. I retreated, therefore, but kept my eye fixed at the same time upon the enemy.

Some ill fate decreed that I should not retreat unobserved. Scarcely had I withdrawn three paces when he started from his seat, and, turning towards me, walked with a quick pace. The shadow of the rock, and the improbability of meeting an enemy here, concealed me for a moment from his observation. I stood still. The slightest motion would have attracted his notice. At present, the narrow space engaged all his vigilance. Cautious footsteps, and attention to the path, were indispensable to his safety. The respite was momentary, and I employed it in my own defense.

How otherwise could I act? The danger that impended aimed at nothing less than my life. To take life of another was the only method of averting it. The means were in my hand, and they were used. In an extremity like this, my muscles would have acted almost in defiance of my will.

The stroke was quick as lightning, and the wound mortal and deep. He had not time to descry the author of his fate, but, sinking on the path, expired without a groan. The hatchet buried itself in his breast, and rolled with him to the bottom of the precipice.

Never before had I taken the life of a human creature. On this head I had, indeed, entertained somewhat of religious scruples. These scruples did not forbid me to defend myself, but they made me cautious and reluctant to decide. Though they could not withhold my hand when urged by a necessity like this, they were sufficient to make me look back upon the deed with remorse and dismay.

I did not escape all compunction in the present instance, but the tumult of my feelings was quickly allayed. To quench my thirst was a considera-tion by which all others were supplanted. I approached the torrent, and not only drank copiously, but laved my head, neck, and arms, in this delicious element.

. . . .

What and where was Deb's hut?

It was a hut in the wilderness, occupied by an old Indian woman, known among her neighbors by the name of Old Deb. Some people called her Queen Mab. Her dwelling was eight long miles from this house.

A thousand questions were precluded and a thousand doubts solved by this information. *Queen Mab* were sounds familiar to my ears; for they originated with myself.

This woman originally belonged to the tribe of Delawares, or Lenni-lennapee. All these districts were once comprised within the dominions of that nation. About thirty years ago, in consequence of perpetual encroach-ments of the English colonists, they abandoned their ancient seats and retired to the banks of the Wabash and Muskingum.

This emigration was concerted in a general council of the tribe, and obtained the concurrence of all but one female. Her birth, talents, and age, gave her much consideration and authority among her countrymen; and all her zeal and eloquence were exerted to induce them to lay aside their scheme. In this, however, she could not succeed. Finding them refractory, she declared her resolution to remain behind and maintain possession of the land which her countrymen should impiously abandon.

The village inhabited by this clan was built upon ground which now constitutes my uncle's barnyard and orchard. On the departure of her countrymen, this female burnt the empty wigwams and retired into the fastnesses of Norwalk. She selected a spot suitable for an Indian dwelling and a small plantation of maize, and in which she was seldom liable to interruption and intrusion.

Her only companions were three dogs, of the Indian or wolf species. These animals differed in nothing from their kinsmen of the forest but in their attachment and obedience to their mistress. She governed them with absolute sway. They were her servants and protectors, and attended her person or guarded her threshold, agreeably to her directions. She fed them with corn, and they supplied her and themselves with meat, by hunting squirrels, raccoons, and rabbits.

To the rest of mankind they were aliens or enemies. They never left the desert but in company with their mistress, and, when she entered a farm-house, waited her return at a distance. They would suffer none to approach them, but attacked no one who did not imprudently crave their acquaintance, or who kept at a respectful distance from their wigwam. That sacred asylum they would not suffer to be violated, and no stranger could enter it but at the imminent hazard of his life, unless accompanied and protected by their dame.

The chief employment of this woman, when at home, besides plucking the weeds from among her corn, bruising the grain between two stones, and setting her snares for rabbits and opossums, was to talk. Though in solitude, her tongue was never at rest but when she was asleep; but her conversation was merely addressed to her dogs. Her voice was sharp and shrill, and her gesticulations were vehement and grotesque. A hearer would naturally imagine that she was scolding; but, in truth, she was merely giving them directions. Having no other object of contemplation or subject of discourse, she always found, in their postures and looks, occasion for praise, or blame, or command. The readiness with which they understood and the docility with which they obeyed her movements and words were truly wonderful.

If a stranger chanced to wander near her hut and overhear her jargon, incessant as it was, and shrill, he might speculate in vain on the reason of these sounds. If he waited in expectation of hearing some reply, he waited in vain. The strain, always voluble and sharp, was never intermitted for a moment, and would continue for hours at a time.

She seldom left the hut but to visit the neighboring inhabitants and demand from them food and clothing, or whatever her necessities required. These were exacted as her due: to have her wants supplied was her prerogative, and to withhold what she claimed was rebellion. She conceived that by remaining behind her countrymen she succeeded to the government and retained the possession of all this region. The English were aliens and sojourners, who occupied the land merely by her connivance and permission, and whom she allowed to remain on no terms but those of supplying her wants.

Being a woman aged and harmless, her demands being limited to that of which she really stood in need, and which her own industry could not procure, her pretensions were a subject of mirth and good-humor, and her injunctions obeyed with seeming deference and gravity. To me she early became an object of curiosity and speculation. I delighted to observe her habits and humor her prejudices. She frequently came to my uncle's house, and I sometimes visited her; insensibly she seemed to contract an affection for me, and regarded me with more complacency and condescension than any other received.

She always disdained to speak English, and custom had rendered her intelligible to most in her native language, with regard to a few simple questions. I had taken some pains to study her jargon, and could make out to discourse with her on the few ideas which she possessed. This circumstance, likewise, wonderfully prepossessed her in my favor.

The name by which she was formerly known was Deb; but her pretensions to royalty, the wildness of her aspect and garb, her shrivelled and diminutive form, a constitution that seemed to defy the ravages of time and the influence of the elements, her age (which some did not scruple to affirm exceeded a hundred years), her romantic solitude and mountainous haunts, suggested to my fancy the appellation of *Queen Mab*. There appeared to me some rude analogy between this personage and her whom the poets of old time have delighted to celebrate: thou perhaps wilt discover nothing but incongruities between them; but, be that as it may, Old Deb and Queen Mab soon came into indiscriminate and general use.

She dwelt in Norwalk upwards of twenty years. She was not forgotten by her countrymen, and generally received from her brothers and sons an autumnal visit; but no solicitations or entreaties could prevail on her to return with them. Two years ago, some suspicion or disgust induced her to forsake her ancient habitation and to seek a new one. Happily she found a more convenient habitation twenty miles to the westward, and in a spot abundantly sterile and rude.

This dwelling was of logs, and had been erected by a Scottish emigrant, who, not being rich enough to purchase land, and entertaining a passion for solitude and independence, cleared a field in the unappropriated wilderness and subsisted on its produce. After some time he disappeared. Various conjectures were formed as to the cause of his absence. None of them were satisfactory; but that which obtained most credit was that he had been murdered by the Indians, who, about the same period, paid their annual visit to the *Queen.* This conjecture acquired some force by observing that the old woman shortly after took possession of his hut, his implements of tillage, and his corn-field.

She was not molested in her new abode, and her life passed in the same quiet tenor as before. Her periodical rambles, her regal claims, her guardian wolves, and her uncouth volubility were equally remarkable; but her circuits were new. Her distance made her visits to Solesbury more rare, and had prevented me from ever extending my pedestrian excursions to her present abode.

These recollections were now suddenly called up by the information of my hostess. The hut where I had sought shelter and relief was, it seems, the residence of Queen Mab. Some fortunate occurrence had called her away during my visit. Had she and her dogs been at home, I should have been set upon by these ferocious sentinels, and, before their dame could have interfered, have been, together with my helpless companion, mangled or killed. These animals never barked; I should have entered unaware of my danger, and my fate could scarcely have been averted by my fusil.

Her absence at this unseasonable hour was mysterious. It was now the time of year when her countrymen were accustomed to renew their visit. Was there a league between her and the plunderers whom I had encountered?

JAMES NELSON BARKER
(1784–1858)

James Nelson Barker, dramatist and public figure, drew on John Smith's *Generall History of Virginia* for the materials of *The Indian Princess; or La Belle Sauvage,* first performed in Philadelphia in 1808. The second Indian play to be written in America *(Ponteach* was the first), it became a popular example of a curious genre; antebellum Americans had a special taste for seeing exciting moments of Indian-white contact on their stage. It is estimated that nearly sixty of such plays were written or produced.

Indian drama treated three stereotyped figures: gentle maidens, very susceptible to the white man's influence; brave heroes, usually based on historical figures, sometimes friendly to the whites, but more often ready to die with their doomed people; and crafty, villainous warriors, usually priests, who see whites as a threat and plan their destruction, and who have no redeeming personal qualities.

Barker's "operatic melo-drame" exploits all three stereotypes of the Indian drama, and is particularly important for its contribution to the mythification of Pocahontas. Sometimes treated historically, under her own name, and sometimes represented by any hospitable Indian maiden, Pocahontas came to represent the fertile, welcoming aspect of the American landscape.

Barker's treatment of her, in this comedy that pairs lovers as lightly as *A Midsummer Night's Dream,* is influenced by his chivalrous glorification of woman. Through the gentleness and susceptibility of her sex, Pocahontas prepares the way for the "godlike" white men, or white civilization and Christianity.

The first extract that follows is Act II, Scene 1, in which Pocahontas saves Smith's life. The second is Act III, Scene 2, in which Pocahontas declares her indebtedness to Rolfe's Christian tutelage.

149

From **The Indian Princess; or, La Belle Sauvage,** *1808*

Scene I. *Inside the palace at Werocomoco.* Powhatan *in state,* Grimosco, etc., *his wives, and warriors, ranged on each side. Music.*

Powhatan. My people, strange beings have appeared among us; they come from the bosom of the waters, amid fire and thunder; one of them has our war-god delivered into our hands: behold the white being!

Music. Smith *is brought in; his appearance excites universal wonder;* Pocahontas *expresses peculiar admiration.*

Pocahontas. O Nima! is it not a God!

Powhatan. Miami, though thy years are few, thou art experienced as age; give us thy voice of counsel.

Miami. Brothers, this stranger is of a fearful race of beings; their barren hunting grounds lie beneath the world, and they have risen, in monstrous canoes, through the great water, to spoil and ravish from us our fruitful inheritance. Brothers, this stranger must die; six of our brethren have fall'n by his hand. Before we lay their bones in the narrow house, we must avenge them: their unappeased spirits will not go to rest beyond the mountains; they cry out for the stranger's blood.

Nantaquas. Warriors, listen to my words; listen, my father, while your son tells the deeds of the brave white man. I saw him when 300 of our fiercest chiefs formed the warring around him. But he defied their arms; he held lightning in his hand. Wherever his arm fell, there sunk a warrior: as the tall tree falls, blasted and riven, to the earth, when the angry Spirit darts his fires through the forest. I thought him a God; my feet grew to the ground; I could not move!

Pocahontas. Nima, dost thou hear the words of my brother.

Nantaquas. The battle ceased, for courage left the bosom of our warriors; their arrows rested in their quivers; their bowstrings no longer sounded; the tired chieftains leaned on their war-clubs, and gazed at the terrible stranger, whom they dared not approach. Give an ear to me, king: 't was then I held out the hand of peace to him, and he became my brother; he forgot

---

James Nelson Barker, "The Indian Princess; or, La Belle Sauvage," in *Representative Plays by American Dramatists, 1715–1819,* ed. Montrose J. Moses (New York, 1918), vol. 1, pp. 593–596 and 610–612.

his arms, for he trusted to his brother: he was discoursing wonders to his friend, when our chiefs rushed upon him, and bore him away. But oh! my father, he must not die; for he is not a war captive; I promised that the chain of friendship should be bright between us. Chieftains, your prince must not falsify his word; father, your son must not be a liar!

Pocahontas. Listen, warriors; listen, father; the white man is my brother's brother!

Grimosco. King! when last night our village shook with the loud noise, it was the Great Spirit who talk'd to his priest; my mouth shall speak his commands: King, we must destroy the strangers, for they are not our God's children; we must take their scalps, and wash our hands in the white man's blood, for he is an enemy to the Great Spirit.

Nantaquas. O priest, thou hast dreamed a false dream; Miami, thou tellest the tale that is not. Hearken, my father, to my true words! the white man is beloved by the Great Spirit; his king is like you, my father, good and great; and he comes from a land beyond the wide water, to make us wise and happy!

Powhatan *deliberates. Music.*

Powhatan. Stranger, thou must prepare for death. Six of our brethren fell by thy hand. Thou must die.

Pocahontas. Father, O father!

Smith. Had not your people first beset me, king,
I would have prov'd a friend and brother to them;
Arts I'd have taught, that should have made them gods,
And gifts would I have given to your people,
Richer than red men ever yet beheld.
Think not I fear to die. Lead to the block.
The soul of the white warrior shall shrink not.
Prepare the stake! amidst your fiercest tortures,
You'll find its fiery pains as nobly scorned,
As when the red man sings aloud his death-song.

Pocahontas. Oh! shall that brave man die!

Music. The King *motions with his hand, and* Smith *is led to the block.*

Miami. [To executioners.] Warriors, when the third signal strikes, sink your tomahawks in his head.

Pocahontas. Oh, do not, warriors, do not! Father, incline your heart to mercy; he will win your battles, he will vanquish your enemies! *[First signal.]* Brother, speak! save your brother! Warriors, are you brave? preserve

151

the brave man! *[Second signal.]* Miami, priest, sing the song of peace; ah! strike not, hold! mercy!

Music. The third signal is struck, the hatchets are lifted up: when the Princess, *shrieking, runs distractedly to the block, and presses* Smith's *head to her bosom.*

White man, thou shalt not die; or I will die with thee!

Music. She leads Smith *to the throne, and kneels.*

My father, dost thou love thy daughter? listen to her voice; look upon her tears: they ask for mercy to the captive. Is thy child dear to thee, my father? Thy child will die with the white man.

Plaintive music. She bows her head to his feet. Powhatan, *after some deliberation, looking on his daughter with tenderness, presents her with a string of white wampum.* Pocahontas, *with the wildest expression of joy, rushes forward with* Smith, *presenting the beads of peace.*

Captive! thou art free!—

*Music. General joy is diffused—*Miami *and* Grimosco *only appear discontented. The prince* Nantaquas *congratulates* Smith. *The* Princess *shows the most extravagant emotions of rapture.*

Smith. O woman! angel sex! where'er thou art,
Still art thou heavenly. The rudest clime
Robs not thy glowing bosom of its nature.
Thrice blessed lady, take a captive's thanks!
                    [He bows upon her hand.]

Pocahontas. My brother!—

                    [Music. Smith *expresses his gratitude.]*

Nantaquas. Father, hear the design that fills my breast. I will go among the white men; I will learn their arts; and my people shall be made wise and happy.

Pocahontas. I too will accompany my brother.

Miami. Princess!—

Pocahontas. Away, cruel Miami; you would have murdered my brother!—

Powhatan. Go, my son; take thy warriors, and go with the white men. Daughter, I cannot lose thee from mine eyes; accompany thy brother but a little on his way. Stranger, depart in peace; I entrust my son to thy friendship.

Smith. Gracious sir,
He shall return with honors and with wonders;
My beauteous sister! noble brother, come!

Music. Exeunt, on one side, Smith, Princess, Nantaquas, Nima, *and train. On the other,* King, Priest, Miami, etc. *The two latter express angry discontent.*

From ACT III, Scene 2

Enter Rolfe *and* Pocahontas.

Princess. Nay, let me on—

Rolfe. No further, gentle love;
The rugged way has wearied you already.

Princess. Feels the wood pigeon weariness, who flies,
Mated with her beloved? Ah! lover, no.

Rolfe. Sweet! in this grove we will exchange adieus;
My steps should point straight onward; were thou with me,
Thy voice would bid me quit the forward path
At every pace, or fix my side-long look,
Spell-bound, upon thy beauties.

Princess. Ah! you love not
The wild-wood prattle of the Indian maid,
As once you did.

Rolfe. By heaven! my thirsty ear,
Could ever drink its liquid melody.
Oh! I could talk with thee, till hasty night,
Ere yet the sentinel day had done his watch;
Veil'd like a spy, should steal on printless feet,
To listen to our parley! Dearest love!
My captain has arrived, and I do know,
When honor and when duty call upon me,
Thou wouldst not have me chid for tardiness.
But, ere the matin of tomorrow's lark,
Do echo from the roof of nature's temple,
Sweetest, expect me.

Princess. Wilt thou surely come?

Rolfe. To win thee from thy father will I come;
And my commander's voice shall join with mine,
To woo Powhatan to resign his treasure.

Princess. Go then, but ah! forget not—

Rolfe. I'll forget
All else, to think on thee!

Princess. Thou art my life!
I lived not till I saw thee, love; and now,
I live not in thine absence. Long, Oh! long
I was the savage child of savage Nature;
And when her flowers sprang up, while each green bough
Sang with the passing west wind's rustling breath;
When her warm visitor, flush'd Summer, came,
Or Autumn strew'd her yellow leaves around,
Or the shrill north wind pip'd his mournful music,
I saw the changing brow of my wild mother
With neither love nor dread. But now, Oh! now,
I could entreat her for eternal smiles,
So thou might'st range through groves of loveliest flowers,
Where never Winter, with his icy lip,
Should dare to press thy cheek.

Rolfe. My sweet enthusiast!

Princess. O! 'tis from thee that I have drawn my being:
Thou'st ta'en me from the path of savage error,
Blood-stain'd and rude, where rove my countrymen,
And taught me heavenly truths, and fill'd my heart
With sentiments sublime, and sweet, and social.
Oft has my winged spirit, following thine,
Cours'd the bright day-beam, and the star of night,
And every rolling planet of the sky,
Around their circling orbits. O my love!
Guided by thee, has not my daring soul,
O'ertopt the far-off mountains of the east,
Where, as our fathers' fable, shad'wy hunters
Pursue the deer, or clasp the melting maid,
'Mid ever blooming spring? Thence, soaring high
From the deep vale of legendary fiction,
Hast thou not heaven-ward turn'd my dazzled sight,
Where sing the spirits of the blessed good
Around the bright throne of the Holy One?
This thou hast done; and ah! what couldst thou more,
Belov'd preceptor, but direct that ray,
Which beams from Heaven to animate existence,
And bid my swelling bosom beat with love!

Rolfe. O, my dear scholar!

Princess. Prithee, chide me, love:
My idle prattle holds thee from thy purpose.

Rolfe. O! speak more music! and I'll listen to it,
Like stilly midnight to sweet Philomel.

Princess. Nay, now begone; for thou must go: ah! fly,
The sooner to return—

Rolfe. Thus, then, adieu!   *[Embrace.]*
But, ere the face of morn blush rosy red,
To see the dew-besprent, cold virgin ground
Stain'd by licentious step; Oh, long before
The foot of th' earliest furred forrester,
Do mark its imprint on morn's misty sheet,
With sweet good morrow will I wake my love.

Princess. To bliss thou'lt wake me, for I sleep till then
Only with sorrow's poppy on my lids.

Music. Embrace; and exit Rolfe, *followed by* Robin; Princess *looks around despondingly.*

But now, how gay and beauteous was this grove!
Sure ev'ning's shadows have enshrouded it,
And 'tis the screaming bird of night I hear,
Not the melodious mock-bird. Ah! fond girl!
'Tis o'er thy soul the gloomy curtain hangs;
'Tis in thy heart the rough-toned raven sings.
O lover! haste to my benighted breast;
Come like the glorious sun, and bring me day!

155

ALEXANDER HENRY

(1739-1824)

Alexander Henry's *Adventures in Canada* is a model of narrative style. In a clear and suspenseful manner, the author tells of his attempt to become a fur trader in the Great Lakes area, just after the English had expelled the French from this territory. The Indians found it difficult to transfer their allegiance, particularly since the French intermarried with them and engaged in social and business life on more equal terms than did the race-conscious English. As an English trader, Henry was the unoffending victim of Chippewa resentment, and escaped alive from the massacre at Michilimackinac only through the intercession of Wawatam, an Indian who developed brotherly feelings toward him. The friendship of Wawatam and Henry is commented upon in the "Wednesday" chapter of Thoreau's *A Week on the Concord and Merrimack Rivers.*

Henry seems to regard Indians objectively, as human beings who differ in intelligence and sensitivity. Unembittered by his imprisonment, he writes in a direct, understated style, filling his narrative with careful pictures of Indians and their activities. The final effect of his book, however, is not that of a collection of data, but of a work of literary art. It is unified and enlivened by a constant sense of the narrator's point of view. His moments of terror remind us of similar moments in the works of Charles Brockden Brown and Edgar Allan Poe; in his capacity for friendship and sympathy for Indians, he stands in a very small company. The passage that follows describes the massacre at Michilimackinac, and Henry's attempts to escape.

From *Travels and Adventures in Canada and the Indian Territories, 1809*

The morning was sultry. A Chipeway came to tell me that his nation was going to play at *bag' gat'iway* with the Sacs or Saäkies, another Indian nation, for a high wager. He invited me to witness the sport, adding that the commandant was to be there and would bet on the side of the Chipeways. In consequence of this information, I went to the commandant and expostulated with him a little, representing that the Indians might possibly have some sinister end in view; but the commandant only smiled at my suspicions.

Bag' gat'iway, called by the Canadians *le jeu de la crosse*, is played with a bat and ball. The bat is about four feet in length, curved, and terminating in a sort of racket. Two posts are planted in the ground at a considerable distance from each other, as a mile or more. Each party has its post, and the game consists in throwing the ball up to the post of the adversary. The ball, at the beginning, is placed in the middle of the course, and each party endeavors as well to throw the ball out of the direction of its own post, as into that of the adversary's.

I did not go myself to see the match which was now to be played without the fort, because, there being a canoe prepared to depart on the following day for Montreal, I employed myself in writing letters to my friends; and even when a fellow-trader, Mr. Tracy, happened to call upon me, saying that another canoe had just arrived from Detroit, and proposing that I should go with him to the beach to inquire the news, it so happened that I still remained to finish my letters, promising to follow Mr. Tracy in the course of a few minutes. Mr. Tracy had not gone more than twenty paces from my door when I heard an Indian war-cry, and a noise of general confusion.

Going instantly to my window, I saw a crowd of Indians within the fort, furiously cutting down and scalping every Englishman they found. In particular, I witnessed the fate of Lieutenant Jemette.

I had, in the room in which I was, a fowling-piece, loaded with swan-shot. This I immediately seized, and held it for a few minutes, waiting to hear the drum beat to arms. In this dreadful interval, I saw several of my countrymen fall, and more than one struggling between the knees of an Indian, who, holding him in this manner, scalped him while yet living.

Alexander Henry, *Travels and Adventures in Canada and the Indian Territories, between the Years 1760 and 1776* (New York, 1809), pp. 77–84.

At length, disappointed in the hope of seeing resistance made to the enemy, and sensible, of course, that no effort of my own unassisted arm could avail against four hundred Indians, I thought only of seeking shelter. Amid the slaughter which was raging, I observed many of the Canadian inhabitants of the fort calmly looking on, neither opposing the Indians nor suffering injury; and, from this circumstance, I conceived a hope of finding security in their houses.

Between the yard-door of my own house, and that of M. Langlade, my next neighbor, there was only a low fence, over which I easily climbed. At my entrance, I found the whole family at the windows, gazing at the scene of blood before them. I addressed myself immediately to M. Langlade, begging that he would put me into some place of safety until the heat of the affair should be over; an act of charity by which he might perhaps preserve me from the general massacre; but, while I uttered my petition, M. Langlade, who had looked for a moment at me, turned again to the window, shrugging his shoulders and intimating that he could do nothing for me: —*"Que voudriez-vous que j'en ferais?"*

This was a moment for despair; but, the next, a Pani woman, a slave of M. Langlade's, beckoned to me to follow her. She brought me to a door, which she opened, desiring me to enter, and telling me that it led to the garret, where I must go and conceal myself. I joyfully obeyed her directions; and she, having followed me up to the garret-door, locked it after me, and with great presence of mind took away the key.

This shelter obtained, if shelter I could hope to find it, I was naturally anxious to know what might still be passing without. Through an aperture, which afforded me a view of the area of the fort, I beheld, in shapes the foulest and most terrible, the ferocious triumphs of barbarian conquerors. The dead were scalped and mangled; the dying were writhing and shrieking under the unsatiated knife and tomahawk; and from the bodies of some, ripped open, their butchers were drinking the blood, scooped up in the hollow of joined hands, and quaffed amid shouts of rage and victory. I was shaken, not only with horror, but with fear. The sufferings which I witnessed, I seemed on the point of experiencing. No long time elapsed before, every one being destroyed who could be found, there was a general cry of "All is finished!" At the same instant, I heard some of the Indians enter the house in which I was.

The garret was separated from the room below only by a layer of single boards, at once the flooring of the one and the ceiling of the other. I could therefore hear everything that passed; and, the Indians no sooner came in than they inquired whether or not any Englishman were in the house. M. Langlade replied that "He could not say—he "did not know of any";— answers in which he did not exceed the truth; for the Pani woman had not only hidden me by stealth, but kept my secret, and her own. M. Langlade was therefore, as I presume, as far from a wish to destroy me as he was careless about saving me, when he added to these answers that "They might examine for themselves, and would soon be satisfied, as to the object of their question." Saying this, he brought them to the garret-door.

The state of my mind will be imagined. Arrived at the door, some delay was occasioned by the absence of the key, and a few moments were thus allowed me, in which to look around for a hiding-place. In one corner of the garret was a heap of those vessels of birch-bark used in maple-sugar making, as I have recently described.

The door was unlocked and opening, and the Indians ascending the stairs, before I had completely crept into a small opening which presented itself at one end of the heap. An instant after, four Indians entered the room, all armed with tomahawks, and all besmeared with blood, upon every part of their bodies.

The die appeared to be cast. I could scarcely breathe; but I thought that the throbbing of my heart occasioned a noise loud enough to betray me. The Indians walked in every direction about the garret, and one of them approached me so closely that at a particular moment, had he put forth his hand, he must have touched me. Still, I remained undiscovered; a circumstance to which the dark color of my clothes, and the want of light, in a room which had no window, and in the corner in which I was, must have contributed. In a word, after taking several turns in the room, during which they told M. Langlade how many they had killed, and how many scalps they had taken, they returned downstairs, and I, with sensations not to be expressed, heard the door, which was the barrier between me and my fate, locked for the second time.

There was a feather-bed on the floor; and, on this, exhausted as I was by the agitation of my mind, I threw myself down and fell asleep. In this state I remained till the dusk of the evening, when I was awakened by a second opening of the door. The person that now entered was M. Langlade's wife, who was much surprised at finding me, but advised me not to be uneasy, observing, that the Indians had killed most of the English, but that she hoped I might myself escape.—A shower of rain having begun to fall, she had come to stop a hole in the roof. On her going away, I begged her to send me a little water to drink, which she did.

As night was now advancing, I continued to lie on the bed, ruminating on my condition, but unable to discover a resource, from which I could hope for life. A flight to Detroit had no probable chance of success. The distance from Michilimackinac was four hundred miles; I was without provisions; and the whole length of the road lay through Indian countries, countries of an enemy in arms, where the first man whom I should meet would kill me. To stay where I was, threatened nearly the same issue. As before, fatigue of mind, and not tranquillity, suspended my cares, and procured me further sleep.

WASHINGTON IRVING

(1783–1859)

In spite of Irving's seventeen years in Europe, his search for native themes led him to contribute importantly to portraiture of the American Indian. Although his firsthand observation of Indians was limited, he was liberated from the pioneer's need to justify Indian displacement. He was able to view Indians sympathetically, bringing the perspective of a worldly man to questions of civilization and savagery.

In his first book, *A History of New-York from the Beginning of the World to the End of the Dutch Dynasty,* by Dietrich Knickerbocker (1809), he satirizes pretentious historians and wittily deflates some shibboleths of American history. In Chapter Five Dietrich Knickerbocker pretends to justify the rights of European colonists to the land they "discovered." He succeeds, of course, in revealing the falsity and injustice of their claims. At the end of the chapter, Irving offers a Swiftian summary of colonization; this passage is reprinted below.

In a more straightforward way, but not more devastatingly, Irving takes up the topic of displaced Indians again in two sketches added to *The Sketch Book of Geoffrey Crayon, Gent.,* in 1820. In "Traits of Indian Character," Irving expresses succinctly that sympathy for wronged Indians implied in *Knickerbocker's History:*

It has been the lot of the unfortunate aborigines of America, in the early periods of colonization, to be doubly wronged by the white men. They have been dispossessed of their hereditary possessions by mercenary and frequently wanton warfare; and their characters have been traduced by bigoted and interested writers.

In this essay, Irving praises the Indians for courage and magnanimity, and explains their deep resentment of white injuries; he calls it "the dark story of their wrongs and wretchedness." In the next sketch, "Philip of Pokanoket," he brings together materials for the many nineteenth-century treatments of Philip (most notably, Cooper's and Stone's). Irving's recognition of the heroism of this "true-born prince" in trying to save his people is in sharp contrast to earlier views of Philip as devilish.

In these comic and serious meditations on history, Irving helped to establish the idealized Indian; he worked from secondary sources, the northeastern Indians having been conquered and displaced by the 1820s. But Irving's treatment of the Indian does not end with these books. In 1832 he travelled across Indian territory, and recorded his glimpses of western tribes in *A Tour on the Prairies* (1835). His most intimate contact with Indians was gathered through his acquaintance with a half-breed guide on this trip. In two succeeding volumes, *Astoria* (1836) and *The Adventures of Captain Bonneville* (1837), he continued to bring to his materials a strong sense of the beauty and dignity of Indians and an awareness of the wrongs they suffered. These two books, like other western narratives of the nineteenth century, have great importance as sources for writers of fiction, among them Poe, Melville, Hawthorne.

From A *History of New York, 1809*

Let us suppose, then, that the inhabitants of the moon, by astonishing advancement in science, and by profound insight into that lunar philosophy, the mere flickerings of which have of late years dazzled the feeble optics, and addled the shallow brains of the good people of our globe—let us suppose, I say, that the inhabitants of the moon, by these means, had arrived at such a command of their *energies,* such an enviable state of *perfectibility,* as to control the elements, and navigate the boundless regions of space. Let us suppose a roving crew of these soaring philosophers, in the course of an aerial voyage of discovery among the stars, should chance to alight upon this outlandish planet.

And here I beg my readers will not have the uncharitableness to smile, as is too frequently the fault of volatile readers when perusing the grave speculations of philosophers. I am far from indulging in any sportive vein at present; nor is the supposition I have been making so wild as many may deem it. It has long been a very serious and anxious question with me, and many a time and oft, in the course of my overwhelming cares and contrivances for the welfare and protection of this my native planet, have I lain awake whole nights debating in my mind, whether it were most probable

Washington Irving, *A History of New-York,* vol. 1 of *The Works of Washington Irving* (New York, 1848), chapter 5, pp. 59–74.

we should first discover and civilize the moon, or the moon discover and civilize our globe. Neither would the prodigy of sailing in the air and cruising among the stars be a whit more astonishing and incomprehensible to us than was the European mystery of navigating floating castles, through the world of waters, to the simple natives. We have already discovered the art of coasting along the aerial shores of our planet, by means of balloons, as the savages had of venturing along their sea-coasts in canoes; and the disparity between the former, and the aerial vehicles of the philosophers from the moon, might not be greater than that between the bark canoes of the savages, and the mighty ships of their discoverers. I might here pursue an endless chain of similar speculations; but as they would be unimportant to my subject, I abandon them to my reader, particularly if he be a philosopher, as matters well worthy of his attentive consideration.

To return then to my supposition—let us suppose that the aerial visitants I have mentioned, possessed of vastly superior knowledge to ourselves; that is to say, possessed of superior knowledge in the art of extermination—riding on hyppogriffs—defended with impenetrable armor—armed with concentrated sunbeams, and provided with vast engines, to hurl enormous moon-stones: in short, let us suppose them, if our vanity will permit the supposition, as superior to us in knowledge, and consequently in power, as the Europeans were to the Indians, when they first discovered them. All this is very possible; it is only our self-sufficiency that makes us think otherwise; and I warrant the poor savages, before they had any knowledge of the white men, armed in all the terrors of glittering steel and tremendous gunpowder, were as perfectly convinced that they themselves were the wisest, the most virtuous, powerful, and perfect of created beings as are, at this present moment, the lordly inhabitants of old England, the volatile populace of France, or even the self-satisfied citizens of this most enlightened republic.

Let us suppose, moreover, that the aerial voyagers, finding this planet to be nothing but a howling wilderness, inhabited by us poor savages and wild beasts, shall take formal possession of it, in the name of his most gracious and philosophic excellency, the man in the moon. Finding, however, that their numbers are incompetent to hold it in complete subjection, on account of the ferocious barbarity of its inhabitants, they shall take our worthy President, the King of England, the Emperor of Hayti, the mighty Bonaparte, and the Great King of Bantam, and returning to their native planet, shall carry them to court, as were the Indian chiefs led about as spectacles in the courts of Europe.

Then, making such obeisance as the etiquette of the court requires, they shall address the puissant man in the moon, in, as near as I can conjecture, the following terms:

"Most serene and mighty Potentate, whose dominions extend as far as eye can reach, who rideth on the Great Bear, useth the sun as a looking-glass, and maintaineth unrivaled control over tides, madmen, and sea-crabs. We thy liege subjects have just returned from a voyage of discovery, in the course of which we have landed and taken possession of that obscure little dirty planet, which thou beholdest rolling at a distance. The five uncouth monsters, which we have brought into this august presence, were once very important chiefs among their fellow savages, who are a race of beings totally destitute of the common attributes of humanity; and differing in every-thing from the inhabitants of the moon, inasmuch as they carry their heads upon their shoulders, instead of under their arms—have two eyes instead of one—are utterly destitute of tails, and of a variety of unseemly complexions, particularly of horrible whiteness—instead of pea-green.

"We have moreover found these miserable savages sunk into a state of the utmost ignorance and depravity, every man shamelessly living with his own wife, and rearing his own children, instead of indulging in that community of wives enjoined by the law of nature, as expounded by the philosophers of the moon. In a word, they have scarcely a gleam of true philosophy among them, but are, in fact, utter heretics, ignoramuses, and barbarians. Taking compassion, therefore, on the sad condition of these sublunary wretches, we have endeavored, while we remained on their planet, to intro-duce among them the light of reason—and the comforts of the moon. We have treated them to mouthfuls of moonshine, and draughts of nitrous oxide which they swallowed with incredible voracity, particularly the females; and we have likewise endeavored to instill into them the precepts of lunar philosophy. We have insisted upon their renouncing the contemptible shackles of religion and common sense, and adoring the profound, omnip-otent, and all perfect energy, and the ecstatic, immutable, immovable perfection. But such was the unparalleled obstinacy of these wretched savages, that they persisted in cleaving to their wives, and adhering to their religion, and absolutely set at naught the sublime doctrines of the moon—nay, among other abominable heresies, they even went so far as blasphemously to declare, that this ineffable planet was made of nothing more nor less than green cheese!"

At these words, the great man in the moon (being a very profound philosopher) shall fall into a terrible passion, and possessing equal authority over things that do not belong to him, as did whilom his holiness the Pope, shall forthwith issue a formidable bull, specifying, "That, whereas a certain crew of Lunatics have lately discovered, and taken possession of a newly discovered planet called *the earth*—and that whereas it is inhabited by none but a race of two-legged animals that carry their heads on their shoulders instead of under their arms; cannot talk the lunatic language; have two eyes

instead of one; are destitute of tails, and of a horrible whiteness, instead
of pea-green—therefore, and for a variety of other excellent reasons, they
are considered incapable of possessing any property in the planet they infest,
and the right and title to it are confirmed to its original discoverers.—And
furthermore, the colonists who are now about to depart to the aforesaid
planet are authorized and commanded to use every means to convert these
infidel savages from the darkness of Christianity, and make them thorough
and absolute lunatics."

In consequence of this benevolent bull, our philosophic benefactors go
to work with hearty zeal. They seize upon our fertile territories, scourge us
from our rightful possessions, relieve us from our wives, and when we are
unreasonable enough to complain, they will turn upon us and say, Miserable
barbarians! ungrateful wretches! have we not come thousands of miles to
improve your worthless planet; have we not fed you with moonshine; have
we not intoxicated you with nitrous oxides; does not our moon give you
light every night, and have you the baseness to murmur, when we claim a
pitiful return for all these benefits? But finding that we not only persist in
absolute contempt of their reasoning and disbelief in their philosophy, but
even go so far as daringly to defend our property, their patience shall be
exhausted, and they shall resort to their superior powers of argument; hunt
us with hyppogriffs, transfix us with concentrated sunbeams, demolish our
cities with moonstones; until having, by main force, converted us to the
true faith, they shall graciously permit us to exist in the torrid deserts of
Arabia, or the frozen regions of Lapland, there to enjoy the blessings of
civilization and the charms of lunar philosophy, in much the same manner
as the reformed and enlightened savages of this country are kindly suffered
to inhabit the inhospitable forests of the north, or the impenetrable wilder-
nesses of South America.

Thus, I hope, I have clearly proved, and strikingly illustrated, the right
of the early colonists to the possession of this country; and thus is this
gigantic question completely vanquished: so having manfully surmounted
all obstacles, and subdued all opposition, what remains but that I should
forthwith conduct my readers into the city which we have been so long in a
manner besieging? But hold; before I proceed another step, I must pause to
take breath, and recover from the excessive fatigue I have undergone, in
preparing to begin this most accurate of histories. And in this I do but imitate the example of a renowned Dutch tumbler of antiquity, who took a
start of three miles for the purpose of jumping over a hill, but having run
himself out of breath by the time he reached the foot, sat himself quietly
down for a few moments to blow, and then walked over it at his leisure.

LYDIA MARIA CHILD

(1802–1880)

Lydia Maria Francis Child began her literary career with *Hobomok;* influenced by the reception of the long narrative poem *Yamoyden: A Tale of the Wars of King Philip* (1820), by James Eastburn and Robert C. Sands, she wrote this sentimental novel at the age of twenty-two. Subsequently, she turned her energies to philanthropy and reform and became a leading abolitionist. Among her other works are *Appeal in Favor of that Class of Americans Called Africans* (1833), *The Rebels; or, Boston Before the Revolution* (1825), and *Philothea: A Romance of Classical Greece* (1836).

Lydia Child's humanitarian spirit led her to portray, in Hobomok, a most noble savage. Friend of the English, he remains loyal to members of the small white settlement at Salem despite stirrings of Indian hostility; he expresses his love for Mary Conant only when she is desolated by the loss of her mother and her white lover. Mary marries Hobomok while she is in a state of grief bordering on insanity, but after the birth of a son and the passage of two years, she begins to recognize and admire his manly qualities. The purportedly drowned lover returns at this time; Hobomok calls up all of his nobility and sacrifices his happiness. He goes west alone to die, foreshadowing the fate of his whole race. Despite her liberalism, Child makes it clear that Mary has lowered herself in marrying Hobomok; her "savage" husband's nobility is measured by his self-abasement. The chapter reprinted below describes the marriage and Hobomok's final generous act.

The book dramatizes the theory of the inevitable, benevolent displacement of the Indian; it is equally severe to rigid Puritanism and to Indian resistance. Child prefers to have her Indians survive in memory, rather than physical reality. Hobomok's child, conveniently given his mother's patronym, after the matrilineal style of the Indians, becomes a Cambridge graduate. Child notes, with some relief, "His father was seldom spoken of; and by degrees his Indian appellation was silently omitted."

From *Hobomok: A Tale of Early Times. . ., 1824*

For several weeks Mary remained in the same stupefied state in which
she had been at the time of her marriage. She would lie through the live-
long day, unless she was requested to rise; and once risen, nothing could
induce her to change her posture. Language has no power to shadow forth
her feelings as she gradually awoke to a sense of her situation. But there is
a happy propensity in the human mind to step as lightly as possible on the
thorns which infest a path we are compelled to tread. It is only when there
is room for hope that evils are impatiently borne. Desolate as Mary's lot
might seem, it was not without its alleviations. All the kind attentions
which could suggest themselves to the mind of a savage, were paid by her
Indian mother. Hobomok continued the same tender reverence he had
always evinced, and he soon understood the changing expression of her
countenance, till her very looks were a law. So much love could not but
awaken gratitude; and Mary by degrees gave way to its influence, until she
welcomed his return with something like affection. True, in her solitary
hours there were reflections enough to make her wretched. Kind as
Hobomok was, and rich as she found his uncultivated mind in native imagination, still the contrast between him and her departed lover would often
be remembered with sufficient bitterness. Besides this, she knew that her
own nation looked upon her as lost and degraded; and, what was far worse,
her own heart echoed back the charge. Hobomok's connection with her was
considered the effect of witchcraft on his part, and even he was generally
avoided by his former friends. However, this evil brought its own cure.
Every wound of this kind, every insult which her husband courageously
endured for her sake, added romantic fervor to her increasing affection, and
thus made life something more than endurable. While all her English
acquaintances more or less neglected her, her old associate, Mrs. Collier,
firmly and boldly stemmed the tide, and seemed resolved to do all in her
power to relieve the hardships of her friends. For a long time her overtures
were proudly refused; for Mary could not endure that the visits of one who
had been so vastly her inferior should now be considered an honor and
obligation. However, persevering kindness did in time overcome this feeling,

Lydia Maria Child, *Hobomok: A Tale of Early Times, by an American* (Boston,
1824), chapter 19, pp. 168–176.

and in less than a year, Sally became a frequent inmate of her wigwam. To this was soon likely to be added another source of enjoyment. Before two years passed away, she became the mother of a hopeful son. Under such circumstances, his birth was no doubt entwined with many mournful associations; still, the smiles of her infant son brought more of pleasure than of pain. As Mary looked on the little being, which was "bone of her bone, and flesh of her flesh," she felt more love for the innocent object than she thought she should ever again experience.

. . . .

After this general view of things, we must now pass over to the 16th of September, 1633, and leave the interim to the reader's imagination. The old squaw had lately died of a fever, and symptoms of the same disorder began to appear in her little grandson, now nearly two years old. On the morning we have mentioned, Mrs. Collier took her own little blooming daughter in her arms, and went into the wigwam to inquire concerning the health of the boy. No sooner was she seated than the children, accustomed to see each other, began to peep in each other's faces, and look up to their mothers, their bright, laughing eyes beaming with cherub love. Hobomok entered, and for a moment stood watching with delighted attention the bewitching sports of childhood. He caught up the infant, and placing his little feet in the center of his hand, held him high above his head.

"My boy, my brave hunter's boy," said he, and pressing him in his arms he half suffocated him with caresses. He placed him in his mother's lap, and took down his quiver, as he said, "Hobomok must be out hunting the deer." The child jumped down upon the floor, and tottling up to him, took hold of his blanket and looked in his face, as he lisped, "Fader come back gin to see 'ittle Hobomok."

Again the father stooped and kissed him, as he answered,

"Hobomok very much bad, if he didn't come back always to see little Hobomok, and his good Mary."

He went out, but soon returned and, lifting the blanket, which served for a door, he again looked at his boy, who would alternately hide his head, and then reach forward to catch another glimpse of his father.

"Good bye, Hobomok—Good bye, Mary"—said the Indian. "Before the sun hides his face, I shall come home loaded with deer."

"Take care of yourself," said his wife, affectionately; "and see that Corbitant be not in your path."

"Sally, you have never said one word about my marrying Hobomok," continued she; "and I have no doubt you think I must be very miserable; but I speak truly when I say that every day I live with that kind, noble-hearted creature, the better I love him."

"I always thought he was the best Indian I ever knew," answered Sally; "and within these three years he has altered so much that he seems almost like an Englishman. After all, I believe matches are foreordained."

"I don't know concerning that," rejoined Mary. "I am sure I am happier than I ever expected to be after Charles's death, which is more than I deserve, considering I broke my promise to my dying mother and deserted my father in his old age."

While conversation of this nature was going on at home, Hobomok was pursuing his way through the woods, whistling and singing as he went, in the joyfulness of his heart. He had proceeded near half a mile in this way, when he espied an eagle, soaring with a flight so lofty, that he seemed almost like a speck in the blue abyss above. The Indian fixed his keen eye upon him, and as he gradually lowered his flight, he made ready his arrow, and a moment after the noble bird lay fluttering at his feet.

"A true aim that, Hobomok," said a voice which sounded familiar to his ears. He raised his head to see from whence it proceeded. Charles Brown stood by his side! The countenance of the savage assumed at once the terrible, ashen hue of Indian paleness. His wounded victim was left untouched, and he hastily retreated into the thicket, casting back a fearful glance on what he supposed to be the ghost of his rival. Brown attempted to follow; but the farther he advanced, the farther the Indian retreated, his face growing paler and paler, and his knees trembling against each other in excessive terror.

"Hobomok," said the intruder, "I am a man like yourself. I suppose three years agone you heard I was dead, but it has pleased the Lord to spare me in captivity until this time, and to lead me once more to New England. The vessel which brought me hither lieth down a mile below, but I chose the rather to be put on shore, being impatient to inquire concerning the friends I left behind. You used to be my good friend, Hobomok, and many a piece of service have you done for me. I beseech you feel of my hand, that you may know I am flesh and blood even as yourself."

After repeated assurances, the Indian timidly approached—and the certainty that Brown was indeed alive was more dreadful to him than all the ghosts that could have been summoned from another world.

"You look as if you were sorry your old friend had returned," said the Englishman: "but do speak and tell me one thing—is Mary Conant yet alive?"

Hobomok fixed his eyes upon him with such a strange mixture of sorrow and fierceness that Brown laid his hand upon his rifle, half fearful his intentions were evil. At length, the Indian answered with deliberate emphasis,

"She is both alive and well."

"I thank God," rejoined his rival. "I need not ask whether she is married?"

The savage looked earnestly and mournfully upon him, and sighed deeply, as he said,

"The handsome English bird hath for three years lain in my bosom; and her milk hath nourished the son of Hobomok."

The Englishman cast a glance of mingled doubt and despair towards the Indian, who again repeated the distressing truth.

Disappointed love, a sense of degradation, perhaps something of resentment were all mingled in a dreadful chaos of agony within the mind of the unfortunate young man, and at that moment it was difficult to tell to which of the two anguish had presented her most unmingled cup. The Indian gazed upon his rival, as he stood leaning his aching head against a tree; and once and again he indulged in the design of taking his life.

"No," thought he. "She was first his. Mary loves him better than she does me; for even now she prays for him in her sleep. The sacrifice must be made to her."

For a long time, however, it seemed doubtful whether he could collect sufficient fortitude to fulfill his resolution. The remembrance of the smiling wife and the little prattling boy, whom he had that morning left, came too vividly before him. It recks not now what was the mighty struggle in the mind of that dark man. He arose and touched Brown's arm, as he said,

"'Tis all true which I have told you. It is three snows since the bird came to my nest; and the Great Spirit only knows how much I have loved her. Good and kind she has been; but the heart of Mary is not with the Indian. In her sleep she talks with the Great Spirit, and the name of the white man is on her lips. Hobomok will go far off among some of the red men in the west. They will dig him a grave, and Mary may sing the marriage song in the wigwam of the Englishman."

"No," answered his astonished companion. "She is your wife. Keep her, and cherish her with tenderness. A moment ago, I expected your arrow would rid me of the life which has now become a burden. I will be as generous as you have been. I will return from whence I came, and bear my sorrows as I may. Let Mary never know that I am alive. Love her, and be happy."

"The purpose of an Indian is seldom changed," replied Hobomok. "My tracks will soon be seen far beyond the back-bone of the Great Spirit. For Mary's sake I have borne the hatred of the Yengees, the scorn of my tribe, and the insults of my enemy. And now I will be buried among strangers, and none shall black their faces for the unknown chief. When the light sinks behind the hills, see that Corbitant be not near my wigwam; for that hawk has often been flying round my nest. Be kind to my boy."—His voice choked, and the tears fell bright and fast. He hastily wiped them away as he added, "You have seen the first and last tears that Hobomok will ever shed. Ask Mary to pray for me—that when I die, I may go to the English-man's God, where I may hunt beaver with little Hobomok, and count my beavers for Mary."

Before Brown had time to reply, he plunged into the thicket and dis-appeared. He moved on with astonishing speed, till he was aware that he must be beyond the reach of pursuit; then throwing himself upon the grass, most earnestly did he hope that the arrow of Corbitant would do the office it had long sought, and wreak upon his head deep and certain venge-ance. But the weapon of his enemy came not. He was reserved for a fate that had more of wretchedness. He lay thus inactive for several hours, musing on all he had enjoyed and lost. At last, he sprung upon his feet, as if stung with torture he could no longer endure, and seizing his bow, he pursued with delirious eagerness every animal which came within his view.

The sun was verging toward the western horizon, when he collected his game in one spot, and selecting the largest deer, and several of the hand-somest smaller animals, he fastened them upon a pole and proceeded to-wards Plymouth.

It was dark, and the tapers were lighted throughout the village, when he entered Governor Winslow's dwelling. Whatever was the purpose of his visit, it was not long continued; and soon after, the deer was noiselessly deposited by the side of Mr. Collier's house, with a slip of paper fastened on his branching horns. Hobomok paused before the door of his wigwam, looked in at a small hole which admitted the light, saw Mary feeding her Indian boy from his little wooden bowl, and heard her beloved voice, as she said to her child, "Father will come home and see little Hobomok presently."

How much would that high-souled child of the forest have given for one parting embrace—one kind assurance that he should not be forgotten. Affection was tugging hard at his heart strings, and once his foot was almost on the threshold.

"No," said he; "it will distress her. The Great Spirit bless 'em both."

Without trusting another look, he hurried forward. He paused on a neighboring hill, looked toward his wigwam till his strained vision could hardly discern the object, with a bursting heart again murmured his farewell and blessing, and forever passed away from New England.

JOHN AUGUSTUS STONE

(1800–1834)

In 1828, the actor Edwin Forrest advertised a five-hundred-dollar reward for the best play in which an American Indian would be the major character. Forrest offered rewards throughout his prosperous career; they resulted in roles that earned him great wealth while they stimulated the use of native materials in American drama. In this case, he awarded the prize to *Metamora; or, The Last of the Wampanoags,* written by a young actor-playwright named John Augustus Stone. Stone, who was born in Concord, Massachusetts, in 1800, made an early debut as a character actor; after a short career, during which he wrote more plays, but no notable ones, he committed suicide in 1834.

Metamora became an important vehicle for Forrest, who performed in it for forty years; the play drew record audiences wherever it was staged. It created a vogue for Indian dramas, more than fifty of which were written during the nineteenth century, including some, like John Brougham's *Po-ca-hon-tas* (1855), that burlesqued the "noble savage" theme.

In Stone's play there is a double plot; first, the white lovers, Walter and Oceana, struggle to overcome her father's tyranny and Walter's unknown paternity; second, Metamora analyzes the force arrayed against his people and tries to save them. The two plots intertwine in the figure of Oceana, who, like Shakespeare's Miranda, is pure, innocent and loyal. Because her dead mother nursed Massasoit, Metamora's father, the chief gives Oceana an eagle feather which will save her from Indian wrath during the war to come. Although Oceana and the other whites are stock figures, she, at least, seems to symbolize the human qualities that might have averted deadly conflict. There is no danger, however, that any part in the play will outshine Metamora's. He alone is given memorable speeches and suitably tragic action.

Reprinted below is act 5, scene 5, including the death of Metamora and his wife, Nahmeokee. Although Metamora is as noble a savage as can be imagined, a model of physical strength, natural piety and self-sacrifice, he also has a bitter prophetic vision. In act 2, scene 1, he predicts the future of his people with an accuracy that has contemporary reverberations.

Nahmeokee suggests, with all the pathos of a fearful mother, that the whites will spare her people. Metamora replies:

Yes, when our fires are no longer red on the high places of our fathers; when the bones of our kindred make fruitful the fields of the stranger, which he has planted amidst the ashes of our wigwams; when we are hunted back like the wounded elk far toward the going down of the sun, our hatchets broken, our bows unstrung and war whoop hushed; then will the stranger spare, for we will be too small for his eye to see.

From *Metamora, or the Last of the Wampanoags*, 1829

Scene 5: *Metamora's stronghold. Rocks, bridge and waterfall. Nahmeokee discovered listening. The child lies under a tree, R., covered with furs. Slow music, four bars.*

Nah. He comes not, yet the sound of the battle has died away like the last breath of a storm! Can he be slain? O cruel white man, this day will stain your name forever. *[Slow music, sixteen bars. Metamora enters on bridge. Crosses and enters L.]*

Meta. Nahmeokee, I am weary of the strife of blood. Where is our little one? Let me take him to my burning heart and he may quell its mighty torrent.

Nah. *[With broken utterance]* He is here! *[Lifts the furs and shows the child dead]*

Meta. Ha! Dead! Dead! Cold!

Nah. Nahmeokee could not cover him with her body, for the white men were around her and over her. I plunged into the stream and the unseen shafts of the fire weapons flew with a great noise over my head. One smote my babe and he sunk into the deep water; the foe shouted with a mighty shout, for he thought Nahmeokee and her babe had sunk to rise no more.

Eugene R. Page, ed., *Metamora and Other Plays* (Princeton, 1941), vol. 14 in *America's Lost Plays*, pp. 38–40.

Meta. His little arms will never clasp thee more; his little lips will never press the pure bosom which nourished him so long! Well, is he not happy? Better to die by the stranger's hand than live his slave.

Nah. O Metamora! *[Falls on his neck]*

Meta. Nay, do not bow down thy head; let me kiss off the hot drops that are running down thy red cheeks. Thou wilt see him again in the peaceful land of spirits, and he will look smilingly as—as—as I do now, Nahmeokee.

Nah. Metamora, is our nation dead? Are we alone in the land of our fathers?

Meta. The palefaces are all around us, and they tread in blood. The blaze of our burning wigwams flashes awfully in the darkness of their path. We are destroyed—not vanquished; we are no more, yet we are forever—Nahmeokee!

Nah. What wouldst thou?

Meta. Dost thou not fear the power of the white man?

Nah. No.

Meta. He may come hither in his might and slay thee.

Nah. Thou art with me.

Meta. He may seize thee, and bear thee off to the far country, bind these arms that have so often clasped me in the dear embrace of love, scourge thy soft flesh in the hour of his wrath, and force thee to carry burdens like the beasts of the fields.

Nah. Thou wilt not let them.

Meta. We cannot fly, for the foe is all about us; we cannot fight, for this is the only weapon I have saved from the strife of blood.

Nah. It was my brother's—Coanchett's.

Meta. It has tasted the white man's blood, and reached the cold heart of the traitor; it has been our truest friend; it is our only treasure.

Nah. Thine eye tells me the thought of thy heart, and I rejoice at it. *[Sinks on his bosom]*

Meta. Nahmeokee, I look up through the long path of thin air, and I think I see our infant borne onward to the land of the happy, where the fair hunting grounds know no storms or snows, and where the immortal brave feast in the eyes of the giver of good. Look upwards, Nahmeokee, the spirit of thy murdered father beckons thee.

Nah. I will go to him.

Meta. Embrace me, Nahmeokee—'twas like the first you gave me in the days of our strength and joy—they are gone. *[Places his ear to the ground]* Hark! In the distant wood I faintly hear the cautious tread of men! They are upon us, Nahmeokee—the home of the happy is made ready for thee. *[Stabs her, she dies]* She felt no white man's bondage—free as the air she lived—pure as the snow she died! In smiles she died! Let me taste it, ere her lips are cold as the ice. *[Loud shouts. Roll of drums. Kaweshine leads Church and Soldiers on bridge, R.]*

Church. He is found! Philip is our prisoner.

Meta. No! He lives—last of his race—but still your enemy—lives to defy you still. Though numbers overpower me and treachery surround me, though friends desert me, I defy you still! Come to me—come singly to me! And this true knife that has tasted the foul blood of your nation and now is red with the purest of mine, will feel a grasp as strong as when it flashed in the blaze of your burning dwellings, or was lifted terribly over the fallen in battle.

Church. Fire upon him!

Meta. Do so, I am weary of the world for ye are dwellers in it; I would not turn upon my heel to save my life.

Church. Your duty, soldiers. *[They fire. Metamora falls. Enter Walter, Oceana, Wolfe, Sir Arthur, Errington, Goodenough, Tramp and Peasants. Roll of drums and trumpet till all on]*

Meta. My curses on you, white men! May the Great Spirit curse you when he speaks in his war voice from the clouds! Murderers! The last of the Wampanoags' curse be on you! May your graves and the graves of your children be in the path the red man shall trace! And may the wolf and panther howl o'er your fleshless bones, fit banquet for the destroyers! Spirits of the grave, I come! But the curse of Metamora stays with the white man! I die! My wife! My queen! My Nahmeokee! *[Falls and dies; a tableau is formed. Drums and trumpet sound a retreat till curtain. Slow curtain]*

WILLIAM GILMORE SIMMS
(1806–1870)

Simms, a South Carolinian, began his literary career as a poet and editor, but became best known for his romantic, historical novels in the tradition of Cooper and Scott. Like Cooper, he was a hasty writer who rarely stopped to revise his prolific output. Today he is admired less for his contrived, sentimental plots than for his rendering of landscape, customs and traditions of the colonial South. His two major subjects were the Revolutionary period in his region *(The Partisan,* 1835; *Mellichampe,* 1836; *Woodcraft,* 1854) and Southern border settlement *(Guy Rivers,* 1834; *The Yemassee,* 1835; *The Cassique of Kiawah,* 1859). Simms was also the author of a *Life of John Smith,* in which he has a moving chapter on Pocahontas. His most important fictional studies of Indians are *The Yemassee, The Cassique of Kiawah,* and the short stories of *The Wigwam and the Cabin.*

As the title of the last-mentioned volume suggests, Simms grouped Indians with blacks, in a theory of white superiority; he predicted the inevitable displacement of the inferior, if sometimes heroic, Indian, and upheld the benevolence of slavery for blacks. In the course of the Civil War, Simms lost his great plantation, Woodlands, and his dream of a Greek democracy in the South.

In the selection that follows from *The Yemassee,* Simm's Southern version of *The Last of the Mohicans,* the profligate youth Occonestoga is killed at a forest altar by his own mother. By this means, he escapes banishment from the Yemassee afterlife, to which he has been sentenced by the aroused tribe for his submission to the white man's vices. This is the novel's subplot; its main concern is the successful love affair of the English governor of the Carolina colony, and his proper protection of the small colony from the desperate and doomed Indians.

From **The Yemassee: A Romance of Carolina,** *1835*

It was a gloomy amphitheatre in the deep forests to which the assembled
multitude bore the unfortunate Occonestoga. The whole scene was unique
in that solemn grandeur, that sombre hue, that deep spiritual repose, in
which the human imagination delights to invest the region which has been
rendered remarkable for the deed of punishment or crime. A small swamp
or morass hung upon one side of the wood, from the rank bosom of which,
in numberless millions, the flickering fire-fly perpetually darted upwards,
giving a brilliance and animation to the spot, which, at that moment, no
assemblage of light or life could possibly enliven. The ancient oak, a
bearded Druid, was there to contribute to the due solemnity of all associations—the green but gloomy cedar, the ghostly cypress, and here and there
the overgrown pine,—all rose up in their primitive strength, and with an
undergrowth around them of shrub and flower, that scarcely, at any time,
in that sheltered and congenial habitation, had found it necessary to shrink
from winter. In the center of the area thus invested, rose a high and
venerable mound, the tumulus of many preceding ages, from the washed
sides of which might now and then be seen protruding the bleached bones
of some ancient warrior or sage. A circle of trees, at a little distance, hedged
it in,—made secure and sacred by the performance there of many of their
religious rites and offices,—themselves, as they bore the broad arrow of the
Yemassee, being free from all danger of overthrow or desecration by Indian
hands.

Amid the confused cries of the multitude, they bore the captive to the
foot of the tumulus, and bound him backward, half reclining upon a tree.
An hundred warriors stood around, armed according to the manner of the
nation, each with a tomahawk and knife and bow. They stood up as for
battle, but spectators simply, and took no part in a proceeding which
belonged entirely to the priesthood. In a wider and denser circle, gathered
hundreds more—not the warriors, but the people—the old, the young, the
women, and the children, all fiercely excited and anxious to see a ceremony,
so awfully exciting to an Indian imagination; involving, as it did, not only
the perpetual loss of human caste and national consideration, but the eternal

William Gilmore Simms, *The Yemassee: A Romance of Carolina*, new and revised
edition (New York, 1878), pp. 210–224.

177

doom, the degradation, the denial of, and the exile from, their simple forest heaven. Interspersed with this latter crowd, seemingly at regular intervals, and with an allotted labor assigned them, came a number of old women, not unmeet representatives, individually, for either of the weird sisters of the Scottish Thane,

"So withered and so wild in their attire—"

and, regarding their cries and actions, of whom we may safely affirm that they looked like anything but inhabitants of earth! In their hands they bore, each of them, a flaming torch of the rich and gummy pine; and these they waved over the heads of the multitude in a thousand various evolutions, accompanying each movement with a fearful cry, which, at regular periods, was chorused by the assembled mass. A bugle, a native instrument of sound, five feet or more in length, hollowed out from the commonest timber—the cracks and breaks of which were carefully sealed up with the resinous gum oozing from their burning torches, and which, to this day, borrowed from the natives, our negroes employ on the southern waters with a peculiar compass and variety of note—was carried by one of the party, and gave forth at intervals, timed with much regularity, a long, protracted, single blast, adding greatly to the wild and picturesque character of the spectacle. At the articulation of these sounds, the circles continued to contract, though slowly; until, at length, but a brief space lay between the armed warriors, the crowd, and the unhappy victim.

The night grew dark of a sudden, and the sky was obscured by one of the brief tempests that usually usher in the summer, and mark the transition, in the south, of one season to another. A wild gust rushed along the wood. The leaves were whirled over the heads of the assemblage, and the trees bent downwards, until they cracked and groaned again beneath the wind. A feeling of natural superstition crossed the minds of the multitude, as the hurricane, though common enough in that region, passed hurriedly along; and a spontaneous and universal voice of chanted prayer rose from the multitude, in their own wild and emphatic language, to the evil deity whose presence they beheld in its progress:

> Thy wing, Opitchi-Manneyto,
> It o'erthrows the tall trees—
> Thy breath, Opitchi-Manneyto,
> Makes the waters tremble—
> Thou art in the hurricane,
> When the wigwam tumbles—
> Thou art in the arrow-fire,

> When the pine is shiver'd—
> But upon the Yemassee,
> Be thy coming gentle—
> Are they not thy well-beloved?
> Bring they not a slave to thee?
> Look! the slave is bound for thee,
> 'Tis the Yemassee that brings him.
> Pass, Opitchi-Manneyto—
> Pass, black spirit, pass from us—
> Be thy passage gentle.

And, as the uncouth strain rose at the conclusion into a diapason of unanimous and contending voices of old and young, male and female, the brief summer tempest had gone by. A shout of self-gratulation, joined with warm acknowledgments, testified the popular sense and confidence in that especial Providence, which even the most barbarous nations claim as forever working in their behalf.

At this moment, surrounded by the chiefs, and preceded by the great prophet or high-priest, Enoree-Mattee, came Sanutee, the well-beloved of the Yemassee, to preside over the destinies of his son. There was a due and becoming solemnity, but nothing of the peculiar feelings of the father, visible in his countenance. Blocks of wood were placed around as seats for the chiefs, but Sanutee and the prophet threw themselves, with more of imposing veneration in the proceeding, upon the edge of the tumulus, just where an overcharged spot, bulging out with the crowding bones of its inmates, had formed an elevation answering the purpose of couch or seat. They sat, directly looking upon the prisoner, who reclined, bound securely upon his back to a decapitated tree, at a little distance before them. A signal having been given, the women ceased their clamors, and approaching him, they waved their torches so closely above his head as to make all his features distinctly visible to the now watchful and silent multitude. He bore the examination with stern, unmoved features, which the sculptor in brass or marble might have been glad to transfer to his statue in the block. While the torches waved, one of the women now cried aloud, in a barbarous chant, above him:—

> Is not this a Yemassee?
> Wherefore is he bound thus—
> Wherefore, with the broad arrow
> On his right arm growing,
> Wherefore is he bound thus—
> Is not this a Yemassee?

A second woman now approached him, waving her torch in like manner, seeming closely to inspect his features, and actually passing her fingers over the emblem upon his shoulder, as if to ascertain more certainly the truth of the image. Having done this, she turned about to the crowd, and in the same barbarous sort of strain with the preceding, replied as follows:—

> It is not the Yemassee,
> But a dog that runs away.
> From his right arm take the arrow,
> He is not the Yemassee.

As these words were uttered, the crowd of women and children around cried out for the execution of the judgment thus given, and once again flamed the torches wildly, and the shoutings were general among the multitude. When they had subsided, a huge Indian came forward, and sternly confronted the prisoner. This man was Malatchie, the executioner; and he looked the horrid trade which he professed. His garments were stained and smeared with blood and covered with scalps, which, connected together by slight strings, formed a loose robe over his shoulders. In one hand he carried a torch, in the other a knife. He came forward, under the instructions of Enoree-Mattee, the prophet, to claim the slave of Opitchi-Manneyto,— that is, in our language, the slave of hell. This he did in the following strain:—

> 'Tis Opitchi-Manneyto
> In Malatchie's ear that cries,
> This is not the Yemassee—
> And the woman's word is true—
> He's a dog that should be mine,
> I have hunted for him long.
> From his master he had run,
> With the stranger made his home,
> Now I have him, he is mine—
> Hear Opitchi-Manneyto.

And, as the besmeared and malignant executioner howled his fierce demand in the very ears of his victim, he hurled the knife which he carried, upwards with such dexterity into the air, that it rested, point downward, and sticking fast on its descent into the tree and just above the head of the doomed Occonestoga. With his hand, the next instant, he laid a resolute grip upon the shoulder of the victim, as if to confirm and strengthen his claim by actual possession; while, at the same time, with a sort of malignant pleasure, he thrust his besmeared and distorted visage close into the face of his prisoner. Writhing against the ligaments which bound him fast, Occonestoga strove to turn his head aside from the disgusting and obtrusive presence; and the desperation of his effort, but that he had been too carefully secured, might have resulted in the release of some of his limbs; for the breast heaved and labored, and every muscle of his arms and legs was wrought, by his severe action, into so many ropes, hard, full, and indicative of prodigious strength.

. . . .

"Is no hatchet sharp for Occonestoga?"—moaned forth the suffering savage. But his trials were only then begun. Enoree-Mattee now approached him with the words, with which, as the representative of the good Manneyto, he renounced him,—with which he denied him access to the Indian heaven, and left him a slave and an outcast, a miserable wanderer amid the shadows and the swamps, and liable to all the dooms and terrors which come with the service of Opitchi-Manneyto.

Thou wast the child of Manneyto—

sung the high priest in a solemn chant, and with a deep-toned voice that thrilled strangely amid the silence of the scene.

> Thou wast a child of Manneyto,
> He gave thee arrows and an eye,—
> Thou wast the strong son of Manneyto,
> He gave thee feathers and a wing—
> Thou wast a young brave of Manneyto,
> He gave thee scalps and a war-song—
> But he knows thee no more—he knows thee no more.

And the clustering multitude again gave back the last line in wild chorus. The prophet continued his chant:

> That Opitchi-Manneyto!—
> He commands thee for his slave—
> And the Yemassee must hear him,
> Hear, and give thee for his slave—
> They will take from thee the arrow,
> The broad arrow of thy people—
> Thou shalt see no blessed valley,
> Where the plum-groves always bloom—
> Thou shalt hear no song of valor,
> From the ancient Yemassee—
> Father, mother, name, and people,

Thou shalt lose with that broad arrow,
Thou art lost to the Manneyto—
He knows thee no more, he knows thee no more.

The despair of hell was in the face of the victim, and he howled forth, in a cry of agony, that, for a moment, silenced the wild chorus of the crowd around, the terrible consciousness in his mind of that privation which the doom entailed upon him. Every feature was convulsed with emotion; and the terrors of Opitchi-Manneyto's dominion seemed already in strong exercise upon the muscles of his heart, when Sanutee, the father, silently approached him, and with a pause of a few moments, stood gazing upon the son from whom he was to be separated eternally—whom not even the uniting, the restoring hand of death could possibly restore to him. And he—his once noble son—the pride of his heart, the gleam of his hope, the triumphant warrior, who was even to increase his own glory, and transmit the endearing title of well-beloved, which the Yemassee had given him, to a succeeding generation—he was to be lost for ever! These promises were all blasted, and the father was now present to yield him up eternally—to deny him—to forfeit him, in fearful penalty to the nation whose genius he had wronged, and whose rights he had violated. The old man stood for a moment, rather, we may suppose, for the recovery of his resolution, than with any desire for the contemplation of the pitiable form before him. The pride of the youth came back to him,—the pride of the strong mind in its desolation—as his eye caught the inflexible gaze of his unswerving father; and he exclaimed bitterly and loud:—

"Wherefore art thou come—thou hast been my foe, not my father—away—I would not behold thee!" and he closed his eyes after the speech, as if to relieve himself from a disgusting presence.

"Thou hast said well, Occonestoga—Sanutee is thy foe—he is not thy father. To say this in thy ears has he come. Look on him, Occonestoga—look up, and hear thy doom. The young and the old of the Yemassee—the warrior and the chief,—they have all denied thee—all given thee up to Opitchi-Manneyto! Occonestoga is no name for the Yemassee. The Yemassee gives it to his dog. The prophet of Manneyto has forgotten thee—thou art unknown to those who were thy people. And I, thy father—with this speech, I yield thee to Opitchi-Manneyto. Sanutee is no longer thy father—thy father knows thee no more"—and once more came to the ears of the victim that melancholy chorus of the multitude—"He knows thee no more—he knows thee no more."

. . . .

"The Yemassee knows thee no more," cried the multitude, and their universal shout was deafening upon the ear. Occonestoga said no word now—he could offer no resistance to the unnerving hands of Malatchie, who now bared the arm more completely of its covering. But his limbs were convulsed with the spasms of that dreadful terror of the future which was racking and raging in every pulse of his heart. He had full faith in the superstitions of his people. His terrors acknowledged the full horrors of their doom. A despairing agony, which no language could describe, had possession of his soul. Meanwhile, the silence of all indicated the general anxiety; and Malatchie prepared to seize the knife and perform the operation, when a confused murmur arose from the crowd around; the mass gave way and parted, and, rushing wildly into the area, came Matiwan, his mother—the long black hair streaming—the features, an astonishing likeness to his own, convulsed like his; and her action that of one reckless of all things in the way of the forward progress she was making to the person of her child. She cried aloud as she came—with a voice that rang like a sudden death-bell through the ring—

"Would you keep the mother from her boy, and he to be lost to her for ever? Shall she have no parting with the young brave she bore in her bosom? Away, keep me not back—I will look upon, I will love him. He shall have the blessing of Matiwan, though the Yemassee and the Manneyto curse."

The victim heard, and a momentary renovation of mental life, perhaps a renovation of hope, spoke out in the simple exclamation which fell from his lips—

"Oh, Matiwan—oh, mother!"

She rushed towards the spot where she heard his appeal, and thrusting the executioner aside, threw her arms desperately about his neck.

"Touch him not, Matiwan," was the general cry from the crowd.—"Touch him not, Matiwan—Manneyto knows him no more."

"But Matiwan knows him—the mother knows her child, though the Manneyto denies him. Oh, boy—oh, boy, boy, boy." And she sobbed like an infant on his neck.

"Thou art come, Matiwan—thou art come, but wherefore?—to curse like the father—to curse like the Manneyto?" mournfully said the captive.

"No, no, no! Not to curse—not to curse. When did mother curse the child she bore? Not to curse, but to bless thee.—To bless thee and forgive."

"Tear her away," cried the prophet; "let Opitchi-Manneyto have his slave."

"Tear her away, Malatchie," cried the crowd, now impatient for the execution. Malatchie approached.

"Not yet—not yet," appealed the woman. "Shall not the mother say farewell to the child she shall see no more?" and she waved Malatchie back, and in the next instant drew hastily from the drapery of her dress a small hatchet, which she had there carefully concealed.

"What wouldst thou do, Matiwan?" asked Occonestoga, as his eye caught the glare of the weapon.

"Save thee, my boy—save thee for thy mother, Occonestoga—save thee for the happy valley."

"Wouldst thou slay me, mother—wouldst strike the heart of thy son?" he asked, with a something of reluctance to receive death from the hands of a parent.

"I strike thee but to save thee, my son:—since they cannot take the totem from thee after the life is gone. Turn away from me thy head—let me not look upon thine eyes as I strike, lest my hands grow weak and tremble. Turn thine eyes away—I will not lose thee."

His eyes closed, and the fatal instrument, lifted above her head, was now visible in the sight of all. The executioner rushed forward to interpose, but he came too late. The tomahawk was driven deep into the skull, and but a single sentence from his lips preceded the final insensibility of the victim.

"It is good, Matiwan, it is good—thou hast saved me—the death is in my heart." And back he sank as he spoke, while a shriek of mingled joy and horror from the lips of the mother announced the success of her effort to defeat the doom, the most dreadful in the imagination of the Yemassee.

"He is not lost—he is not lost. They may not take the child from his mother. They may not keep him from the valley of Manneyto. He is free— he is free." And she fell back in a deep swoon into the arms of Sanutee, who by this time had approached. She had defrauded Opitchi-Manneyto of his victim, for they may not remove the badge of the nation from any but the living victim.

NATHANIEL HAWTHORNE
(1804–1864)

In the dark backgrounds of *The Scarlet Letter* (1850) and *The House of the Seven Gables* (1851), Hawthorne's great romances, a strong tone is contributed by references to Indians. When Roger Chillingworth emerges from the forest to witness Hester's ignominy, he is accompanied by an Indian to whom a ransom must be paid; he soon uses the secrets taught him by Indian medicine men to cure Pearl of her infant distemper. Something of the deviltry of pagans lingers in his character. Later in the novel, at the election-day climax, Indians mingle with the townspeople and take Hester's splendid ornament for a badge of distinction.

In *The House of the Seven Gables,* Hawthorne describes the greed of the Pyncheons. The persecution of poor Clifford is inspired by the hope of finding a lost Indian deed; the reader is invited to associate this transfer of land with the vicious behavior that accomplished the dispossession of Old Maule—to view Indians as victimized by greed.

In his short stories as well, the same flavor of ambivalence hangs over Hawthorne's Indian comment. Examples are "Roger Malvin's Burial," a story of guilt and punishment based, Hawthorne says, on an event following Lovell's Fight; and "Young Goodman Brown," in which the protagonist fears a "devilish Indian" behind each tree and finally attends a witches' Sabbath in the forest, in the company of "Indian priests and powwows, who had often scared their native forest with more hideous incantations than any known to English witchcraft." Hawthorne is not led by his fictional method into an exploration of Indian character; he uses his Indians for color, associating them, as the Puritans did, with the dark forest and the darker aspects of human behavior. His use of Indian material can be further studied by noting the more than twenty references to Indians listed in *An Analytical Index to the Works of Nathaniel Hawthorne,* by E. M. O'Connor.

In the following retelling of a story from Cotton Mather's *Magnalia Christi Americana* (see p. 56), Hawthorne displays his interesting mixture of feelings concerning Indians. The story, originally published in *The American Magazine of Useful and Entertaining Knowledge,* begins with a conventional portrait of vicious Indians dashing out the brains of infants, and ends with a strenuous indictment of the "bloody old hag" who took her revenge.

From *The Duston Family*, *1836*

Goodman Duston and his wife, somewhat less than a century and a half ago, dwelt in Haverhill, at the time a small frontier settlement in the province of Massachusetts Bay. They had already added seven children to the King's liege subjects in America; and Mrs. Duston, about a week before the period of our narrative, had blessed her husband with an eighth. One day in March, 1698, when Mr. Duston had gone forth about his ordinary business, there fell out an event, which had nearly left him a childless man, and a widower besides. An Indian war party, after traversing the trackless forest all the way from Canada, broke in upon their remote and defenceless town. Goodman Duston heard the war-whoop and alarm, and, being on horseback, immediately set off full speed to look after the safety of his family. As he dashed along, he beheld dark wreaths of smoke eddying from the roofs of several dwellings near the roadside; while the groans of dying men, the shrieks of affrighted women, and the screams of children pierced his ear, all mingled with the horrid yell of the raging savages. The poor man trembled, yet spurred on so much the faster, dreading that he should find his own cottage in a blaze, his wife murdered in her bed, and his little ones tossed into the flames. But, drawing near the door, he saw his seven elder children, of all ages between two years and seventeen, issuing out together, and running down the road to meet him. The father only bade them make the best of their way to the nearest garrison, and, without a moment's pause, flung himself from his horse, and rushed into Mrs. Duston's bedchamber.

The good woman, as we have before hinted, had lately added an eighth to the seven former proofs of her conjugal affection; and she now lay with the infant in her arms, and her nurse, the widow Mary Neff, watching by her bedside. Such was Mrs. Duston's helpless state, when her pale and breathless husband burst into the chamber, bidding her instantly to rise and

Nathaniel Hawthorne, "The Duston Family," in *The American Magazine of Useful and Entertaining Knowledge*, vol. 2, no. 9 (Boston, May 9, 1836), pp. 395–397.

flee for her life. Scarcely were the words out of his mouth, when the Indian yell was heard; and staring wildly out of the window, Goodman Duston saw that the bloodthirsty foe was close at hand. At this terrible instant, it appears that the thought of his children's danger rushed so powerfully upon his heart, that he quite forgot the still more perilous situation of his wife; or, as is not improbable, he had such knowledge of the good lady's character as afforded him a comfortable hope that she would hold her own, even in a contest with a whole tribe of Indians. However that might be, he seized his gun and rushed out of doors again, meaning to gallop after his seven children, and snatch up one of them in his flight, lest his whole race and generation should be blotted from the earth in that fatal hour. With this idea, he rode up behind them, swift as the wind. They had, by this time, got about forty rods from the house, all pressing forward in a group; and though the younger children tripped and stumbled, yet the elder ones were not prevailed upon, by the fear of death, to take to their heels and leave these poor little souls to perish. Hearing the tramp of hoofs in their rear, they looked round, and espying Goodman Duston, all suddenly stopped. The little ones stretched out their arms; while the elder boys and girls, as it were, resigned their charge into his hands; and all the seven children seemed to say,—"Here is our father! Now we are safe!"

But if ever a poor mortal was in trouble, and perplexity, and anguish of spirit, that man was Mr. Duston! He felt his heart yearn towards these seven poor helpless children, as if each were singly possessed of his whole affections; for not one among them all but had some peculiar claim to their dear father's love. There was his first-born; there, too, the little one who, till within a week past, had been the baby; there was a girl with her mother's features, and a boy, the picture of himself, and another in whom the looks of both parents were mingled; there was one child, whom he loved for his mild, quiet, and holy disposition, and destined him to be a minister; and another, whom he loved not less for his rough and fearless spirit, and who, could he live to be a man, would do a man's part against these bloody Indians. Goodman Duston looked at the poor things, one by one; and with yearning fondness, he looked at them all, together; then he gazed up to Heaven for a moment, and finally waved his hand to his seven beloved ones. "Go on, my children," said he calmly. "We will live or die together!"

He reined in his horse, and caused him to walk behind the children, who, hand in hand, went onward, hushing their sobs and wailings, lest these sounds should bring the savages upon them. Nor was it long before the fugitives had proof that the red devils had found their track. There was a curl of smoke from behind the huge trunk of a tree, a sudden and sharp report echoed through the woods, and a bullet hissed over Goodman Duston's shoulder and passed above the children's heads. The father, turning half round on his horse, took aim and fired at the skulking foe, with such effect as to cause a momentary delay of the pursuit. Another shot— and another—whistled from the covert of the forest; but still the little band pressed on, unharmed; and the stealthy nature of the Indians forbade them to rush boldly forward, in the face of so firm an enemy as Goodman Duston. Thus he and his seven children continued their retreat, creeping along, as Cotton Mather observes, "at the pace of a child of five years old," till the stockades of a little frontier fortress appeared in view, and the savages gave up the chase.

We must not forget Mrs. Duston, in her distress. Scarcely had her husband fled from the house, ere the chamber was thronged with the horrible visages of the wild Indians, bedaubed with paint and besmeared with blood, brandishing their tomahawks in her face, and threatening to add her scalp to those that were already hanging at their girdles. It was, however, their interest to save her alive, if the thing might be, in order to exact ransom. Our great-great-grandmothers, when taken captive in the old times of Indian warfare, appear, in nine cases out of ten, to have been in pretty much such a delicate situation as Mrs. Duston; notwithstanding which, they were wonderfully sustained through long, rough, and hurried marches, amid toil, weariness, and starvation, such as the Indians themselves could hardly endure. Seeing that there was no help for it, Mrs. Duston rose, and she and the widow Neff, with the infant in her arms, followed their captors out of doors. As they crossed the threshold, the poor babe set up a feeble wail; it was its death cry. In an instant, an Indian seized it by the heels, swung it in the air, dashed out its brains against the trunk of the nearest tree, and threw the little corpse at the mother's feet. Perhaps it was the remembrance of that moment that hardened Hannah Duston's heart, when her time of vengeance came. But now, nothing could be done but to stifle her grief and rage within her bosom, and follow the Indians into the dark gloom of the forest, hardly venturing to throw a parting glance at the blazing cottage, where she had dwelt happily with her husband, and had borne him eight children,—the seven, of whose fate she knew nothing, and the infant, whom she had just seen murdered.

The first day's march was fifteen miles; and during that, and many succeeding days, Mrs. Duston kept pace with her captors; for, had she lagged behind, a tomahawk would at once have been sunk into her brains. More than one terrible warning was given her; more than one of her fellow captives,—of whom there were many,—after tottering feebly, at length sank upon the ground; the next moment, the death groan was breathed, and the scalp was reeking at an Indian's girdle. The unburied corpse was left in the forest, till the rites of sepulture should be performed by the autumnal gales, strewing the withered leaves upon the whitened bones. When out of danger of immediate pursuit, the prisoners, according to Indian custom, were divided among different parties of the savages, each of whom were to shift for themselves. Mrs. Duston, the widow Neff, and an English lad fell to the lot of a family consisting of two stout warriors, three squaws, and seven children. These Indians, like most with whom the French had held intercourse, were Catholics; and Cotton Mather affirms, on Mrs. Duston's authority, that they prayed at morning, noon, and night, nor ever partook of food without a prayer; nor suffered their children to sleep till they had prayed to the Christian's God. Mather, like an old hard-hearted, pedantic bigot as he was, seems trebly to exult in the destruction of these poor wretches, on account of their popish superstitions. Yet what can be more touching than to think of these wild Indians, in their loneliness and their wanderings, wherever they went among the dark, mysterious woods, still keeping up domestic worship, with all the regularity of a household at its peaceful fireside.

They were travelling to a rendezvous of the savages, somewhere in the northeast. One night, being now above a hundred miles from Haverhill, the red men and women, and the red children, and the three palefaces, Mrs. Duston, the widow Neff, and the English lad, made their encampment, and kindled a fire beneath the gloomy old trees, on a small island in Contocook River. The barbarians sat down to what scanty food Providence had sent them, and shared it with their prisoners, as if they had all been the children of one wigwam, and had grown up together on the margin of the same river within the shadow of the forest. Then the Indians said their prayers—the prayers that the Romish priests had taught them—and made the sign of the cross upon their dusky breasts, and composed themselves to rest. But the three prisoners prayed apart; and when their petitions were ended, they likewise lay down, with their feet to the fire. The night wore on; and the light and cautious slumbers of the red men were often broken by the rush and ripple of the stream, or the groaning and moaning of the forest, as if nature were wailing over her wild children; and sometimes, too, the little redskins cried in sleep, and the Indian mothers awoke to hush them. But, a little before break of day, a deep, dead slumber fell upon the Indians. "See," cries Cotton Mather triumphantly, "if it prove not so!"

Up rose Mrs. Duston, holding her own breath, to listen to the long, deep breathing of her captors. Then she stirred the widow Neff, whose place was by her own, and likewise the English lad; and all three stood up, with the doubtful gleam of the decaying fire hovering upon their ghastly visages, as they stared round at the fated slumberers. The next instant each of the three captives held a tomahawk. Hark! that low moan, as of one in a troubled dream—it told a warrior's death pang! Another!—Another!—and the third half-uttered groan was from a woman's lips. But, O, the children!

Their skins are red; yet spare them, Hannah Duston, spare those seven little ones, for the sake of the seven that have fed at your own breast. "Seven," quoth Mrs. Duston to herself. "Eight children have I borne—and where are the seven, and where is the eighth!" The thought nerved her arm; and the copper-colored babes slept the same dead sleep with their Indian mothers. Of all that family, only one woman escaped, dreadfully wounded, and fled shrieking into the wilderness! and a boy, whom, it is said, Mrs. Duston had meant to save alive. But he did well to flee from the raging tigress! There was little safety for a redskin, when Hannah Duston's blood was up.

The work being finished, Mrs. Duston laid hold of the long black hair of the warriors, and the women, and the children, and took all their ten scalps, and left the island, which bears her name to this very day. According to our notion, it should be held accursed, for her sake. Would that the bloody old hag had been drowned in crossing Contocook River, or that she had sunk over head and ears in a swamp, and been there buried, till summoned forth to confront her victims at the Day of Judgment; or that she had gone astray and been starved to death in the forest, and nothing ever seen of her again, save her skeleton, with the ten scalps twisted round it for a girdle! But, on the contrary, she and her companions came safe home, and received the bounty on the dead Indians, besides liberal presents from private gentlemen, and fifty pounds from the Governor of Maryland. In her old age, being sunk into decayed circumstances, she claimed, and, we believe, received a pension, as a further price of blood.

This awful woman, and that tender-hearted yet valiant man, her husband, will be remembered as long as the deeds of old times are told round a New England fireside. But how different is her renown from his!

ROBERT MONTGOMERY BIRD
(1806–1854)

In the preface to the revised edition of *Nick of the Woods* (1853), Bird described his attitude toward Indians very directly:

The Indian is doubtless a gentleman; but he is a gentleman who wears a very dirty shirt, and lives a very miserable life, having nothing to employ him or keep him alive except the pleasures of the chase and of the scalp-hunt—which we dignify with the name of war . . . . The purposes of the author, in his book, confined him to real Indians. He drew them as, in his judgment, they existed—and as, according to all observation, they still exist when not softened by cultivation,—ignorant, violent, debased, brutal . . . .

In this way Bird answered the critics who, influenced by the work of Cooper and Chateaubriand, accused him of showing "antipathy." He took his stand on the word "real," failing to acknowledge the limitations of his own perceptions.

Bird's work is anything but "realistic," whatever that may mean. His main melodramatic plot involves the attempt of a young Virginian to help the cousin he loves to escape a villainous seducer. This requires long wandering on the "dark and bloody ground" of Kentucky, where the Jibbenainosay, a strange creature responsible for the murder and mutilation of Indians, helps white settlers in the dead of night. In the novel's resolution, this figure is discovered to be one with the Quaker Nathan Slaughter, whose family has been murdered and scalped by the Shawnee chief, Wenonga, or Black Vulture. A pacifist during the day, Nathan becomes the "Nick," or devil, of the American forest at night, in a desperate response to the conditions of white settlement. The passage excerpted below contains a characterization of Wenonga, and the supreme example of the Jibbenainosay's revenge.

Bird, a Philadelphia physician, was a playwright as well as a novelist. Several of his tragedies, which included two on Indian subjects, were produced by Edwin Forrest. Other works in which he exploits Indian materials are the plays *Oralloossa* and *King Philip; or, The Sagamore,* and a novel, *The Adventures of Robin Day* (1839).

From *Nick of the Woods; or The Jibbenainosay, A Tale of Kentucky,* *1837*

At nightfall, Nathan was removed to Wenonga's cabin, where the chief, surrounded by a dozen or more warriors, made him a speech in such English phrases as he had acquired, informing the prisoner, as before, that "he, Wenonga, was a great chief and warrior, that the other, the prisoner, was a great medicine-man; and, finally, that he, Wenonga, required of his prisoner, the medicine-man, by his charms, to produce the Jibbenainosay, the unearthly slayer of his people and curse of his tribe, in order that he, the great chief, who feared neither warrior nor devil, might fight him, like a man, and kill him, so that he, the aforesaid destroyer, should destroy his young men in the dark no longer."

Not even to this speech, though received by the warriors with marks of great approbation, did Nathan vouchsafe the least notice; and the savages despairing of moving him to their purpose at that period, but hoping perhaps to find him in a more reasonable mood at another moment, left him, but not until they had again inspected the thongs and satisfied themselves they were tied in knots strong and intricate enough to hold even a conjuror. They, also, before leaving him to himself, placed food and water at his side, and in a way that was perhaps designed to show their opinion of his wondrous powers; for as his arms were pinioned tightly behind his back, it was evident he could feed himself only by magic.

. . . .

The steps approached; they reached the door; Nathan threw himself back, reclining against his pile of furs, and fixed his eye upon the mats at the entrance. They were presently parted; and the old chief Wenonga came halting into the apartment,—halting, yet with a step that was designed to indicate all the pride and dignity of a warrior. And this attempt at state was the more natural and proper, as he was armed and painted as if for war, his grim countenance hideously bedaubed on one side with vermilion, on the other with black; a long scalping-knife, without sheath or cover, swinging from his wampum belt; while a hatchet, the blade and handle both of steel,

Robert Montgomery Bird, *Nick of the Woods; or, The Jibbenainosay, A Tale of Kentucky,* a new edition revised by the author (New York, 1853), pp. 351–359.

was grasped in his hand. In this guise, and with a wild and demoniacal glitter of eye, that seemed the result of mingled drunkenness and insanity, the old chief stalked and limped up to the prisoner, looking as if bent upon his instant destruction. That his passions were up in arms, that he was ripe for mischief and blood, was, indeed, plain and undeniable; but he soon made it apparent that his rage was only conditional and alternative, as regarded the prisoner. Pausing within three or four feet of him, and giving him a look that seemed designed to freeze his blood, it was so desperately hostile and savage, he extended his arm and hatchet,—not, however, to strike, as it appeared, but to do what might be judged almost equally agreeable to nine-tenths of his race,—that is, to deliver a speech.

"I am Wenonga!" he cried, in his own tongue, being perhaps too much enraged to think of any other,—"I am Wenonga, a great Shawnee chief. I have fought the Long-knives, and drunk their blood: when they hear my voice, they are afraid;—they run howling away, like dogs when the squaws beat them from the fire—who ever stood before Wenonga? I have fought my enemies, and killed them. I never feared a white-man: why should I fear a white-man's devil? Where is the Jibbenainosay, the curse of my tribe?—the Shawneewannaween, the howl of my people? He kills them in the dark, he creeps upon them while they sleep; but he fears to stand before the face of a warrior! Am I a dog? or a woman? The squaws and the children curse me, as I go by: they say *I* am the killer of their husbands and fathers; they tell me it was the deed of Wenonga that brought the white-man's devil to kill them; 'if Wenonga is a chief, let him kill the killer of his people!' I am Wenonga; I am a man; I fear nothing: I have sought the Jibbenainosay. But the Jibbenainosay is a coward; he walks in the dark, he kills in the time of sleep—he fears to fight a warrior! My brother is a great medicine-man; he is a white-man, and he knows how to find the white-man's devils. Let my brother speak for me; let him show me where to find the Jibbenainosay; and he shall be a great chief, and the son of a chief: Wenonga will make him his son, and he shall be a Shawnee!"

"Does Wenonga, at last, feel he has brought a devil upon his people?" said Nathan, speaking for the first time since his capture, and speaking in a way well suited to strike the interrogator with surprise. A sneer, as it seemed, of gratified malice crept over his face, and was visible even through the coat of paint that still invested his features; and, to crown all, his words were delivered in the Shawnee tongue, correctly and unhesitatingly pronounced; which was itself, or so Wenonga appeared to hold it, a proof of his superhuman acquirements.

The old chief started, as the words fell upon his ear, and looked around him in awe, as if the prisoner had already summoned a spirit to his elbow.

"I have heard the voice of the dead!" he cried. "My brother is a great

Medicine! But I am a chief;—I am not afraid."

"The chief tells me lies," rejoined Nathan, who, having once unlocked his lips, seemed but little disposed to resume his former silence;—"the chief tells me lies: there is no white-devil hurts his people!"

"I am an old man, and a warrior,—I speak the truth!" said the chief, with dignity; and then added, with sudden feeling,—"I am an old man: I had sons and grandsons—young warriors, and boys that would soon have blacked their faces for battle—where are they? The Jibbenainosay has been in my village, he has been in my wigwam—There are none left—the Jibbenainosay killed them!"

"Ay!" exclaimed the prisoner, and his eyes shot fire as he spoke, "they fell under his hand, man and boy—there was not one of them spared—they were of the blood of Wenonga!"

"Wenonga is a great chief!" cried the Indian: "he is childless; but childless he has made the Long-knife."

"The Long-knife, and the son of Onas!" said Nathan.

The chief staggered back, as if struck by a blow, and stared wildly upon the prisoner.

"My brother is a medicine-man,—he knows all things!" he exclaimed. "He speaks the truth: I am a great warrior; I took the scalp of the Quakel——"

"And of his wife and children—you left not one alive!—Ay!" continued Nathan, fastening his looks upon the amazed chief, "you slew them all! And he that was the husband and father was the Shawnees' friend, the friend even of Wenonga!"

"The white-men are dogs and robbers!" said the chief: "the Quakel was my brother; but I killed him. I am an Indian—I love white-man's blood. My people have soft hearts; they cried for the Quakel: but I am a warrior with no heart. I killed them: their scalps are hanging to my fire-post! I am not sorry; I am not afraid."

The eyes of the prisoner followed the Indian's hand, as he pointed, with savage triumph, to the shrivelled scalps that had once crowned the heads of childhood and innocence, and then sank to the floor, while his whole frame shivered as with an ague-fit.

"My brother is a great medicine-man," iterated the chief: "he shall show me the Jibbenainosay, or he shall die."

"The chief lies!" cried Nathan, with a sudden and taunting laugh: "he can talk big things to a prisoner, but he fears the Jibbenainosay!"

"I am a chief and warrior: I will fight the white-man's devil!"

"The warrior shall see him then," said the captive, with extraordinary fire. "Cut me loose from my bonds, and I will bring him before the chief."

And as he spoke, he thrust out his legs, inviting the stroke of the axe upon the thongs that bound his ankles.

But this was a favor, which, stupid or mad as he was, Wenonga hesitated to grant.

"The chief," cried Nathan, with a laugh of scorn, "would stand face to face with the Jibbenainosay, and yet fears to loose a naked prisoner!"

The taunt produced its effect. The axe fell upon the thong, and Nathan leaped to his feet. He extended his wrists. The Indian hesitated again. "The chief shall see the Jibbenainosay!" cried Nathan; and the cord was cut. The prisoner turned quickly round; and while his eyes fastened with a wild but joyous glare upon his jailer's, a laugh that would have become the jaws of a hyena lighted up his visage, and sounded from his lips. "Look!" he cried, "thee has thee wish! Thee sees the destroyer of thee race,—ay, murdering villain, the destroyer of thee people, and theeself!"

And with that, leaping upon the astounded chief with rather the rancorous ferocity of a wolf than the enmity of a human being, and clutching him by the throat with one hand, while with the other he tore the iron tomahawk from his grasp, he bore him to the earth, clinging to him as he fell, and using the wrested weapon with such furious haste and skill that, before they had yet reached the ground, he had buried it in the Indian's brain. Another stroke, and another, he gave with the same murderous activity and force; and Wenonga trode the path to the spirit-land, bearing the same gory evidences of the unrelenting and successful vengeance of the white-man that his children and grandchildren had borne before him.

"Ay, dog, thee dies at last! at last I have caught thee!"

With these words, Nathan, leaving the shattered skull, dashed the tomahawk into the Indian's chest, snatched the scalping-knife from the belt, and with one grinding sweep of the blade, and one fierce jerk of his arm, the gray scalp-lock of the warrior was torn from the dishonored head. The last proof of the slayer's ferocity was not given until he had twice, with his utmost strength, drawn the knife over the dead man's breast, dividing skin, cartilage, and even bone, before it, so sharp was the blade and so powerful the hand that urged it.

Then, leaping to his feet, and snatching from the post the bundle of withered scalps—the locks and ringlets of his own murdered family,—which he spread a moment before his eyes with one hand, while the other extended, as if to contrast the two prizes together, the reeking scalp-lock of the murderer, he sprang through the door of the lodge, and fled from the village; but not until he had, in the insane fury of the moment, given forth a wild, ear-piercing yell, that spoke the triumph, the exulting transport, of long-baffled but never-dying revenge. The wild whoop, thus rising in the depth and stillness of the night, startled many a wakeful warrior and timorous mother from their repose. But such sounds in a disorderly hamlet of barbarians were too common to create alarm or uneasiness; and the wary and the timid again betook themselves to their dreams, leaving the corpse of their chief to stiffen on the floor of his own wigwam.

EDGAR ALLAN POE
(1809–1849)

Poe's short brilliant writing career was centered in cities of the eastern seaboard—New York, Philadelphia, Richmond; but his literary landscapes were abstract and symbolic. In an era in which writers were turning to the use of native American materials, he generally peopled stories with aristocratic mansion-dwellers, or ladies of exotic name, and set them in prisons, crypts, gothic palaces. When he did reflect the outer features of American life, like the relationship of blacks and whites, he heightened the American situation into a nightmare distortion, always directing his own attention to the psychological struggles of a main character, often a first-person narrator.

Edwin Fussell, in his study of the complex literary West of Poe, points to "The Masque of the Red Death: A Fantasy" (1842) as a parable for the settlement of the American continent: "the west as annihilation, the Indian as retribution." This ambitious, suggestive criticism, and the way it transforms reading Poe, should direct special attention to two specific uses of Indians in Poe's fiction. In *The Narrative of A. Gordon Pym,* an 1838 novella, massive Dirk Peters is described as a half-breed Upsaroka Indian. He is Pym's savior, and he survives him to dwell, silent and enigmatic, in Illinois. Peters, whose beneficence is never explained, displays qualities more often associated with an African slave than with an Indian.

Following his success with this longer narrative form, Poe devised another first-person narrative about exploration. In 1840, *Burton's Gentleman's Magazine* began to serialize his new novel, which drew on the craze for western adventure stimulated by Lewis and Clark and their successors. *The Journal of Julius Rodman* remained unfinished, yet it affords Poe's lengthiest treatment of Indians. Poe invents an editor who presents Rodman's diary and comments on it in a matter-of-fact, informational tone. This editor's information about the Sioux, while distinguished for its fullness, is derived from an uncomplimentary source. Rodman's diary itself portrays the Indians as extremely stupid, easily manipulated by the white man, posing no significant threat. This bland view of Indians naturally undercuts the reader's belief in Rodman's heroism, and finally defeats Poe's ingenuity.

From **The Journal of Julius Rodman,** *1840*

[Fictional Editor's Note] In person, the Sioux generally are an ugly ill-made race, their limbs being much too small for the trunk, according to our ideas of the human form—their cheek bones are high, and their eyes protruding and dull. The heads of the men are shaved, with the exception of a small spot on the crown, whence a long tuft is permitted to fall in plaits upon the shoulders; this tuft is an object of scrupulous care, but is now and then cut off, upon an occasion of grief or solemnity. A full dressed Sioux chief presents a striking appearance. The whole surface of the body is painted with grease and coal. A shirt of skins is worn as far down as the waist, while round the middle is a girdle of the same material, and sometimes of cloth, about an inch in width; this supports a piece of blanket or fur passing between the thighs. Over the shoulders is a white-dressed buffalo mantle, the hair of which is worn next the skin in fair weather, but turned outwards in wet. This robe is large enough to envelop the whole body, and is frequently ornamented with porcupine quills (which make a rattling noise as the warrior moves) as well as with a great variety of rudely painted figures, emblematical of the wearer's military character. Fastened to the top of the head is worn a hawk's feather, adorned with porcupine quills. Leggings of dressed antelope skin serve the purpose of pantaloons, and have seams at the sides, about two inches wide, and bespotted here and there with small tufts of human hair, the trophies of some scalping excursion. The moccasins are of elk or buffalo skin, the hair worn inwards; on great occasions the chief is seen with the skin of a polecat dangling at the heel of each boot. The Sioux are indeed partial to this noisome animal, whose fur is in high favor for tobacco-pouches and other appendages.

The dress of a chieftain's squaw is also remarkable. Her hair is suffered to grow long, is parted across the forehead, and hangs loosely behind, or is collected into a kind of net. Her moccasins do not differ from her husband's; but her leggings extend upwards only as far as the knee, where they are met by an awkward shirt of elk-skin depending to the ankles, and supported above by a string going over the shoulders. This shirt is usually confined to the waist by a girdle, and over all is thrown a buffalo mantle like that of the men. The tents of the Teton Sioux are described as of neat construction, being formed of white-dressed buffalo hide, well secured and supported by poles.

The region infested by the tribe in question extends along the banks of the Missouri for some hundred and fifty miles or more, and is chiefly prairie land, but is occasionally diversified by hills. These latter are always deeply

Edmund Clarence Stedman and George E. Woodberry, eds., *The Works of Edgar Allan Poe,* (Chicago, 1895), pp. 304–317 and 333–334.

cut by gorges or ravines, which in the middle of summer are dry, but form the channels of muddy and impetuous torrents during the season of rain. Their edges are fringed with thick woods, as well at top as at bottom; but the prevalent aspect of the country is that of a bleak low land, with rank herbage, and without trees. The soil is strongly impregnated with mineral substances in great variety—among others with glauber salts, copperas, sulphur, and alum, which tinge the water of the river and impart to it a nauseous odor and taste. The wild animals most usual are the buffalo, deer, elk, and antelope. We again resume the words of the Journal.

September 6. The country was open, and the day remarkably pleasant: so that we were all in pretty good spirits notwithstanding the expectation of attack. So far, we had not caught even a glimpse of an Indian, and we were making rapid way through their dreaded territory. I was too well aware, however, of the savage tactics to suppose that we were not narrowly watched, and had made up my mind that we should hear something of the Tetons at the first gorge which would afford them a convenient lurking-place.

About noon a Canadian bawled out "The Sioux!—the Sioux!"—and directed attention to a long narrow ravine, which intersected the prairie on our left, extending from the banks of the Missouri as far as the eye could reach, in a southwardly course. This gully was the bed of a creek, but its waters were now low, and the sides rose up like huge regular walls on each side. By the aid of a spy-glass I perceived at once the cause of the alarm given by the voyageur. A large party of mounted savages were coming down the gorge in Indian file, with the evident intention of taking us unawares. Their calumet feathers had been the means of their detection; for every now and then we could see some of these bobbing up above the edge of the gulley, as the bed of the ravine forced the wearer to rise higher than usual. We could tell that they were on horseback by the motion of these feathers. The party was coming upon us with great rapidity; and I gave the word to pull on with all haste so as to pass the mouth of the creek before they reached it. As soon as the Indians perceived by our increased speed that they were discovered, they immediately raised a yell, scrambled out of the gorge, and galloped down upon us, to the number of about one hundred.

Our situation was now somewhat alarming. At almost any other part of the Missouri which we had passed during the day, I should not have cared so much for these freebooters; but just here the banks were remarkably steep and high, partaking of the character of the creek banks, and the savages were enabled to overlook us completely, while the cannon, upon which we had placed so much reliance, could not be brought to bear upon them at all. What added to our difficulty was that the current in the middle of the river was so turbulent and strong that we could make no headway against it except by dropping arms, and employing our whole force at the oars.

The water near the northern shore was too shallow even for the piroque, and our only mode of proceeding, if we designed to proceed at all, was by pushing it within a moderate stone's throw of the left or southern bank, where we were completely at the mercy of the Sioux, but where we could make good headway by means of our poles and the wind, aided by the eddy. Had the savages attacked us at this juncture I cannot see how we could have escaped them. They were all well provided with bows and arrows, and small round shields, presenting a very noble and picturesque appearance. Some of the chiefs had spears, with fanciful flags attached, and were really gallant-looking men.

Either good luck upon our own parts, or great stupidity on the part of the Indians, relieved us very unexpectedly from the dilemma. The savages, having galloped up to the edge of the cliff just above us, set up another yell, and commenced a variety of gesticulations, whose meaning we at once knew to be that we should stop and come on shore. I had expected this demand, and had made up my mind that it would be most prudent to pay no attention to it at all, but proceed on our course. My refusal to stop had at least one good effect, for it appeared to mystify the Indians most wonderfully, who could not be brought to understand the measure in the least, and stared at us, as we kept on our way without answering them, in the most ludicrous amazement. Presently they commenced an agitated conversation among themselves, and at last finding that nothing could be made of us, fairly turned their horses' heads to the southward and galloped out of sight, leaving us as much surprised as rejoiced at their departure.

In the meantime we made the most of the opportunity, and pushed on with might and main, in order to get out of the region of steep banks before the anticipated return of our foes. In about two hours we again saw them in the south, at a great distance, and their number much augmented. They came on at full gallop, and were soon at the river; but our position was now much more advantageous, for the banks were sloping, and there were no trees to shelter the savages from our shot. The current, moreover, was not so rapid as before, and we were enabled to keep in mid-channel. The party, it seems, had only retreated to procure an interpreter, who now appeared upon a large gray horse, and, coming into the river as far as he could without swimming, called out to us in bad French to stop, and come on shore. To this I made one of the Canadians reply that, to oblige our friends the Sioux, we would willingly stop, for a short time, and converse, but that it was inconvenient for us to come on shore, as we could not do so without incommoding our great medicine (here the Canadian pointed to the cannon) who was anxious to proceed on his voyage, and whom we were afraid to disobey.

At this they began again their agitated whisperings and gesticulations among themselves, and seemed quite at a loss what to do. In the mean-time the boats had been brought to anchor in a favorable position, and I was resolved to fight now, if necessary, and endeavor to give the freebooters so warm a reception as would inspire them with wholesome dread for the future. I reflected that it was nearly impossible to keep on good terms with these Sioux, who were our enemies at heart, and who could only be restrained from pillaging and murdering us by a conviction of our prowess. Should we comply with their present demands, go on shore, and even succeed in purchasing a temporary safety by concessions and donations, such conduct would not avail us in the end, and would be rather a palliation than a radical cure of the evil. They would be sure to glut their vengeance sooner or later, and, if they suffered us to go on our way now, might here-after attack us at a disadvantage, when it might be as much as we would do to repel them, to say nothing of inspiring them with awe. Situated as we were here, it was in our power to give them a lesson they would be apt to remember; and we might never be in so good a situation again. Thinking thus, and all except the Canadians agreeing with me in opinion, I determined to assume a bold stand, and rather provoke hostilities than avoid them. This was our true policy. The savages had no fire arms which we could discover, except an old carabine carried by one of the chiefs; and their arrows would not prove very effective weapons when employed at so great a distance as that now between us. In regard to their number, we did not care much for that. Their position was one which would expose them to the full sweep of our cannon.

When Jules (the Canadian) had finished his speech about incommoding our great medicine, and when the consequent agitation had somewhat sub-sided among the savages, the interpreter spoke again and propounded three queries. He wished to know, first, whether we had any tobacco, or whiskey, or fire-guns—secondly, whether we did not wish the aid of the Sioux in rowing our large boat up the Missouri as far as the country of the Ricarees, who were great rascals—and, thirdly, whether our great medicine was not a very large and strong green grasshopper.

To these questions, propounded with profound gravity, Jules replied, by my directions, as follows. First, that we had plenty of whiskey, as well as tobacco, with an inexhaustible supply of fire-guns and powder—but that our great medicine had just told us that the Tetons were greater rascals than the Ricarees—that they were our enemies—that they had been lying in wait to intercept and kill us for many days past—that we must give them nothing at all, and hold no intercourse with them whatever; we should therefore be afraid to give them anything, even if so disposed, for fear of the anger of the great medicine, who was not to be trifled with. Secondly, that, after the character just given the Sioux Tetons, we could not think of employing them to row our boat—and, thirdly, that it was a good thing for them (the Sioux) that our great medicine had not overheard their last query, respecting the "large green grasshopper"; for, in that case, it might have gone very hard with them (the Sioux). Our great medicine was anything but a large green grasshopper, and *that* they should soon see, to their cost, if they did not immediately go, the whole of them, about their business.

Notwithstanding the imminent danger in which we were all placed, we could scarcely keep our countenances in beholding the air of profound admiration and astonishment with which the savages listened to these replies; and I believe that they would have immediately dispersed, and left us to proceed on our voyage, had it not been for the unfortunate words in which I informed them that they were greater rascals than the Ricarees. This was, apparently, an insult of the last atrocity, and excited them to an incontrollable degree of fury. We heard the words "Ricaree! Ricaree!" repeated, every now and then, with the utmost emphasis and excitement; and the whole band, as well as we could judge, seemed to be divided into two factions; the one urging the immense power of the great medicine, and the other the outrageous insult of being called greater rascals than the Ricarees. While matters stood thus, we retained our position in the middle of the stream, firmly resolved to give the villains a dose of our cannister-shot, upon the first indignity which should be offered us.

Presently, the interpreter on the gray horse came again into the river, and said that he believed we were no better than we should be—that all the pale faces who had previously gone up the river had been friends of the Sioux, and had made them large presents—that they, the Tetons, were determined not to let us proceed another step unless we came on shore and gave up all our fire-guns and whiskey, with half of our tobacco—that it was plain we were allies of the Ricarees, (who were now at war with the Sioux), and that our design was to carry them supplies, which we should not do—lastly, that they did not think very much of our great medicine, for he had told us a lie in relation to the designs of the Tetons, and was positively nothing but a great green grasshopper, in spite of all that we thought to the contrary. These latter words, about the great green grass-hopper, were taken up by the whole assemblage as the interpreter uttered them, and shouted out at the top of the voice, that the great medicine himself might be sure to hear the taunt. At the same time, they all broke into wild disorder, galloping their horses furiously in short circles, using contemptuous and indecent gesticulations, brandishing their spears, and drawing their arrows to the head.

I knew that the next thing would be an attack, and so determined to anticipate it at once, before any of our party were wounded by the discharge of their weapons—there was nothing to be gained by delay, and everything by prompt and resolute action. As soon as a good opportunity presented itself, the word was given to fire, and instantly obeyed. The effect of the discharge was very severe, and answered all our purposes to the full. Six of the Indians were killed, and perhaps three times as many badly wounded. The rest were thrown into the greatest terror and confusion, and made off into the prairie at full speed, as we drew up our anchors, after reloading the gun, and pulled boldly in for the shore. By the time we had reached it, there was not an unwounded Teton within sight.

I now left John Greely, with three Canadians, in charge of the boats, landed with the rest of the men, and, approaching a savage who was severely but not dangerously wounded, held a conversation with him, by means of Jules. I told him that the whites were well disposed to the Sioux, and to all the Indian nations; that our sole object in visiting his country was to trap beaver, and see the beautiful region which had been given the red men by the Great Spirit; that when we had procured as many furs as we wished, and seen all we came to see, we should return home; that we had heard that the Sioux, and especially the Tetons, were a quarrelsome race, and that therefore we had brought with us our great medicine for protection; that he was now much exasperated with the Tetons on account of their intolerable insult in calling him a green grasshopper (which he was not); that I had had great difficulty in restraining him from a pursuit of the warriors who had fled, and from sacrificing the wounded who now lay around us; and that I had only succeeded in pacifying him by becoming personally responsible for the future good behavior of the savages. At this portion of my discourse the poor fellow appeared much relieved, and extended his hand in token of amity. I took it, and assured him and his friends of my protection as long as we were unmolested, following up this promise by a present of twenty carrots of tobacco, some small hardware, beads, and red flannel, for himself and the rest of the wounded.

While all this was going on, we kept a sharp lookout for the fugitive Sioux. As I concluded making the presents, several gangs of these were observable in the distance, and were evidently seen by the disabled savage; but I thought it best to pretend not to perceive them, and shortly afterwards returned to the boats. The whole interruption had detained us full three hours, and it was after three o'clock when we once more started on our route. We made extraordinary haste, as I was anxious to get as far as possible from the scene of action before night. We had a strong wind at our back, and the current diminished in strength as we proceeded, owing to the widening of the stream. We therefore made great way, and by nine o'clock, had reached a large and thickly wooded island, near the northern bank, and close by the mouth of a creek. Here we resolved to encamp, and had scarcely set foot on shore, when one of the Greelys shot and secured a fine buffalo, many of which were upon the place. After posting our sentries for the night, we had the hump for supper, with as much whiskey as was good for us. Our exploit of the day was then freely discussed, and by most of the men was treated as an excellent joke; but I could by no means enter into any merriment upon the subject. Human blood had never, before this epoch, been shed at my hands; and although reason urged that I had taken the wisest, and what would no doubt prove in the end the most merciful course, still conscience, refusing to hearken even to reason herself, whispered pertinaciously within my ear—"it is human blood which thou hast shed." The hours wore away slowly—I found it impossible to sleep. At length the morning dawned, and with its fresh dews, its fresher breezes, and smiling flowers, there came a new courage, and a bolder tone of thought, which enabled me to look more steadily upon what had been done, and to regard in its only proper point of view the urgent necessity of the deed.

LYDIA HUNTLEY SIGOURNEY
(1791–1865)

Mrs. Sigourney, known as "The Sweet Singer of Hartford," published sixty-seven volumes of poetry. Sentimental and often banal, her poems are more important as indices of popular taste than as literary art. In stanzas seventeen to twenty-two from "Pocahontas," printed below, she dramatizes the rescue of Smith, comparing the Indian maiden to Pharoah's daughter, Smith to Moses. The glorification of Pocahontas, echoed in Whitman and Hart Crane, is an important theme in our literature. The final stanzas of the poem, fifty-three to fifty-six, are interesting as a popular expression of the "vanishing Indian" motif described in the introductory essay to this section.

From **Pocahontas, and Other Poems,** *1841*

XVII.

A forest-child, amid the flowers at play!
　　Her raven locks in strange profusion flowing;
A sweet, wild girl, with eye of earnest ray,
　　And olive cheek, at each emotion glowing;
Yet, whether in her gladsome frolic leaping,
Or 'neath the greenwood shade unconscious sleeping,
　　Or with light oar her fairy pinnace rowing,
Still, like the eaglet on its new-fledged wing,
Her spirit-glance bespoke the daughter of a king.

Lydia Huntley Sigourney, *Pocahontas, and Other Poems* (New York, 1841), pp. 19–20 and 31–32.

XVIII.

But he, that wily monarch, stern and old,
   Mid his grim chiefs, with barbarous trappings bright,
That morn a court of savage state did hold.
   The sentenced captive see—his brow how white!
Stretch'd on the turf his manly form lies low,
The war-club poises for its fatal blow,
   The death-mist swims before his darken'd sight:
Forth springs the child, in tearful pity bold,
Her head on his declines, her arms his neck enfold.

XIX.

"The child! what madness fires her? Hence! Depart!
   Fly, daughter, fly! before the death-stroke rings;
Divide her, warriors, from that English heart."
   In vain! for with convulsive grasp she clings:
She claims a pardon from her frowning sire;
Her pleading tones subdue his gather'd ire;
   And so, uplifting high his feathery dart,
That doting father gave the child her will,
And bade the victim live, and be his servant still.

XX.

Know'st thou what thou hast done, thou dark-hair'd child?
   What great events on thy compassion hung?
What prowess lurks beneath yon aspect mild,
   And in the accents of that foreign tongue?
As little knew the princess who descried
A floating speck on Egypt's turbid tide,
   A bulrush-ark the matted reeds among,
And, yielding to an infant's tearful smile,
Drew forth Jehovah's seer, from the devouring Nile.

XXI.

In many a clime, in many a battle tried,
   By Turkish sabre and by Moorish spear;
Mid Afric's sands, or Russian forests wide,
   Romantic, bold, chivalrous, and sincere,
Keen-eyed, clear-minded, and of purpose pure,
Dauntless to rule, or patient to endure,

Was he whom thou hast rescued with a tear:
Thou wert the saviour of the Saxon vine,
And for this deed alone our praise and love are thine.

XXII.

Nor yet for this alone shall history's scroll
    Embalm thine image with a grateful tear;
For when the grasp of famine tried the soul,
    When strength decay'd, and dark despair was near,
Who led her train of playmates, day by day,
O'er rock, and stream, and wild, a weary way,
    Their baskets teeming with the golden ear?
Whose generous hand vouchsafed its tireless aid
To guard a nation's germ? Thine, thine, heroic maid!

. . . .

LIII.

Like the fallen leaves those forest-tribes have fled:
    Deep 'neath the turf their rusted weapon lies;
No more their harvest lifts its golden head,
    Nor from their shaft the stricken‑red-deer flies:
But from the far, far west, where holds, so hoarse,
The lonely Oregon, its rock-strewn course,
    While old Pacific's sullen surge replies,
Are heard their exiled murmurings deep and low,
Like one whose smitten soul departeth full of wo.

LIV.

I would ye were not, from your fathers' soil,
    Track'd like the dun wolf, ever in your breast
The coal of vengeance and the curse of toil;
    I would we had not to your mad lip prest
The fiery poison-cup, nor on ye turn'd
The blood-tooth'd ban-dog, foaming, as he burn'd
    To tear your flesh; but thrown in kindness bless'd
The brother's arm around ye, as ye trod,
And led ye, sad of heart, to the bless'd Lamb of God.

207

LV.

Forgotten race, farewell! Your haunts we tread,
    Our mighty rivers speak your words of yore,
Our mountains wear them on their misty head,
    Our sounding cataracts hurl them to the shore;
But on the lake your flashing oar is still,
Hush'd is your hunter's cry on dale and hill,
    Your arrow stays the eagle's flight no more;
And ye, like troubled shadows, sink to rest
In unremember'd tombs, unpitied and unbless'd.

LVI.

The council-fires are quench'd, that erst so red
    Their midnight volume mid the groves entwined;
King, stately chief, and warrior-host are dead,
    Nor remnant nor memorial left behind:
But thou, O forest-princess, true of heart,
When o'er our fathers waved destruction's dart,
    Shalt in their children's loving hearts be shrined;
Pure, lonely star, o'er dark oblivion's wave,
It is not meet thy name should moulder in the grave.

MARGARET FULLER
(1810–1850)

Until recent years, Margaret Fuller's eventful life has received more attention than her work. Her prodigious abilities made themselves known early, as she devoted herself to study, teaching, and journalism. She learned German to read Goethe, and became a friend and disciple of Ralph Waldo Emerson. From 1839 to 1844, in Boston, she conducted classes on literature, called Conversations; in 1840, she edited *The Dial*. During these years she published two translations of German correspondence. In 1841 she was a participant in the Transcendentalist utopian experiment at Brook Farm.

In 1843, Margaret Fuller travelled to northern Illinois; from the journal kept at this time she extracted the book *Summer on the Lakes*. On this trip there was much opportunity for firsthand observation of Indians. Unlike her friend Emerson, Fuller avoids general comments on the beneficence of progress and describes the encounters she sought with Indian women. After the publication of this book she became the literary critic of Horace Greeley's *New York Tribune*. In 1845 her controversial volume *Woman in the Nineteenth Century* was published and provoked outrage in the critical establishment.

In 1846 Margaret Fuller sailed for Europe, sending back letters as a travelling correspondent to the *Tribune*. She soon became interested in the Italian liberation movement led by Giuseppe Mazzini. During the Roman Revolution, she married an Italian, Giovanni Angelo, Marchese Ossoli, and bore a son. In the worst of the fighting she endured separation from her husband and child and worked as nurse and director of a hospital. In 1850, returning to America with the completed manuscript of a book on the Italian revolution, Margaret Fuller, her husband and child drowned in a shipwreck near Fire Island.

Notwithstanding the homage paid to women and the consequence
allowed them in some cases, it is impossible to look upon the Indian women
without feeling that they *do* occupy a lower place than women among the
nations of European civilization. The habits of drudgery expressed in their
form and gesture, the soft and wild but melancholy expression of their eye,
reminded me of the tribe mentioned by Mackenzie, where the women
destroy their female children whenever they have a good opportunity; and
of the eloquent reproaches addressed by the Paraguay woman to her mother
that she had not in the same way saved her from the anguish and weariness
of her lot.

More weariness than anguish, no doubt, falls to the lot of most of these
women. They inherit submission, and the minds of the generality accom-
modate themselves more or less to any posture. Perhaps they suffer less
than their white sisters, who have more aspiration and refinement with
little power of self-sustenance. But their place is certainly lower and their
share of the human inheritance less.

Their decorum and delicacy are striking and show that, when these are
native to the mind, no habits of life make any difference. Their whole
gesture is timid, yet self-possessed. They used to crowd round me to
inspect little things I had to show them, but never press near; on the contrary, would reprove and keep off the children. Anything they took from
my hand was held with care, then shut or folded, and returned with an air
of ladylike precision. They would not stare, however curious they might
be, but cast sidelong glances.

A locket that I wore was an object of untiring interest; they seemed to
regard it as a talisman. My little sunshade was still more fascinating to
them; apparently they had never before seen one. For an umbrella they
entertained profound regard, probably looking upon it as the most luxurious
superfluity a person can possess and therefore a badge of great wealth. I
used to see an old squaw, whose sullied skin and coarse, tanned locks told
that she had braved sun and storm without a doubt or care for sixty years
at least, sitting gravely at the door of her lodge with an old green umbrella

Margaret Fuller Ossoli, *At Home and Abroad; or, Things and Thoughts in America and Europe,* ed. Arthur B. Fuller (Boston, 1856), pp. 85–90.

over her head, happy for hours together in the dignified shade. For her happiness pomp came not, as it so often does, too late; she received it with grateful enjoyment.

One day as I was seated on one of the canoes, a woman came and sat beside me, with her baby in its cradle set up at her feet. She asked me by a gesture to let her take my sunshade, and then to show her how to open it. Then she put it into her baby's hand and held it over its head, looking at me the while with a sweet, mischievous laugh, as much as to say, "You carry a thing that is only fit for a baby." Her pantomime was very pretty. She, like the other women, had a glance, and shy, sweet expression in the eye; the men have a steady gaze.

That noblest and loveliest of modern *preux,* Lord Edward Fitzgerald, who came through Buffalo to Detroit and Mackinaw with Brant and was adopted into the Bear tribe by the name of Eghnidal, was struck in the same way by the delicacy of manners in women. He says: "Notwithstanding the life they lead, which would make most women rough and masculine, they are as soft, meek, and modest as the best brought up girls in England. Somewhat coquettish, too! Imagine the manners of Mimi in a poor *squaw* that has been carrying packs in the woods all her life."

McKenney mentions that the young wife during the short bloom of her beauty is an object of homage and tenderness to her husband. One Indian woman, the Flying Pigeon, a beautiful and excellent person of whom he gives some particulars, is an instance of the power uncommon characters will always exert of breaking down the barriers custom has erected round them. She captivated by her charms, and inspired her husband and son with reverence for her character. The simple praise with which the husband indicates the religion, the judgment, and the generosity he saw in her, are as satisfying as Count Zinzendorf's more labored eulogium on his "noble consort." The conduct of her son when, many years after her death, he saw her picture at Washington is unspeakably affecting. Catlin gives anecdotes of the grief of a chief for the loss of a daughter, and the princely gifts he offers in exchange for her portrait, worthy not merely of European but of Troubadour sentiment. It is also evident that, as Mrs. Schoolcraft says, the women have great power at home. It can never be otherwise, men being dependent upon them for the comfort of their lives. Just so among ourselves, wives who are neither esteemed nor loved by their husbands have great power over their conduct by the friction of every day, and over the formation of their opinions by the daily opportunities so close a relation affords of perverting testimony and instilling doubts. But these sentiments should not come in brief flashes, but burn as a steady flame; then there would be more women worthy to inspire them. This power is good for nothing, unless the woman be wise to use it aright. Has the Indian, has the

211

white woman, as noble a feeling of life and its uses, as religious a self-respect, as worthy a field of thought and action, as man? If not, the white woman, the Indian woman, occupies a position inferior to that of man. It is not so much a question of power as of privilege.

The men of these subjugated tribes, now accustomed to drunkenness and every way degraded, bear but a faint impress of the lost grandeur of the race. They are no longer strong, tall, or finely proportioned. Yet as you see them stealing along a height or striding boldly forward, they remind you of what *was* majestic in the red man.

On the shores of Lake Superior, it is said, if you visit them at home, you may still see a remnant of the noble blood. The Pillagers *(Pilleurs),* a band celebrated by the old travelers, are still existent there.

> Still some, "the eagles of their tribe," may rush.

I have spoken of the hatred felt by the white man for the Indian: with white women it seems to amount to disgust, to loathing. How I could endure the dirt, the peculiar smell of the Indians and their dwellings was a great marvel in the eyes of my lady acquaintance; indeed I wonder why they did not quite give me up, as they certainly looked on me with great distaste for it. "Get you gone, you Indian dog," was the felt, if not the breathed, expression towards the hapless owners of the soil—all their claims, all their sorrows quite forgot in abhorrence of their dirt, their tawny skins, and the vices the whites have taught them.

A person who had seen them during the great part of a life expressed his prejudices to me with such violence that I was no longer surprised that the Indian children threw sticks at him as he passed. A lady said: "Do what you will for them, they will be ungrateful. The savage cannot be washed out of them. Bring up an Indian child, and see if you can attach it to you." The next moment she expressed, in the presence of one of those children whom she was bringing up, loathing at the odor left by one of her people, and one of the most respected, as he passed through the room. When the child is grown she will be considered basely ungrateful not to love the lady, as she certainly will not; and this will be cited as an instance of the impossibility of attaching the Indian.

Whether the Indian could, by any efforts of love and intelligence from the white man, have been civilized and made a valuable ingredient in the new state, I will not say; but this we are sure of—the French Catholics at least did not harm them or disturb their minds merely to corrupt them. The French they loved. But the stern Presbyterian with his dogmas and his task-work, the city circle and the college with their niggard concessions and unfeeling stare, have never tried the experiment. It has not been tried. Our people and our government have sinned alike against the first-born of the soil, and if they are the fated agents of a new era, they have done nothing— have invoked no god to keep them sinless while they do the hest of fate.

Worst of all is it when they invoke the holy power only to mask their iniquity; when the felon trader, who all the week has been besotting and degrading the Indian with rum mixed with red pepper and damaged tobacco, kneels with him on Sunday before a common altar to tell the rosary which recalls the thought of Him crucified for love of suffering men, and to listen to sermons in praise of "purity"!!

"My savage friends," cries the old, fat priest, "you must, above all things, aim at *purity.* "

Oh! my heart swelled when I saw them in a Christian church. Better their own dog-feasts and bloody rites than such mockery of that other faith.

"The dog," said an Indian, "was once a spirit; he has fallen for his sin, and was given by the Great Spirit in this shape to man as his most intelligent companion. Therefore we sacrifice it in highest honor to our friends in this world—to our protecting geniuses in another."

There was religion in that thought. The white man sacrifices his own brother and to Mammon, yet he turns in loathing from the dog-feast.

"You say," said the Indian of the South to the missionary, "that Christianity is pleasing to God. How can that be? Those men at Savannah are Christians."

Yes, slavedrivers and Indian traders are called Christians, and the Indian is to be deemed less like the Son of Mary than they! Wonderful is the deceit of man's heart!

WILLIAM CULLEN BRYANT
(1794–1878)

Bryant's poetry was influenced both by the pre-Romantic English Graveyard School and by the burgeoning movement toward the use of native American materials in literature. Poets like Edward Young encouraged Bryant to consider questions of death, immortality, and the solace of eternal nature; Philip Freneau, Charles Brockden Brown, James Fenimore Cooper and others suggested that the American landscape and its original inhabitants could provide important new literary sensations.

Unlike Walt Whitman, Bryant worked in traditional forms. In poems written between 1824 and 1844, he shows his interest in Indian legend, his awareness of the guilt incurred by whites, and his belief in Indian harmony with nature. A startlingly contemporary note is his comment on the white man's depredations on nature. This theme is treated symbolically in "The White-Footed Deer," printed below. Other poems by Bryant that use Indian materials are "The Disinterred Warrior," (1827) and "The Indian at the Burial-Place of his Fathers" (1824). Bryant's portraits of Indians as faceless, brutal warriors and as doomed, noble figures sum up the contradictions in the nineteenth-century image.

From **Poetical Works,** *1883*

The White-Footed Deer, 1844

It was a hundred years ago,
　　When, by the woodland ways,
The traveller saw the wild-deer drink,
　　Or crop the birchen sprays.

Parke Godwin, ed., *The Poetical Works of William Cullen Bryant* (New York, 1883), p. 321.

"THE WHITE-FOOTED DEER"

Beneath a hill, whose rocky side
    O'erbrowed a grassy mead,
And fenced a cottage from the wind,
    A deer was wont to feed.

She only came when on the cliffs
    The evening moonlight lay,
And no man knew the secret haunts
    In which she walked by day.

White were her feet, her forehead showed
    A spot of silvery white,
That seemed to glimmer like a star
    In autumn's hazy night.

And here, when sang the whippoorwill,
    She cropped the sprouting leaves,
And here her rustling steps were heard
    On still October eves.

But when the broad midsummer moon
    Rose o'er that grassy lawn,
Beside the silver-footed deer
    There grazed a spotted fawn.

The cottage dame forbade her son
    To aim the rifle here;
"It were a sin," she said, "to harm
    Or fright that friendly deer.

"This spot has been my pleasant home
    Ten peaceful years and more;
And ever, when the moonlight shines,
    She feeds before our door.

"The red-men say that here she walked
    A thousand moons ago;
They never raise the war-whoop here,
    And never twang the bow.

"I love to watch her as she feeds,
And think that all is well
While such a gentle creature haunts
The place in which we dwell."

The youth obeyed, and sought for game
In forests far away,
Where, deep in silence and in moss,
The ancient woodland lay.

But once, in autumn's golden time
He ranged the wild in vain,
Nor roused the pheasant nor the deer
And wandered home again.

The crescent moon and crimson eve
Shone with a mingling light;
The deer, upon the grassy mead,
Was feeding full in sight.

He raised the rifle to his eye,
And from the cliffs around
A sudden echo, shrill and sharp,
Gave back its deadly sound.

Away, into the neighboring wood,
The startled creature flew,
And crimson drops at morning lay
Amid the glimmering dew.

Next evening shone the waxing moon
As brightly as before;
The deer upon the grassy mead
Was seen again no more.

But ere that crescent moon was old,
By night the red-men came.
And burnt the cottage to the ground,
And slew the youth and dame.

"THE WHITE-FOOTED DEER"

Now woods have overgrown the mead,
  And hid the cliffs from sight;
There shrieks the hovering hawk at noon,
  And prowls the fox at night.

FRANCIS PARKMAN

(1823-1893)

As a Harvard undergraduate, Francis Parkman had already decided on his life's work—a history of the French, British and Indians in America. In the summer of 1845 he travelled west with a friend; among Pawnees and Sioux, he hoped to gather firsthand impressions for his history. In 1849 he published *The Oregon Trail*, an account of this trip based on his journals. Despite a lifetime of physical suffering—nervous ailments, lameness, increasing blindness—Parkman persisted in his task, turning out eight volumes of his history, a book on rose culture, and a novel. He was professor of horticulture at Harvard and a founder of the Archaeological Institute of America.

By birth and education Parkman was a Boston Brahmin; his youthful arrogance and detachment kept him from fully expressing the pleasure he took in living among the Sioux. Marked in all of his work, even as early as *The Oregon Trail*, is a quality of unromantic pessimism. This book illustrates the strength of his objective description of Indian manners, his snobbism, and his attraction to wilderness scenes.

The selection excerpted below is from *The Conspiracy of Pontiac;* it ends the first chapter of that work with Parkman's influential attack on the "noble savage" of literature.

From **The Conspiracy of Pontiac** . . . , *1851*

Of the Indian character, much has been written foolishly, and credulously believed. By the rhapsodies of poets, the cant of sentimentalists, and the extravagance of some who should have known better, a counterfeit image has been tricked out, which might seek in vain for its likeness through every corner of the habitable earth; an image bearing no more resemblance to its original than the monarch of the tragedy and the hero of the epic poem

Francis Parkman, *The Conspiracy of Pontiac and the Indian War after the Conquest of Canada,* in *The Works of Francis Parkman,* vol. 1 (Boston, 1898), pp. 43–49.

bear to their living prototypes in the palace and the camp. The shadows of his wilderness home, and the darker mantle of his own inscrutable reserve, have made the Indian warrior a wonder and a mystery. Yet to the eye of rational observation there is nothing unintelligible in him. He is full, it is true, of contradiction. He deems himself the center of greatness and renown; his pride is proof against the fiercest torments of fire and steel; and yet the same man would beg for a dram of whiskey, or pick up a crust of bread thrown to him like a dog, from the tent door of the traveller. At one moment, he is wary and cautious to the verge of cowardice; at the next, he abandons himself to a very insanity of recklessness; and the habitual self-restraint which throws an impenetrable veil over emotion is joined to the wild, impetuous passions of a beast or a madman.

Such inconsistencies, strange as they seem in our eyes, when viewed under a novel aspect, are but the ordinary incidents of humanity. The qualities of the mind are not uniform in their action through all the relations of life. With different men, and different races of men, pride, valor, prudence, have different forms of manifestation, and where in one instance they lie dormant, in another they are keenly awake. The conjunction of greatness and littleness, meanness and pride, is older than the days of the patriarchs; and such antiquated phenomena, displayed under a new form in the unreflecting, undisciplined mind of a savage, call for no special wonder, but should rather be classed with the other enigmas of the fathomless human heart. The dissecting knife of a Rochefoucault might lay bare matters of no less curious observation in the breast of every man.

Nature has stamped the Indian with a hard and stern physiognomy. Ambition, revenge, envy, jealousy, are his ruling passions; and his cold temperament is little exposed to those effeminate vices which are the bane of milder races. With him revenge is an overpowering instinct; nay, more, it is a point of honor and a duty. His pride sets all language at defiance. He loathes the thought of coercion; and few of his race have ever stooped to discharge a menial office. A wild love of liberty, an utter intolerance of control, lie at the basis of his character, and fire his whole existence. Yet, in spite of this haughty independence, he is a devout hero-worshipper; and high achievement in war or policy touches a chord to which his nature never fails to respond. He looks up with admiring reverence to the sages and heroes of his tribe; and it is this principle, joined to the respect for age, which springs from the patriarchal element in his social system, which, beyond all other, contributes union and harmony to the erratic members of an Indian community. With him the love of glory kindles into a burning passion; and to allay its cravings, he will dare cold and famine, fire, tempest, torture, and death itself.

These generous traits are overcast by much that is dark, cold, and sinister, by sleepless distrust, and rankling jealousy. Treacherous himself, he is always suspicious of treachery in others. Brave as he is,—and few of mankind are braver,—he will vent his passion by a secret stab rather than an open blow. His warfare is full of ambuscade and strategem; and he never rushes into battle with that joyous self-abandonment, with which the warriors of the Gothic races flung themselves into the ranks of their enemies. In his feasts and his drinking-bouts we find none of that robust and full-toned mirth which reigned at the rude carousals of our barbaric ancestry. He is never jovial in his cups, and maudlin sorrow or maniacal rage is the sole result of his potations.

Over all emotion he throws the veil of an iron self-control, originating in a peculiar form of pride, and fostered by rigorous discipline from childhood upward. He is trained to conceal passion, and not to subdue it. The inscrutable warrior is aptly imaged by the hackneyed figure of a volcano covered with snow; and no man can say when or where the wild-fire will burst forth. This shallow self-mastery serves to give dignity to public deliberation, and harmony to social life. Wrangling and quarrel are strangers to an Indian dwelling; and while an assembly of the ancient Gauls was garrulous as a convocation of magpies, a Roman senate might have taken a lesson from the grave solemnity of an Indian council. In the midst of his family and friends, he hides affections, by nature none of the most tender, under a mask of icy coldness; and in the torturing fires of his enemy, the haughty sufferer maintains to the last his look of grim defiance.

His intellect is as peculiar as his moral organization. Among all savages, the powers of perception preponderate over those of reason and analysis; but this is more especially the case with the Indian. An acute judge of character, at least of such parts of it as his experience enables him to comprehend; keen to a proverb in all exercises of war and the chase, he seldom traces effects to their causes, or follows out actions to their remote results. Though a close observer of external nature, he no sooner attempts to account for her phenomena than he involves himself in the most ridiculous absurdities; and quite content with these puerilities, he has not the least desire to push his inquiries further. His curiosity, abundantly active within its own narrow circle, is dead to all things else; and to attempt rousing it from its torpor is but a bootless task. He seldom takes cognizance of general or abstract ideas; and his language has scarcely the power to express them, except through the medium of figures drawn from the external world, and often highly picturesque and forcible. The absence of reflection makes him grossly improvident, and unfits him for pursuing any complicated scheme of war or policy.

Some races of men seem molded in wax, soft and melting, at once plastic and feeble. Some races, like some metals, combine the greatest flexibility with the greatest strength. But the Indian is hewn out of a rock. You cannot change the form without destruction of the substance. Such, at least, has too often proved the case. Races of inferior energy have possessed a power of expansion and assimilation to which he is a stranger; and it is this fixed and rigid quality which has proved his ruin. He will not learn the arts of civilization, and he and his forest must perish together. The stern, unchanging features of his mind excite our admiration, from their very immutability; and we look with deep interest on the fate of this irreclaimable son of the wilderness, the child who will not be weaned from the breast of his rugged mother. And our interest increases when we discern in the unhappy wanderer, mingled among his vices, the germs of heroic virtues—a hand bountiful to bestow, as it is rapacious to seize, and, even in extremest famine, imparting its last morsel to a fellow-sufferer; a heart which, strong in friendship as in hate, thinks it not too much to lay down life for its chosen comrade; a soul true to its own idea of honor, and burning with an unquenchable thirst for greatness and renown.

The imprisoned lion in the showman's cage differs not more widely from the lord of the desert, than the beggarly frequenter of frontier garrisons and dramshops differs from the proud denizen of the woods. It is in his native wilds alone that the Indian must be seen and studied. Thus to depict him is the aim of the ensuing History; and if, from the shades of rock and forest, the savage features should look too grimly forth, it is because the clouds of a tempestuous war have cast upon the picture their murky shadows and lurid fires.

HERMAN MELVILLE
(1819–1891)

Although Melville's greatest achievement is a novel of the sea, readers of *Moby-Dick* have been struck by its many allusions to the West. To critics, it has seemed that Melville was writing, in terms of the whale hunt, of the whole American assault on nature in the names of materialism and egocentricity. In the wreck of tragic Ahab, Melville dramatized his country-men's perversion of their noblest capacities; the white man's control of that "rare old craft," the *Pequod,* named after an extinct tribe of Massachusetts Indians, leads to the destruction of all by a massive whale whose beauty, intelligence, and seeming malignity make him an awesome symbol of God-in-Nature.

A central issue of the novel is the physical and moral superiority of three pagan harpooners. One of these, Tashtego, a Gay Head Indian, assumes special importance in the novel. It is Tashtego who sights the whale a split second after Ahab, who exemplifies the interrelatedness of men in the chapter in which Queequeg rescues him from the whale's "Heidelburgh Tun," who terrifies poor Doughboy with a pantomime of scalping, and who shows his confusion in his own three-line chapter. At the end, when our sympathies are thoroughly aroused for the crew so madly endangered by Ahab, Tashtego is the emblem of loyalty and unflagging energy in Melville's compassionate last paragraph. Reprinted below are the description of Tashtego from "Knights and Squires," and this final paragraph.

Just how deeply knowledge of the western frontier and its interesting inhabitants affected Melville can be seen in the rich allusions that lard Melville's books before and after *Moby-Dick.* In *Redburn,* for example, the evil sailor Jackson, prefiguring Ahab, is described as a "horrid desperado, and like a wild Indian, whom he resembled . . . he seemed to run amuck at heaven and earth." Opposing this stereotyped allusion is another, more interesting one, in *White-Jacket.* Melville's narrator is reminded of a Sioux Indian he once met on the Mississippi, who exhibited, on the back of his blanket, a group of painted red hands, each hand representing a scalped enemy.

Poor savage: thought I; and is this the cause of your lofty gait? Do you straighten yourself to think that you have committed a murder, when a chance falling stone has often done the same? Is it a proud thing to topple down six feet perpendicular of immortal manhood, though that lofty living tower needed perhaps thirty good growing summers to bring it to maturity? Poor savage! And you account it so glorious, do you, to mutilate and destroy what God himself was more than a quarter of a century in building?

And yet, fellow-Christians, what is the American frigate *Macedonian,* or the English frigate *President,* but as two bloody red hands painted on this poor savage's blanket?

Are there no Moravians in the Moon, that not a missionary has yet visited this poor pagan planet of ours, to civilise civilisation and christianise Christendom?

Melville also refers at length to the Indian and his white antagonist in *The Confidence-Man* (1857). In this experimental novel, in place of one or two central protagonists Melville introduces a series of men who play upon the weakness, innocence and gullibility of their fellow-passengers aboard a Mississippi steamboat ironically named *Fidele.* Revealed are the greed, cruelty and egotism that underlie benevolent appearances. In chapters 26 and 27 Melville borrows a story from Judge James Hall, whose *Sketches of the West* celebrated the heroism and endurance of frontiersmen. Melville obscures his attitude toward the story by choosing as narrator an ambiguous, otherwise unidentified "man in a violet vest," who tells it to a "cosmopolitan," identified by his wider role in the book as a shallow deceiver. Although the passage is subject to varied interpretations, it may be said that Melville rejects Hall's defense of the frontiersman along with the cosmopolitan's sentimental belief in a "ruling principle of Love." Thoroughly skeptical himself, Melville sees Moredock as a version of Ahab—a man who sacrifices his humanity in an overwhelming desire for certainty.

From Moby Dick; *or The Whale,* 1851

Next was Tashtego, an unmixed Indian from Gay Head, the most west-
erly promontory of Martha's Vineyard, where there still exists the last
remnant of a village of red men, which has long supplied the neighboring
island of Nantucket with many of her most daring harpooneers. In the
fishery, they usually go by the generic name of Gay-Headers. Tashtego's
long, lean, sable hair, his high cheek bones, and black rounding eyes—for
an Indian, Oriental in their largeness, but Antarctic in their glittering
expression—all this sufficiently proclaimed him an inheritor of the
unvitiated blood of those proud warrior hunters, who, in quest of the great
New England moose, had scoured, bow in hand, the aboriginal forests of
the main. But no longer snuffing in the trail of the wild beasts of the woodland, Tashtego now hunted in the wake of the great whales of the sea; the
unerring harpoon of the son fitly replacing the infallible arrow of the sires.
To look at the tawny brawn of his lithe snaky limbs, you would almost
have credited the superstitions of some of the earlier Puritans, and half
believed this wild Indian to be a son of the Prince of the Powers of the Air.
Tashtego was Stubb the second mate's squire.

. . . .

But as the last whelmings intermixingly poured themselves over the
sunken head of the Indian at the main-mast, leaving a few inches of the
erect spar yet visible, together with long streaming yards of the flag, which
calmly undulated, with ironical coincidings, over the destroying billows
they almost touched;—at that instant, a red arm and a hammer hovered back-
wardly uplifted in the open air, in the act of nailing the flag faster and yet
faster to the subsiding spar. A sky-hawk that tauntingly had followed the
main-truck downwards from its natural home among the stars, pecking at
the flag, and incommoding Tashtego there; this bird now chanced to
intercept its broad fluttering wing between the hammer and the wood; and
simultaneously feeling that ethereial thrill, the submerged savage beneath,
in his death-gasp, kept his hammer frozen there; and so the bird of heaven,

Herman Melville, *Moby-Dick; or, The Whale* (New York, 1851), pp. 131–132,
634.

with archangelic shrieks, and his imperial beak thrust upwards, and his whole captive form folded in the flag of Ahab, went down with his ship, which, like Satan, would not sink to hell till she had dragged a living part of heaven along with her, and helmeted herself with it.

Now small fowls flew screaming over the yet yawning gulf; a sullen white surf beat against its steep sides; then all collapsed, and the great shroud of the sea rolled on as it rolled five thousand years ago.

CHAPTER 26

Containing the Metaphysics of Indian-hating,
According to the Views of One Evidently not so
Prepossessed as Rousseau in Favor of Savages

"The judge always began in these words: 'The backwoodsman's hatred of the Indian has been a topic for some remark. In the earlier times of the frontier the passion was thought to be readily accounted for. But Indian rapine having mostly ceased through regions where it once prevailed, the philanthropist is surprised that Indian-hating has not in like degree ceased with it. He wonders why the backwoodsman still regards the red man in much the same spirit that a jury does a murderer, or a trapper a wild cat—a creature, in whose behalf mercy were not wisdom; truce is vain; he must be executed.

" 'A curious point,' the judge would continue, 'which perhaps not everybody, even upon explanation, may fully understand; while, in order for anyone to approach to an understanding, it is necessary for him to learn, or if he already know, to bear in mind, what manner of man the backwoodsman is; as for what manner of man the Indian is, many know, either from history or experience.

" 'The backwoodsman is a lonely man. He is a thoughtful man. He is a man strong and unsophisticated. Impulsive, he is what some might call

---

Herman Melville, *The Confidence-Man: His Masquerade* (New York, 1857), chapters 26 and 27, pp. 224–236 and 237–243.

unprincipled. At any rate, he is self-willed; being one who less hearkens to what others may say about things, than looks for himself, to see what are things themselves. If in straits, there are few to help; he must depend upon himself; he must continually look to himself. Hence self-reliance, to the degree of standing by his own judgment, though it stand alone. Not that he deems himself infallible; too many mistakes in following trails prove the contrary; but he thinks that nature destines such sagacity as she has given him, as she destines it to the 'possum. To these fellow-beings of the wilds their untutored sagacity is their best dependence. If with either it proved faulty, if the 'possum's betray it to the trap; or the backwoodsman's mislead him into ambuscade, there are consequences to be undergone, but no self-blame. As with the 'possum, instincts prevail with the backwoodsman over precepts. Like the 'possum, the backwoodsman presents the spectacle of a creature dwelling exclusively among the works of God, yet these, truth must confess, breed little in him of a godly mind. Small bowing and scraping is his, further than when with bent knee he points his rifle, or picks its flint. With few companions, solitude by necessity his lengthened lot, he stands the trial—no slight one, since, next to dying, solitude, rightly borne, is perhaps of fortitude the most rigorous test. But not merely is the backwoodsman content to be alone, but in no few cases is anxious to be so. The sight of smoke ten miles off is provocation to one more remove from man, one step deeper into nature. Is it that he feels that whatever man may be, man is not the universe? that glory, beauty, kindness, are not all engrossed by him? that as the presence of man frights birds away, so, many bird-like thoughts? Be that how it will, the backwoodsman is not without some fineness to his nature. Hairy Orson as he looks, it may be with him as with the Shetland seal—beneath the bristles lurks the fur.

" 'Though held in a sort a barbarian, the backwoodsman would seem to America what Alexander was to Asia—captain in the vanguard of conquering civilization. Whatever the nation's growing opulence or power, does it not lackey his heels? Pathfinder, provider of security to those who come after him, for himself he asks nothing but hardship. Worthy to be compared with Moses in the Exodus, or the Emperor Julian in Gaul, who on foot, and barebrowed, at the head of covered or mounted legions, marched so through the elements, day after day. The tide of emigration, let it roll as it will, never overwhelms the backwoodsman into itself; he rides upon advance, as the Polynesian upon the comb of the surf.

" 'Thus, though he keep moving on through life, he maintains with respect to nature much the same unaltered relation throughout; with her creatures, too, including panthers and Indians. Hence, it is not unlikely that, accurate as the theory of the Peace Congress may be with respect to those two varieties of beings, among others, yet the backwoodsman might be qualified to throw out some practical suggestions.
226

" 'As the child born to a backwoodsman must in turn lead his father's life—a life which, as related to humanity, is related mainly to Indians—it is thought best not to mince matters, out of delicacy; but to tell the boy pretty plainly what an Indian is, and what he must expect from him. For however charitable it may be to view Indians as members of the Society of Friends, yet to affirm them such to one ignorant of Indians, whose lonely path lies a long way through their lands, in the event, might prove not only injudicious but cruel. At least something of this kind would seem the maxim upon which backwoods education is based. Accordingly if in youth the backwoodsman incline to knowledge, as is generally the case, he hears little from his schoolmasters, the old chroniclers of the forest, but histories of Indian lying, Indian theft, Indian double-dealing, Indian fraud and perfidy, Indian want of conscience, Indian blood-thirstiness, Indian diabolism— histories which, though of wild woods, are almost as full of things unangelic as the Newgate Calendar or the Annals of Europe. In these Indian narra- tives and traditions the lad is thoroughly grounded. "As the twig is bent the tree's inclined." The instinct of antipathy against an Indian grows in the backwoodsman with the sense of good and bad, right and wrong. In one breath he learns that a brother is to be loved, and an Indian to be hated.

" 'Such are the facts,' the judge would say, 'upon which, if one seek to moralize, he must do so with an eye to them. It is terrible that one creature should so regard another, should make it conscience to abhor an entire race. It is terrible; but is it surprising? Surprising, that one should hate a race which he believes to be red from a cause akin to that which makes some tribes of garden insects green? A race whose name is upon the fron- tier a *memento mori;* painted to him in every evil light; now a horse-thief like those in Moyamensing; now an assassin like a New York rowdy; now a treaty-breaker like an Austrian; now a Palmer with poisoned arrows; now a judicial murderer and Jeffries, after a fierce farce of trial condemning his victim to bloody death; or a Jew with hospitable speeches cozening some fainting stranger into ambuscade, there to burk him, and account it a deed grateful to Manitou, his god.

" 'Still, all this is less advanced as truths of the Indians than as examples of the backwoodsman's impression of them—in which the charitable may think he does them some injustice. Certain it is, the Indian themselves think so; quite unanimously, too. The Indians, indeed, protest against the backwoodsman's view of them; and some think that one cause of their returning his antipathy so sincerely as they do, is their moral indignation at being so libeled by him, as they really believe and say. But whether, on this or any point, the Indians should be permitted to testify for themselves, to the exclusion of other testimony, is a question that may be left to the Supreme Court. At any rate, it has been observed that when an Indian becomes a genuine proselyte to Christianity (such cases, however, not being very many; though, indeed, entire tribes are sometimes nominally brought to the true light), he will not in that case conceal his enlightened conviction, that his race's portion by nature is total depravity; and, in that way, as much as admits that the backwoodsman's worst idea of it is not very far from true; while, on the other hand, those red men who are the greatest sticklers for the theory of Indian virtue, and Indian loving-kindness, are sometimes the arrantest horse-thieves and tomahawkers among them. So, at least, avers the backwoodsman. And though, knowing the Indian nature, as he thinks he does, he fancies he is not ignorant that an Indian may in some points deceive himself almost as effectually as in bush-tactics he can another, yet his theory and his practice as above contrasted seem to involve an inconsistency so extreme, that the backwoodsman only accounts for it on the supposition that when a tomahawking red man advances the notion of the benignity of the red race, it is but part and parcel with that subtle strategy which he finds so useful in war, in hunting, and the general conduct of life.'

"In further explanation of that deep abhorrence with which the back-woodsman regards the savage, the judge used to think it might perhaps a little help, to consider what kind of stimulus to it is furnished in those forest histories and traditions before spoken of. In which behalf, he would tell the story of the little colony of Wrights and Weavers, originally seven cousins from Virginia who, after successive removals with their families, at last established themselves near the southern frontier of the Bloody Ground, Kentucky: 'They were strong, brave men; but, unlike many of the pioneers in those days, theirs was no love of conflict for conflict's sake. Step by step they had been lured to their lonely resting-place by the ever-beckoning seductions of a fertile and virgin land, with a singular exemption, during the march, from Indian molestation. But clearings made and houses built, the bright shield was soon to turn its other side. After repeated persecutions and eventual hostilities, forced on them by a dwindled tribe in their neighborhood—persecutions resulting in loss of crops and cattle; hostilities in which they lost two of their number, illy to be spared, besides others getting painful wounds—the five remaining cousins made, with some serious concessions, a kind of treaty with Mocmohoc, the chief, being to this induced by the harryings of the enemy, leaving them no peace. But they were further prompted, indeed, first incited, by the suddenly changed ways of Mocmohoc, who, though hitherto deemed a savage almost perfidious as Caesar Borgia, yet now put on a seeming the reverse of this, engaging to bury the hatchet, smoke the pipe, and be friends forever; not friends in the mere sense of renouncing enmity, but in the sense of kindliness, active and familiar.

" 'But what the chief now seemed, did not wholly blind them to what the chief had been; so that, though in no small degree influenced by his change of bearing, they still distrusted him enough to covenant with him, among other articles on their side, that though friendly visits should be exchanged between the wigwams and the cabins, yet the five cousins should never, on any account, be expected to enter the chief's lodge together. The intention was, though they reserved it, that if ever, under the guise of amity, the chief should mean them mischief, and effect it, it should be but partially; so that some of the five might survive, not only for their families' sake, but also for retribution's. Nevertheless, Mocmohoc did, upon a time, with such fine art and pleasing carriage win their confidence, that he brought them all together to a feast of bear's meat, and there, by stratagem, ended them. Years after, over their calcined bones and those of all their families, the chief, reproached for his treachery by a proud hunter whom he had made captive, jeered out, "Treachery? pale face! 'Twas they who broke their covenant first, in coming all together; they that broke it first, in trusting Mocmohoc." '

"At this point the judge would pause, and lifting his hand, and rolling his eyes, exclaim in a solemn enough voice, 'Circling wiles and bloody lusts. The acuteness and genius of the chief but make him the more atrocious.'

"After another pause, he would begin an imaginary kind of dialogue between a backwoodsman and a questioner:

" 'But are all Indians like Mocmohoc?—Not all have proved such; but in the least harmful may lie his germ. There is an Indian nature. "Indian blood is in me," is the half-breed's threat.—But are not some Indians kind?—Yes, but kind Indians are mostly lazy, and reputed simple—at all events, are seldom chiefs; chiefs among the red men being taken from the active, and those accounted wise. Hence, with small promotion, kind Indians have but proportionate influence. And kind Indians may be forced to do unkind biddings. So "beware the Indian kind or unkind," said Daniel Boone, who lost his sons by them.—But, have all you backwoodsmen been some way victimized by Indians?—No.—Well, and in certain cases may not at least some few of you be favored by them?—Yes, but scarce one among us so self-important, or so selfish-minded, as to hold his personal exemption from Indian outrage such a set off against the contrary experience of so many others, as that he must needs, in a general way, think well of Indians; or, if he do, an arrow in his flank might suggest a pertinent doubt.

" 'In short,' according to the judge, 'if we at all credit the backwoodsman, his feeling against Indians, to be taken aright, must be considered as being not so much on his own account as on others', or jointly on both accounts. True it is, scarce a family he knows but some member of it, or connection, has been by Indians maimed or scalped. What avails, then, that some one

Indian, or some two or three, treat a backwoodsman friendly-like? He fears me, he thinks. Take my rifle from me, give him motive, and what will come? Or if not so, how know I what involuntary preparations may be going on in him for things as unbeknown in present time to him as me—a sort of chemical preparation in the soul for malice, as chemical preparation in the body for malady.'

"Not that the backwoodsman ever used those words, you see, but the judge found him expression for his meaning. And this point he would conclude with saying, that, 'what is called a "friendly Indian" is a very rare sort of creature; and well it was so, for no ruthlessness exceeds that of a "friendly Indian" turned enemy. A coward friend, he makes a valiant foe.

" 'But, thus far the passion in question has been viewed in a general way as that of a community. When to his due share of this the backwoodsman adds his private passion, we have then the stock out of which is formed, if formed at all, the Indian-hater *par excellence.*'

"The Indian-hater *par excellence* the judge defined to be one 'who, having with his mother's milk drank in small love for red men, in youth, or early manhood, ere the sensibilities become osseous, receives at their hand some signal outrage, or, which in effect is much the same, some of his kin have, or some friend. Now, nature all around him by her solitudes wooing or bidding him muse upon this matter, he accordingly does so, till the thought develops such attraction, that much as straggling vapors troop from all sides to a storm-cloud, so straggling thoughts of other outrages troop to the nucleus thought, assimilate with it, and swell it. At last, taking counsel with the elements, he comes to his resolution. An intenser Hannibal, he makes a vow, the hate of which is a vortex from whose suction scarce the remotest chip of the guilty race may reasonably feel secure. Next, he declares himself and settles his temporal affairs. With the solemnity of a Spaniard turned monk, he takes leave of his kin; or rather, these leave-takings have something of the still more impressive finality of death-bed adieux. Last, he commits himself to the forest primeval; there, so long as life shall be his, to act upon a calm, cloistered scheme of strategical, implacable, and lonesome vengeance. Ever on the noiseless trail; cool, collected, patient; less seen than felt; snuffing, smelling—a Leather-stocking Nemesis. In the settlements he will not be seen again; in eyes of old companions tears may start at some chance thing that speaks of him; but they never look for him, nor call; they know he will not come. Suns and seasons fleet; the tiger-lily blows and falls; babes are born and leap in their mothers' arms; but, the Indian-hater is good as gone to his long home, and "Terror" is his epitaph.'

"Here the judge, not unaffected, would pause again, but presently resume: 'How evident that in strict speech there can be no biography of an Indian-hater *par excellence,* any more than one of a sword-fish, or other deep-sea denizen; or, which is still less imaginable, one of a dead man. The career of the Indian-hater *par excellence* has the impenetrability of the fate of a lost steamer. Doubtless, events, terrible ones, have happened, must have happened; but the powers that be in nature have taken order that they shall never become news.

" 'But, luckily for the curious, there is a species of diluted Indian-hater, one whose heart proves not so steely as his brain. Soft enticements of domestic life too often draw him from the ascetic trail; a monk who apostatizes to the world at times. Like a mariner, too, though much abroad, he may have a wife and family in some green harbor which he does not forget. It is with him as with the Papist converts in Senegal; fasting and mortification prove hard to bear.'

"The judge, with his usual judgment, always thought that the intense solitude to which the Indian-hater consigns himself, has, by its overawing influence, no little to do with relaxing his vow. He would relate instances where, after some months' lonely scoutings, the Indian-hater is suddenly seized with a sort of calenture; hurries openly toward the first smoke, though he knows it is an Indian's, announces himself as a lost hunter, gives the savage his rifle, throws himself upon his charity, embraces him with much affection, imploring the privilege of living a while in his sweet companionship. What is too often the sequel of so distempered a procedure may be best known by those who best know the Indian. Upon the whole, the judge, by two-and-thirty good and sufficient reasons, would maintain that there was no known vocation whose consistent following calls for such self-containings as that of the Indian-hater *par excellence.* In the highest view, he considered such a soul one peeping out but once an age.

"For the diluted Indian-hater, although the vacations he permits himself impair the keeping of the character, yet, it should not be overlooked that this is the man who, by his very infirmity, enables us to form surmises, however inadequate, of what Indian-hating in its perfection is."

"One moment," gently interrupted the cosmopolitan here, "and let me refill my calumet."

Which being done, the other proceeded:

CHAPTER 27

Some Account of a Man of Questionable Morality,
but who, nevertheless, would seem Entitled to the
Esteem of that Eminent English Moralist who said
He Liked a Good Hater

"Coming to mention the man to whose story all thus far said was but the introduction, the judge, who, like you, was a great smoker, would insist upon all the company taking cigars, and then lighting a fresh one himself, rise in his place, and, with the solemnest voice, say—'Gentlemen, let us smoke to the memory of Colonel John Moredock'; when, after several whiffs taken standing in deep silence and deeper reverie, he would resume his seat and his discourse, something in these words:

" 'Though Colonel John Moredock was not an Indian-hater *par excellence*, he yet cherished a kind of sentiment toward the red man, and in that degree, and so acted out his sentiment as sufficiently to merit the tribute just rendered to his memory.

" 'John Moredock was the son of a woman married thrice, and thrice widowed by a tomahawk. The three successive husbands of this woman had been pioneers, and with them she had wandered from wilderness to wilderness, always on the frontier. With nine children, she at last found herself at a little clearing, afterwards Vincennes. There she joined a company about to remove to the new country of Illinois. On the eastern side of Illinois there were then no settlements; but on the west side, the shore of the Mississippi, there were, near the mouth of the Kaskaskia, some old hamlets of French. To the vicinity of those hamlets, very innocent and pleasant places, a new Arcadia, Mrs. Moredock's party was destined; for thereabouts, among the vines, they meant to settle. They embarked upon the Wabash in boats, proposing descending that stream into the Ohio, and the Ohio into the Mississippi, and so, northwards, toward the point to be reached. All went well till they made the rock of the Grand Tower on the Mississippi, where they had to land and drag their boats round a point swept by a strong current. Here a party of Indians, lying in wait, rushed out and murdered nearly all of them. The widow was among the victims with her children, John excepted, who, some fifty miles distant, was following with a second party.

" 'He was just entering upon manhood, when thus left in nature sole survivor of his race. Other youngsters might have turned mourners; he turned avenger. His nerves were electric wires—sensitive, but steel. He was one who, from self-possession, could be made neither to flush nor pale. It is said that when the tidings were brought him, he was ashore sitting beneath a hemlock eating his dinner of venison—and as the tidings were told him, after the first start he kept on eating, but slowly and deliberately, chewing the wild news with the wild meat, as if both together, turned to chyle, together should sinew him to his intent. From that meal he rose an Indian-hater. He rose; got his arms, prevailed upon some comrades to join him, and without delay started to discover who were the actual transgressors. They proved to belong to a band of twenty renegades from various tribes, outlaws even among Indians, and who had formed themselves into a marauding crew. No opportunity for action being at the time presented, he dismissed his friends; told them to go on, thanking them, and saying he would ask their aid at some future day. For upwards of a year, alone in the wilds, he watched the crew. Once, what he thought a favorable chance having occurred—it being midwinter, and the savages encamped, apparently to remain so—he anew mustered his friends, and marched against them; but getting wind of his coming, the enemy fled and in such panic that everything was left behind but their weapons. During the winter, much the same thing happened upon two subsequent occasions. The next year he sought them at the head of a party pledged to serve him for forty days. At last the hour came. It was on the shore of the Mississippi. From their covert, Moredock and his men dimly descried the gang of Cains in the red dusk of evening, paddling over to a jungled island in mid-stream, there the more securely to lodge; for Moredock's retributive spirit in the wilderness spoke ever to their trepidations now, like the voice calling through the garden. Waiting until dead of night, the whites swam the river, towing after them a raft laden with their arms. On landing, Moredock cut the fastenings of the enemy's canoes, and turned them, with his own raft, adrift; resolved that there should be neither escape for the Indians, nor safety, except in victory, for the whites. Victorious the whites were; but three of the Indians saved themselves by taking to the stream. Moredock's band lost not a man.

" 'Three of the murderers survived. He knew their names and persons. In the course of three years each successively fell by his own hand. All were now dead. But this did not suffice. He made no avowal, but to kill Indians had become his passion. As an athlete, he had few equals; as a shot, none; in single combat, not to be beaten. Master of that woodland cunning enabling the adept to subsist where the tyro would perish, and expert in all those arts by which an enemy is pursued for weeks, perhaps months, without once suspecting it, he kept to the forest. The solitary Indian that met him died. When a murder was descried, he would either secretly pursue their track for some chance to strike at least one blow; or if, while thus engaged, he himself was discovered, he would elude them by superior skill.

" 'Many years he spent thus; and though after a time he was, in a degree, restored to the ordinary life of the region and period, yet it is believed that John Moredock never let pass an opportunity of quenching an Indian. Sins of commission in that kind may have been his, but none of omission.

" 'It were to err to suppose,' the judge would say, 'that this gentleman was naturally ferocious, or peculiarly possessed of those qualities, which, unhelped by provocation of events, tend to withdraw man from social life. On the contrary, Moredock was an example of something apparently self-contradicting, certainly curious, but, at the same time, undeniable; namely, that nearly all Indian-haters have at bottom loving hearts; at any rate, hearts, if anything, more generous than the average. Certain it is, that, to the degree in which he mingled in the life of the settlements, Moredock showed himself not without humane feelings. No cold husband or colder father, he; and, though often and long away from his household, bore its needs in mind, and provided for them. He could be very convivial; told a good story (though never of his more private exploits), and sung a capital song. Hospitable, not backward to help a neighbor; by report, benevolent, as retributive, in secret; while, in a general manner, though sometimes grave— as is not unusual with men of his complexion, a sultry and tragical brown— yet with nobody, Indians excepted, otherwise than courteous in a manly fashion; a moccasined gentleman, admired and loved. In fact, no one more popular, as an incident to follow may prove.

" 'His bravery, whether in Indian fight, or any other, was unquestionable. An officer in the ranging service during the war of 1812, he acquitted himself with more than credit. Of his soldierly character, this anecdote is told: Not long after Hull's dubious surrender at Detroit, Moredock with some of his rangers rode up at night to a log-house, there to rest till morning. The horses being attended to, supper over, and sleeping-places assigned the troop, the host showed the colonel his best bed, not on the ground like the rest, but a bed that stood on legs. But out of delicacy, the guest declined to monopolize it, or indeed, to occupy it at all; when, to increase the inducement, as the host thought, he was told that a general officer had once slept in that bed. "Who, pray?" asked the colonel. "General Hull." "Then you must not take offence," said the colonel, buttoning up his coat, "but really, no coward's bed for me, however comfortable." Accordingly he took up with valor's bed—a cold one on the ground.

" 'At one time the colonel was a member of the territorial council of Illinois, and at the formation of the state government, was pressed to become a candidate for governor, but begged to be excused. And, though he declined to give his reasons for declining yet by those who best knew him the cause was not wholly unsurmised. In his official capacity he might be called upon to enter into friendly treaties with Indian tribes, a thing not to be thought of. And even did no such contingency arise, yet he felt there would be impropriety in the Governor of Illinois stealing out now and then, during a recess of the legislative bodies, for a few days' shooting at human beings, within the limits of his paternal chief-magistracy. If the governorship offered large honors, from Moredock it demanded larger sacrifices. These were incompatibles. In short, he was not unaware that to be a consistent Indian-hater involves the renunciation of ambition, with its objects—the pomps and glories of the world; and since religion, pronouncing such things vanities, accounts it merit to renounce them, therefore, so far as this goes, Indian-hating, whatever may be thought of it in other respects, may be regarded as not wholly without the efficacy of a devout sentiment.' "

Here the narrator paused. Then, after his long and irksome sitting, started to his feet, and regulating his disordered shirt-frill, and at the same time adjustingly shaking his legs down in his rumpled pantaloons, concluded: "There, I have done; having given you, not my story, mind, or my thoughts, but another's. And now, for your friend Coonskins, I doubt not, that, if the judge were here, he would pronounce him a sort of comprehensive Colonel Moredock, who, too much spreading his passion, shallows it."

HENRY WADSWORTH
LONGFELLOW (1807-1882)

The most famous and admired poet of his time, Longfellow has seemed a considerably less significant figure in the twentieth century. Descendent of prominent New Englanders, professor of Romance languages at Harvard, he nourished his poetry on scholarship. "The Song of Hiawatha" (1855), his long Indian narrative poem, is based on scholarly research. The legends and language come, primarily, from Longfellow's reading of Henry Rowe Schoolcraft, an American geologist and ethnologist who lived among the Chippewa, in Michigan. Married to the daughter of a chief, Schoolcraft translated Indian poetry and legend, and compiled his research in several important volumes; the best known are *Algic Researches: Comprising Inquiries Respecting the Mental Characteristics of the North American Indian* (1839), *Oneota; or, Characteristics of the Red Race of America* (1844), and *History, Condition and Prospects of the Indian Tribes of the United States* (1851-1857).

If the matter of Longfellow's work came from reading ethnology, the meter came from that of the Finnish epic, *Kalevala*. Longfellow faced charges of plagiarism, when lines and incidents in his work seemed to echo the *Kalevala* too closely; moreover, critics have often complained that he followed Schoolcraft even into error by confusing the Chippewa magic figure Manabozho with the Iroquois statesman Hiawatha. But whatever the blunders and great tedious stretches of the poem, it served to teach generations of American schoolchildren the meaning of narrative poetry and to foster some interest in Indian legend.

Hiawatha strikes the contemporary reader as an attempt to exploit Indian legend without fully respecting it, to justify white dispossession of Indians by representing their spokesman as Christian and acquiescent. However, even the sentimental end of the poem cannot destroy one's pleasure in Canto XIII's images of fruitfulness and its tactful use of Indian language. No one claims now that "The Song of Hiawatha" adequately represents Indian legend or is, as Albert Keiser calls it, "America's most notable poem." It does testify, however, to the need white Americans had to simplify and sentimentalize the history of this continent.

From **The Song of Hiawatha,** *1855*

XIII.

Blessing the Corn-Fields

Sing, O Song of Hiawatha,
Of the happy days that followed,
In the land of the Ojibways,
In the pleasant land and peaceful!
Sing the mysteries of Mondamin,
Sing the Blessing of the Corn-fields!
Buried was the bloody hatchet,
Buried was the dreadful war-club,
Buried were all warlike weapons,
And the war-cry was forgotten.
There was peace among the nations;
Unmolested roved the hunters,
Built the birch canoe for sailing,
Caught the fish in lake and river,
Shot the deer and trapped the beaver;
Unmolested worked the women,
Made their sugar from the maple,
Gathered wild rice in the meadows,
Dressed the skins of deer and beaver.
All around the happy village
Stood the maize-fields, green and shining,
Waved the green plumes of Mondamin,
Waved his soft and sunny tresses,
Filling all the land with plenty.
'Twas the women who in Spring-time
Planted the broad fields and fruitful,
Buried in the earth Mondamin;
'Twas the women who in Autumn
Stripped the yellow husks of harvest,
Stripped the garments from Mondamin,
Even as Hiawatha taught them.
Once, when all the maize was planted,
Hiawatha, wise and thoughtful,

Henry Wadsworth Longfellow, "The Song of Hiawatha," in *The Poetical Works of Henry Wadsworth Longfellow,* vol. 2 (Boston, 1882), pp. 122–130.

Spake and said to Minnehaha,
To his wife, the Laughing Water:
"You shall bless to-night the corn-fields,
Draw a magic circle round them,
To protect them from destruction,
Blast of mildew, blight of insect,
Wagemin, the thief of corn-fields,
Paimosaid, who steals the maize-ear!
   "In the night, when all is silence,
In the night, when all is darkness,
When the Spirit of Sleep, Nepahwin,
Shuts the doors of all the wigwams,
So that not an ear can hear you,
So that not an eye can see you,
Rise up from you bed in silence,
Lay aside your garments wholly,
Walk around the fields you planted,
Round the borders of the corn-fields,
Covered by your tresses only,
Robed with darkness as a garment.
   "Thus the fields shall be more fruitful,
And the passing of your footsteps
Draw a magic circle round them,
So that neither blight nor mildew,
Neither burrowing worm nor insect,
Shall pass o'er the magic circle;
Not the dragon-fly, Kwo-ne-she,
Nor the spider, Subbe-kashe,
Nor the grasshopper, Pah-puk-keena,
Nor the mighty caterpillar,
Way-muk-kwana, with the bear-skin,
King of all the caterpillars!"
   On the tree-tops near the corn-fields
Sat the hungry crows and ravens,
Kahgahgee, the King of Ravens,
With his band of black marauders.
And they laughed at Hiawatha,
Till the tree-tops shook with laughter,
With their melancholy laughter
At the words of Hiawatha.
"Hear him!" said they; "hear the Wise Man,
Hear the plots of Hiawatha!"

When the noiseless night descended
Broad and dark o'er field and forest,
When the mournful Wawonaissa,
Sorrowing sang among the hemlocks,
And the Spirit of Sleep, Nepahwin,
Shut the doors of all the wigwams,
From her bed rose Laughing Water,
Laid aside her garments wholly,
And with darkness clothed and guarded
Unashamed and unaffrighted,
Walked securely round the corn-fields,
Drew the sacred, magic circle
Of her footprints round the corn-fields.
　No one but the Midnight only
Saw her beauty in the darkness,
No one but the Wawonaissa
Heard the panting of her bosom;
Guskewau, the darkness, wrapped her
Closely in his sacred mantle,
So that none might see her beauty,
So that none might boast, "I saw her!"
　On the morrow, as the day dawned,
Kahgahgee, the King of Ravens,
Gathered all his black marauders,
Crows and black-birds, jays and ravens,
Clamorous on the dusky tree-tops,
And descended, fast and fearless,
On the fields of Hiawatha,
On the grave of the Mondamin.
　"We will drag Mondamin," said they,
"From the grave where he is buried,
Spite of all the magic circles
Laughing Water draws around it,
Spite of all the sacred footprints
Minnehaha stamps upon it!"
　But the wary Hiawatha
Ever thoughtful, careful, watchful,
Had o'erheard the scornful laughter
When they mocked him from the tree-tops.
"Kaw!" he said, "my friends the ravens!
Kahgahgee, my King of Ravens!
I will teach you all a lesson

That shall not be soon forgotten!"
He had risen before the daybreak,
He had spread o'er all the corn-fields
Snares to catch the black marauders,
And was lying now in ambush
In the neighboring grove of pine-trees,
Waiting for the crows and blackbirds,
Waiting for the jays and ravens.

Soon they came with caw and clamor,
Rush of wings and cry of voices,
To their work of devastation,
Settling down upon the corn-fields,
Delving deep with beak and talon,
For the body of Mondamin.
And with all their craft and cunning,
All their skill in wiles of warfare,
They perceived no danger near them,
Till their claws became entangled,
Till they found themselves imprisoned
In the snares of Hiawatha.

From his place of ambush came he,
Striding terrible among them,
And so awful was his aspect
That the bravest quailed with terror.
Without mercy he destroyed them
Right and left, by tens and twenties,
And their wretched, lifeless bodies
Hung aloft on poles for scarecrows
Round the consecrated corn-fields,
As a signal of his vengeance,
As a warning to marauders.

Only Kahgahgee, the leader,
Kahgahgee, the King of Ravens,
He alone was spared among them
As a hostage for his people.
With his prisoner-string he bound him,
Led him captive to his wigwam,
Tied him fast with cords of elm-bark
To the ridge-pole of his wigwam.

"Kahgahgee, my raven!" said he,
"You the leader of the robbers,
You the plotter of this mischief,

The contriver of this outrage,
I will keep you, I will hold you,
As a hostage for your people,
As a pledge of good behavior!"
And he left him, grim and sulky,
Sitting in the morning sunshine
On the summit of the wigwam,
Croaking fiercely his displeasure,
Flapping his great sable pinions,
Vainly struggling for his freedom,
Vainly calling on his people!
Summer passed, and Shawondasse
Breathed his sighs o'er all the landscape,
From the South-land sent his ardors,
Wafted kisses warm and tender;
And the maize-field grew and ripened,
Till it stood in all the splendor
Of its garments green and yellow,
Of its tassels and its plumage,
And the maize-ears full and shining
Gleamed from bursting sheaths of verdure.
Then Nokomis, the old woman,
Spake, and said to Minnehaha:
" 'Tis the Moon when leaves are falling;
All the wild-rice has been gathered,
And the maize is ripe and ready;
Let us gather in the harvest,
Let us wrestle with Mondamin,
Strip him of his plumes and tassels,
Of his garments green and yellow!"
And the merry Laughing Water
Went rejoicing from the wigwam,
With Nokomis, old and wrinkled,
And they called the women round them,
Called the young men and the maidens,
To the harvest of the corn-fields,
To the husking of the maize-ear.
On the border of the forest,
Underneath the fragrant pine-trees,
Sat the old men and the warriors
Smoking in the pleasant shadow.
In uninterrupted silence

Looked they at the gamesome labor
Of the young men and the women;
Listened to their noisy talking,
To their laughter and their singing,
Heard them chattering like the magpies,
Heard them laughing like the blue-jays,
Heard them singing like the robins.

And whene'er some lucky maiden
Found a red ear in the husking,
Found a maize-ear red as blood is,
"Nushka!" cried they all together,
"Nushka! you shall have a sweetheart,
You shall have a handsome husband!"
"Ugh!" the old men all responded
From their seats beneath the pine-trees.

And whene'er a youth or maiden
Found a crooked ear in husking,
Found a maize-ear in the husking
Blighted, mildewed, or misshapen,
Then they laughed and sang together,
Crept and limped about the corn-fields,
Mimicked in their gait and gestures
Some old man, bent almost double,
Singing singly or together:
"Wagemin, the thief of corn-fields!
Paimosaid, who steals the maize-ear!"

Till the corn-fields rang with laughter,
Till from Hiawatha's wigwam
Kahgahgee, the King of Ravens,
Screamed and quivered in his anger,
And from all the neighboring tree-tops
Cawed and croaked the black marauders.
"Ugh!" the old men all responded,
From their seats beneath the pine-trees!

WALT WHITMAN

(1819–1892)

Whitman, who reached out imaginatively to embrace all Americans, included portraits of Indians in prose and poetry, but he never directed mature, sustained effort at rendering his sense of them. In an early set piece, "The Inca's Daughter," he describes the suicide of an Indian princess:

> Her snake-like eye, her cheek of fire
> Glowed with intenser, deeper hue;
> She smiled in scorn, and from her robe
> A poisoned arrow drew.

The twenty-one-year-old poet, still working in conventional rhyme, gives no hint of his later development here, except to suggest that the figure of the Indian woman would haunt his imagination.

In the first two selections that follow, from *Leaves of Grass* (1855), Whitman gives us brief but fresh images of Indian women. In the red bride of "Song of Myself" he suggests great sexual vitality; surprisingly, the story is cut off by an account of the poet's nursing a runaway slave. This section seems to look forward, without explicit moralizing, to the fathering of a new race, the erasure of old racist brutalities. Later in the first edition of *Leaves of Grass,* in the midst of a dream of death, and after a sudden remembrance of Washington's worst defeat, the image of an Indian woman is again invoked. This time, in a poem later called "The Sleepers," the "red squaw" is associated with Whitman's beloved mother; she represents, to mother and son, a comforting vision of "beauty and purity." She and the red bride are spirits of the land, figures who embody the Pocahontas myth. Throughout *Leaves of Grass,* in catalogues of Indian place names, in allusions to earth as "old top-knot," in late poems on Red Jacket and Osceola, even in the "barbaric yawp" that ends "Song of Myself," Whitman testifies to the powerful effect that the American Indian had on his poetic imagination.

In prose, too, Whitman sought to make use of Indian materials. Early in his writing career, he tried his hand at moralistic fiction. In *Franklin*

Evans; or, The Inebriate (1842), a bathetic temperance novel, the Devil Rum teaches his lessons through the experience of the Indians. In order to hold the reader's interest in his tract, Whitman incorporates a story-within-the-story. "The Death of Wind Foot" is a conventional tale of Indian revenge set in pre-white times. Its effect, like that of *The Last of the Mohicans,* is to provide a fable of Indian destruction which ennobles that which is lost.

A more effective and original Indian tale is Whitman's "The Half-Breed: A Tale of the Western Frontier." The young author published this novelette under the title of "Arrow-Tip" in 1845; it reappeared in the Brooklyn *Eagle* under its present title in 1846. A crude and undeveloped story, "The Half-Breed" canonizes the noble full-blooded Indian chief, although it sacrifices his life to mistaken white suspicion. Its villain is a half-breed hunchback, whose malice causes the chief's death; contrary to Whitman's poetic vision, this "monstrous abortion" is a symbol of the failure of racial mixture. The portrait of the villain, Boddo, is excerpted below.

In an interesting piece of reminiscence, written in February, 1884, Whitman admits his failure to give more satisfying portraits of the Indian. He reveals here, more artlessly than in his fiction or poetry, his own awareness of Indian greatness and beauty. In "An Indian Bureau Reminiscence," the last selection below, Whitman eloquently questions his countrymen's application of the terms "civilized" and "savage."

From *Leaves of Grass,* 1855

I saw the marriage of the trapper in the open air in the far west . . . .
    the bride was a red girl,
Her father and his friends sat near by crosslegged and dumbly
    smoking . . . . they had moccasins to their feet and large thick
    blankets hanging from their shoulders;
On a bank lounged the trapper . . . . he was dressed mostly in skins
    . . . . his luxuriant beard and curls protected his neck,
One hand rested on his rifle . . . . the other hand held firmly the wrist
    of the red girl,
She had long eyelashes . . . . her head was bare . . . . her coarse straight
    locks descended upon her voluptuous limbs and reached to her
    feet.   . . . .

Walt Whitman, *Leaves of Grass* (Brooklyn, New York, 1855), pp. 18–19, 74.

Now I tell what my mother told me today as we sat at dinner
together,
Of when she was a nearly grown girl living home with her parents on
the old homestead.

A red squaw came one breakfasttime to the old homestead,
On her back she carried a bundle of rushes for rushbottoming chairs;
Her hair straight shiny coarse black and profuse halfenveloped her
face,
Her step was free and elastic . . . . her voice sounded exquisitely as
she spoke.
My mother looked in delight and amazement at the stranger,
She looked at the beauty of her tallborne face and full and pliant
limbs,
The more she looked upon her she loved her,
Never before had she seen such wonderful beauty and purity;
She made her sit on a bench by the jamb of the fireplace . . . . she
cooked food for her,
She had no work to give her but she gave her remembrance and
fondness.

The red squaw staid all the forenoon, and toward the middle of the
afternoon she went away;
O my mother was loth to have her go away,
All the week she thought of her . . . . she watched for her many a
month,
She remembered her many a winter and many a summer,
But the red squaw never came nor was heard of there again.

From *The Half-Breed: A Tale of the Western Frontier, 1846*

"Boddo! Boddo!" they cried, "Boddo is coming!" And they pointed
with their mischievous fingers, to a turn in the road, at about ten rods
distance, where a figure was seen slowly walking, or rather limping, towards
them.

More than half the party started off on a gallop, and in a few moments

Walt Whitman, "The Half-Breed: A Tale of the Western Frontier" *Brooklyn Daily
Eagle,* vol. 5, no. 133 (June 1, 1846).

they were at the side of him who had attracted their attention. Boddo, as the youngsters called him—and that was the name he went by all over the settlement—appeared to be a man of about seven-and-twenty years of age. He was deformed in body—his back being mounted with a mighty hunch, and his long neck bent forward, in a peculiar and disagreeable manner. In height he was hardly taller than the smallest of the children who clustered tormentingly around him.—His face was the index to many bad passions—which were only limited in the degree of their evil, because his intellect itself was not very bright; though the sedulous care of someone had taught him even more than the ordinary branches of education. Among the most powerful of his bad points was a malignant peevishness, dwelling on every feature of his countenance. Perhaps it was this latter trait which caused the wild boys of the place ever to take great comfort in making him the subject of their vagaries. The gazer would have been at some doubt whether to class this strange and hideous creature with the race of Red Men or White—for he was a half-breed, his mother an Indian squaw, and his father some unknown member of the race of the settlers.

"Why, Boddo," said the elf, Bill, "how-d'e-do? You lovely creature I hav'nt seen you for a week!"

And the provoking boy took the hunchback's hand, and shook it as heartily as if they had been old friends forever. Boddo scowled, but it was of no avail. He was in the power of the lawless ones, and could not escape.

"What's the price of soap, Boddo?" said another urchin, pointing to the filthy hands and face of the Indian. And they all laughed merrily.

"Devils!" exclaimed the passionate half-breed, making an impotent attempt at blows, which they easily foiled; "why do you pester me? Go! —go away—or I shall turn upon you."

"O, Boddo! dear Boddo! do not let your sweet temper rise!" said little Bill, and he patted the Indian on his head, as a man would do to a child.

Boddo glanced *up* to him with an expression of hate which might have appalled any but the heedless one on whom he gazed. He turned round and round, like a wild beast in the toils; but wherever he cast his look, he saw nothing but villainous little fingers extended, and roguish eyes flashing. The poor fellow was indeed sadly beset, and was rapidly working himself up to a pitch of rage, which might have cost some of the thoughtless crew a broken head. At this moment, the tall boy who had reproved Bill in front of the schoolhouse, came up, and, beholding the plight of the tormented one, offered his gentle interference.

From **An Indian Bureau Reminiscence,** *1884*

After the close of the Secession War in 1865, I worked several months (until Mr. Harlan turned me out for having written "Leaves of Grass") in the Interior Department at Washington, in the Indian Bureau. Along this time there came to see their Great Father an unusual number of aboriginal visitors, delegations for treaties, settlement of lands, etc.—some young or middle-aged, but mainly old men, from the West, North, and occasionally from the South—parties of from five to twenty each—the most wonderful proofs of what Nature can produce, (the survival of the fittest, no doubt—all the frailer samples dropped, sorted out by death)— as if to show how the earth and woods, the attrition of storms and elements, and the exigencies of life at first hand, can train and fashion men, indeed *chiefs,* in heroic massiveness, imperturbability, muscle, and that last and highest beauty consisting of strength—the full exploitation and fruitage of a human identity, not from the culmination-points of "culture" and artificial civilization, but tallying our race, as it were, with giant, vital, gnarled, enduring trees, or monoliths of separate hardiest rocks, and humanity holding its own with the best of the said trees or rocks, and outdoing them.

There were Omahas, Poncas, Winnebagoes, Cheyennes, Navahos, Apaches, and many others. Let me give a running account of what I see and hear through one of these conference collections at the Indian Bureau, going back to the present tense. Every head and face is impressive, even artistic; Nature redeems herself out of her crudest recesses. Most have red paint on their cheeks, however, or some other paint. ("Little Hill" makes the opening speech, which the interpreter translates by scraps.) Many wear head tires of gaudy-color'd braid, wound around thickly— some with circlets of eagles' feathers. Necklaces of bears' claws are plenty around their necks. Most of the chiefs are wrapped in large blankets of the brightest scarlet. Two or three have blue, and I see one black. (A wise man called "the Flesh" now makes a short speech, apparently asking something. Indian Commissioner Dole answers him, and the interpreter translates in scraps again.) All the principal chiefs have tomahawks or

---

Walt Whitman, "An Indian Bureau Reminiscence," *November Boughs* (London, 1889), pp. 73–75.

hatchets, some of them very richly ornamented and costly. Plaid shirts are to be observed—none too clean. Now a tall fellow, "Hole-in-the-Day," is speaking. He has a copious head-dress composed of feathers and narrow ribbon, under which appears a countenance painted all over a bilious yellow. Let us note this young chief. For all his paint, "Hole-in-the-Day" is a handsome Indian, mild and calm, dressed in drab buckskin leggings, dark gray surtout, and a soft black hat. His costume will bear full observation, and even fashion would accept him. His apparel is worn loose and scant enough to show his superb physique, especially in neck, chest, and legs. ("The Apollo Belvidere!" was the involuntary exclamation of a famous European artist when he first saw a full-grown young Choctaw.)

One of the red visitors—a wild, lean-looking Indian, the one in the black woolen wrapper—has an empty buffalo head, with the horns on, for his personal surmounting. I see a markedly Bourbonish countenance among the chiefs—(it is not very uncommon among them, I am told.) Most of them avoided resting on chairs during the hour of their "talk" in the Commissioner's office; they would sit around on the floor, leaning against something, or stand up by the walls, partially wrapped in their blankets. Though some of the young fellows were, as I have said, magnificent and beautiful animals, I think the palm of unique picturesqueness, in body, limb, physiognomy, etc., was borne by the old or elderly chiefs, and the wise men.

My here-alluded-to experience in the Indian Bureau produced one very definite conviction, as follows: There is something about these aboriginal Americans, in their highest characteristic representations, essential traits, and the ensemble of their physique and physiognomy—something very remote, very lofty, arousing comparisons with our own civilized ideals—something that our literature, portrait painting, etc., have never caught, and that will almost certainly never be transmitted to the future, even as a reminiscence. No biographer, no historian, no artist, has grasped it—perhaps could not grasp it. It is so different, so far outside our standards of eminent humanity. Their feathers, paint—even the empty buffalo skull—did not, to say the least, seem any more ludicrous to me than many of the fashions I have seen in civilized society. I should not apply the word savage (at any rate, in the usual sense) as a leading word in the description of those great aboriginal specimens, of whom I certainly saw many of the best. There were moments, as I looked at them or studied them, when our own exemplification of personality, dignity, heroic presentation anyhow (as in the conventions of society, or even the accepted poems and plays,) seemed sickly, puny, inferior.

The interpreters, agents of the Indian Department, or other whites accompanying the bands, in positions of responsibility, were always interesting to me; I had many talks with them. Occasionally I would go to the hotels where the bands were quartered, and spend an hour or two informally. Of course we could not have much conversation—though (through the interpreters) more of this than might be supposed—sometimes quite animated and significant. I had the good luck to be invariably received and treated by all of them in their most cordial manner.

JAMES FENIMORE COOPER
(1789–1851)

When Franz Schubert asked for Cooper's novels as he lay dying in 1829, he was expressing the enthusiasm many of his European and American contemporaries felt as the first works of this gentleman-of-leisure-turned-novelist appeared. *The Pioneers* (1823), *The Last of the Mohicans* (1826), and *The Prairie* (1827), the first three volumes of the Leatherstocking series, are the books Schubert wanted; in them, Cooper offered his mastery of narrative, his concern for the development of American democracy, his description of wilderness scenes, and his characterization of the frontiersman and the Indian. It would be no exaggeration to say that, in Europe and in the eastern states (from which Indians had already been removed), many readers formulated their own visions of Indians after reading Cooper's exciting novels.

Relying on some research, Cooper turned, for his Indian material, to the work of John Heckewelder, a Moravian missionary among the Delaware Indians. In his *Account of the History, Manners and Customs of the Indian Nations, Who Once Inhabited Pennsylvania and the Neighboring States* (1819), Heckewelder supports the Delawares in their grievance against the Iroquois. Cooper assimilated and romanticized this preference, and it supported the shape of all of his Indian plots: in each novel there are "noble savages" and savage demons; sometimes these are the Mohicans (Cooper's misspelling) and Mingoes or Iroquois; on the prairie, they become Pawnees (good) and Sioux (evil). The most famous examples of Cooper's two Indian personalities are noble young Uncas, of *The Last of the Mohicans,* and his antagonist, the crafty, vicious Magua, a renegade Huron.

It is important to note, when reading of Cooper's Indians, that although good and bad Indians are carefully differentiated, both are finally doomed to extinction. Cooper symbolized this idea in a later novel, *Wyandotté* (1847), in which he combines the good and evil natures in one character variously known by his tribal name and the contemptuous sobriquet Saucy Nick. Regarded as a friend of the whites, Nick falsely stabs the novel's white protagonist, and later drops dead of contrition when his split

personality is healed by Christianity. Cooper, however he values the
characteristics that the noble red man embodies, sees him as succumbing
to civilization. In *The Pioneers,* for example, Chingachgook, the father of
Uncas, becomes Injun Joe, a despairing survivor; in his end, the author
prophesies that the forests and wildlife of New York State will disappear
before the greed of the colonists.

The selection excerpted below is from *The Wept of Wish-ton-Wish,* an
historical novel written after Cooper had completed the Leatherstocking
series. In this book a small group of Connecticut Puritans, in 1675, are
attacked by Narragansetts and Wampanoags, under the leadership of King
Philip; the Indians are retaliating for the colonists' encroachment on their
lands. Cooper creates a complex captivity tale, for the daughter of the
Heathcotes, a leading white family, is kidnapped during an Indian raid by
a young Narragansett boy who had earlier been held in kindly captivity
by the whites. Believing that her family perished in the massacre, the noble
Conanchet marries the white girl, who is given the name of Narra-mattah.
The following extract comes from the chapter in which, during a subsequent
battle, Conanchet reunites his wife with her people. "The troubled spirit
of the Indians of those regions" is Philip, or Metamora, who has been angered
by Conanchet's refusal to permit the massacre of the Heathcotes. In this
novel, we can see Cooper applying his favorite methods to historical person-
ages and events. Again his imagination has been most deeply stirred by the
heroic resignation of a man whose people have been sacrificed to make way
for the growing white population. Whatever the author's conscious ration-
alization may be, Uncas and Conanchet represent the best of the "new
world." For their loss there is little real consolation.

From *The Wept of Wish-ton-Wish,* 1855

"Why has Conanchet sent for a woman from the woods?" repeated the
same soft voice, nearer to the elbow of the young Sachem, and which
spoke with less of the timidity of the sex, now that the troubled spirit of
the Indians of those regions had disappeared.

"Narra-mattah, come near," returned the young chief, changing the deep
and proud tones in which he had addressed his restless and bold companion

James Fenimore Cooper, *The Wept of Wish-ton-Wish: A Tale* (New York, 1855), pp.
380–387.

in arms, to those which better suited the gentle ear for which his words were intended. "Fear not, daughter of the morning, for those around us are of a race used to see women at the council-fires. Now look, with an open eye—is there anything among these trees that seemeth like an ancient tradition? Hast ever beheld such a valley, in thy dreams? Have yonder Pale-faces, whom the tomahawks of my young men spared, been led before thee by the Great Spirit, in the dark night?"

The female listened, in deep attention. Her gaze was wild and uncertain, and yet it was not absolutely without gleamings of a half-reviving intelligence. Until that moment, she had been too much occupied in conjecturing the subject of her visit to regard the natural objects by which she was surrounded; but with her attention thus directly turned upon them, her organs of sight embraced each and all, with the discrimination that is so remarkable in those whose faculties are quickened by danger and necessity. Passing from side to side, her swift glances ran over the distant hamlet, with its little fort; the buildings in the near grounds; the soft and verdant fields; the fragrant orchard, beneath whose leafy shades she stood, and the blackened tower, that rose in its centre, like some gloomy memorial, placed there to remind the spectator not to trust too fondly to the signs of peace and loveliness that reigned around. Shaking back the ringlets that had blown about her temples, the wondering female returned thoughtfully and in silence to her place.

" 'Tis a village of the Yengeese!" she said, after a long and expressive pause. "A Narragansett woman does not love to look at the lodges of the hated race."

"Listen.—Lies have never entered the ears of Narra-mattah. My tongue hath spoken like the tongue of a chief. Thou didst not come of the sumach, but of the snow. This hand of thine is not like the hands of the women of my tribe; it is little, for the Great Spirit did not make it for work; it is of the color of the sky in the morning, for thy fathers were born near the place where the sun rises. Thy blood is like spring-water. All this thou knowest, for none have spoken false in thy ear. Speak—dost thou never see the wigwam of thy father? Does not his voice whisper to thee, in the language of his people?"

The female stood in the attitude which a sibyl might be supposed to assume, while listening to the occult mandates of the myterious oracle, every faculty entranced and attentive.

"Why does Conanchet ask these questions of his wife? He knows what she knows; he sees what she sees; his mind is her mind. If the Great Spirit made her skin of a different color, he made her heart the same. Narramattah will not listen to the lying language; she shuts her ears, for there is deceit in its sounds. She tries to forget it. One tongue can say all she wishes to speak to Conanchet; why should she look back in dreams, when a great chief is her husband?"

The eye of the warrior, as he looked upon the ingenuous and confiding face of the speaker, was kind to fondness. The firmness had passed away and in its place was left the winning softness of affection, which, as it belongs to nature, is seen, at times, in the expression of an Indian's eye, as strongly as it is ever known to sweeten the intercourse of a more polished condition of life.

"Girl," he said with emphasis, after a moment of thought, as if he would recall her and himself to more important duties, "this is a warpath; all on it are men. Thou wast like the pigeon before its wing opens, when I brought thee from the nest; still the winds of many winters had blown upon thee. Dost never think of the warmth and of the food of the lodge in which thou hast passed so many seasons?"

"The wigwam of Conanchet is warm; no woman of the tribe hath as many furs as Narra-mattah."

"He is a great hunter! when they hear his moccasin, the beavers lie down to be killed! But the men of the Pale-faces hold the plow. Does not 'the driven snow' think of those who fenced the wigwam of her father from the cold, or of the manner in which the Yengeese live?"

His youthful and attentive wife seemed to reflect; but raising her face, with an expression of content that could not be counterfeited, she shook her head in the negative.

"Does she never see a fire kindled among the lodges, or hear the whoops of warriors as they break into a settlement?"

"Many fires have been kindled before her eyes. The ashes of the Narragansett town are not yet cold."

"Does not Narra-mattah hear her father speaking to the God of the Yengeese? Listen—he is asking favor for his child!"

"The Great Spirit of the Narragansett has ears for his people."

"But I hear a softer voice! 'Tis a woman of the Pale-faces among her children: cannot the daughter hear?"

Narra-mattah, or "the driven snow," laid her hand lightly on the arm of the chief, and she looked wistfully and long into his face, without an answer. The gaze seemed to deprecate the anger that might be awakened by what she was about to reveal.

"Chief of my people," she said, encouraged by his still calm and gentle brow to proceed, "what a girl of the clearings sees in her dreams shall not be hid. It is not the lodges of her race, for the wigwam of her husband is warmer. It is not the food and clothes of a cunning people, for who is richer than the wife of a great chief? It is not her fathers speaking to their Spirit, for there is none stronger than Manitou. Narra-mattah has forgotten all: she does not wish to think of things like these. She knows how to hate a hungry and craving race. But she sees one that the wives of the Narragansetts do not see. She sees a woman with a white skin; her eye looks softly on her child in her dreams; it is not an eye, it is a tongue! It says, what does the wife of Conanchet wish?—is she cold? here are furs—is she hungry? here is venison—is she tired? The arms of the pale woman open, that an Indian girl may sleep. When there is silence in the lodges, when Conanchet and his young men lie down, then does this pale woman speak. Sachem, she does not talk of the battles of her people, nor of the scalps that her warriors have taken, nor of the manner in which the Pequots and Mohicans fear her tribe. She does not tell how a young Narragansett should obey her husband, nor how the women must keep food in the lodges for the hunters that are wearied; her tongue useth strange words. It names a Mighty and Just Spirit, it telleth of peace, and not of war; it soundeth as one talking from the clouds; it is like the falling of the water among rocks. Narra-mattah loves to listen, for the words seem to her like the Wish-Ton-Wish, when he whistles in the woods."

Conanchet had fastened a look of deep and affectionate interest on the wild and sweet countenance of the being who stood before him. She had spoken in that attitude of earnest and natural eloquence that no art can equal; and when she ceased, he laid a hand, in kind but melancholy fondness, on the half-inclined and motionless head, as he answered.

"This is the bird of night, singing to its young! The Great Spirit of thy fathers is angry, that thou livest in the lodge of a Narragansett. His sight is too cunning to be cheated. He knows that the moccasin, and the wampum, and the robe of fur, are liars; he sees the color of the skin beneath."

"Conanchet, no," returned the female hurriedly, and with a decision her timidity did not give reason to expect. "He seeth farther than the skin, and knoweth the color of the mind. He hath forgotten that one of his girls is missing."

"It is not so. The eagle of my people was taken into the lodges of the Pale-faces. He was young, and they taught him to sing with another tongue. The colors of his feathers were changed, and they thought to cheat the Manitou. But when the door was open, he spread his wings and flew back to his nest. It is not so. What hath been done is good, and what will be done is better. Come; there is a straight path before us."

Thus saying, Conanchet motioned to his wife to follow towards the group of captives. The foregoing dialogue had occurred in a place where the two parties were partially concealed from each other by the ruin; but as the distance was so trifling, the Sachem and his companion were soon confronted with those he sought. Leaving his wife a little without the circle, Conanchet advanced, and taking the unresisting and half-unconscious

Ruth by the arm, he led her forward. He placed the two females in attitudes where each might look the other full in the face. Strong emotion struggled in a countenance which, in spite of its fierce mask of war-paint, could not entirely conceal its workings.

"See," he said in English, looking earnestly from one to the other. "The Good Spirit is not ashamed of his work. What he hath done, he hath done; Narragansett nor Yengeese can alter it. This is the white bird that came from the sea," he added, touching the shoulder of Ruth lightly with a finger, "and this the young, that she warmed under her wing."

Then, folding his arms on his naked breast, he appeared to summon his energy, lest, in the scene that he knew must follow, his manhood might be betrayed into some act unworthy of his name.

The captives were necessarily ignorant of the meaning of the scene which they had just witnessed. So many strange and savage-looking forms were constantly passing and repassing before their eyes, that the arrival of one, more or less, was not likely to be noted. Until she heard Conanchet speak in her native tongue, Ruth had lent no attention to the interview between him and his wife. But the figurative language and no less remarkable action of the Narragansett, had the effect to arouse her suddenly, and in the most exciting manner, from her melancholy.

No child of tender age ever unexpectedly came before the eyes of Ruth Heathcote, without painfully recalling the image of the cherub she had lost. The playful voice of infancy never surprised her ear, without the sound conveying a pang to the heart; nor could allusion, ever so remote, be made to persons or events that bore resemblance to the sad incidents of her own life, without quickening the never-dying pulses of maternal love. No wonder, then, that when she found herself in the situation and under the circumstances described, nature grew strong within her, and that her mind caught glimpses, however dim and indistinct they might be, of a truth that the reader has already anticipated. Still, a certain and intelligible clue was wanting. Fancy had ever painted her child in the innocence and infancy in which it had been torn from her arms; and here, while there was so much to correspond with reasonable expectation, there was little to answer to the long and fondly-cherished picture. The delusion, if so holy and natural a feeling may thus be termed, had been too deeply seated to be dispossessed at a glance. Gazing long, earnestly, and with features that varied with every changing feeling, she held the stranger at the length of her two arms, alike unwilling to release her hold, or to admit her closer to a heart which might rightfully be the property of another.

"Who art thou?" demanded the mother, in a voice that was tremulous with the emotions of that sacred character. "Speak, mysterious and lovely being—who art thou?"

Narra-mattah had turned a terrified and imploring look at the immovable and calm form of the chief, as if she sought protection from him at whose hands she had been accustomed to receive it. But a different sensation took possession of her mind, when she heard sounds which had too often soothed the ear of infancy ever to be forgotten. Struggling ceased, and her pliant form assumed the attitude of intense and entranced attention. Her head was bent aside, as if the ear were eager to drink in a repetition of the tones, while her bewildered and delighted eye still sought the countenance of her husband.

"Vision of the woods!—wilt thou not answer?" continued Ruth. "If there is reverence for the Holy One of Israel in thine heart, answer, that I may know thee!"

"Hist! Conanchet!" murmured the wife, over whose features the glow of pleased and wild surprise continued to deepen. "Come near, Sachem, the Spirit that talketh to Narra-mattah in her dreams, is nigh."

"Woman of the Yengeese!" said the husband, advancing with dignity to the spot, "let the clouds blow from thy sight. Wife of a Narragansett! see clearly. The Manitou of your race speaks strong. He telleth a mother to know her child!"

Ruth could hesitate no longer; neither sound nor exclamation escaped her, but as she strained the yielding frame of her recovered daughter to her heart, it appeared as if she strove to incorporate the two bodies into one. A cry of pleasure and astonishment drew all around her. Then came the evidence of the power of nature when strongly awakened. Age and youth alike acknowledged its potency, and recent alarms were overlooked in the pure joy of such a moment. The spirit of even the lofty-minded Conanchet was shaken. Raising the hand, at whose wrist still hung the bloody tomahawk, he veiled his face, and, turning aside, that none might see the weakness of so great a warrior, he wept.

HORACE GREELEY
(1811–1872)

A New York editor and politician, Greeley was famous for directing his countrymen westward. Although he was a liberal, in favor of abolition, universal suffrage, and amnesty after the Civil War, his view of the Indian partakes of every frontier prejudice. It is striking to note the similarities in the excerpt below from Greeley's travel diary and the commentary of Cotton Mather, in his "Life of John Eliot," written one hundred fifty years earlier. Greeley's contemptuous images of Indian men and women deserve consideration for their succinct expression of an influential nineteenth-century point of view.

From *An Overland Journey From New York to San Francisco* . . . , *1860*

I have learned to appreciate better than hitherto, and to make more allowance for, the dislike, aversion, contempt, wherewith Indians are usually regarded by their white neighbors, and have been since the days of the Puritans. It needs but little familiarity with the actual, palpable aborigines to convince any one that the poetic Indian—the Indian of Cooper and Longfellow—is only visible to the poet's eye. To the prosaic observer, the average Indian of the woods and prairies is a being who does little credit to human nature—a slave of appetite and sloth, never emancipated from the tyranny of one animal passion save by the more ravenous demands of another. As I passed over those magnificent bottoms of the Kansas which form the reservations of the Delawares, Potawatamies, etc., constituting the very best corn-lands on earth, and saw their owners sitting around the doors

Horace Greeley, *An Overland Journey, from New York to San Francisco in the Summer of 1859* (New York, 1860), pp. 151–156.

of their lodges at the height of the planting season and in as good, bright planting weather as sun and soil ever made, I could not help saying, "These people must die out—there is no help for them. God has given this earth to those who will subdue and cultivate it, and it is vain to struggle against His righteous decree." And I yesterday tried my powers of persuasion on Left-Hand—the only Arapaho chief who talks English—in favor of an Arapaho tribal farm—say of two hundred acres for a beginning—to be broken and fenced by the common efforts of the tribe, and a patch therein allotted to each head of a family who would agree to plant and till it—I apprehend to very little purpose. For Left-Hand, though shrewd in his way, is an Indian, and every whit as conservative as Boston's Beacon Street or our Fifth Avenue. He knows that there is a certain way in which his people have lived from time immemorial, and in which they are content still to live, knowing and seeking no better. He may or may not have heard that it is the common lot of prophets to be stoned and of reformers to be crucified; but he probably comprehends that squaws cannot fence and plow, and that "braves" are disinclined to any such steady, monotonous exercise of their muscles. I believe there is no essential difference in this respect between "braves" of the red and those of the white race, since even our country's bold defenders have not been accustomed to manifest their intrepidity in the cornfields along their line of march, save in the season of roasting-ears; and the verb "to soldier" has acquired, throughout Christendom in all its moods and tenses, a significance beyond the need of a glossary. Briefly, the "brave," whether civilized or savage, is not a worker, a producer; and where the men are all "braves," with a war always on hand, the prospect for productive industry is gloomy indeed. If, then, the hope of Indian renovation rested mainly on the men, it would be slender enough. There is little probability that the present generation of "braves" can be weaned from the traditions and the habits in which they find a certain personal consequence and immunity from daily toil, which stand them instead of intelligence and comfort. Squalid and conceited, proud and worthless, lazy and lousy, they will strut out or drink out their miserable existence, and at length afford the world a sensible relief by dying out of it.

But it is otherwise with the women. Degraded and filthy as they are, beyond description or belief, they bear the germ of renovation for their race, in that they are neither too proud nor too indolent to labor. The squaw accepts work as her destiny from childhood. In her father's lodge, as in that wherein she comes in turn to hold a fifth or sixth interest in a husband (for all Indians are polygamists in theory, and all who have means or energy become such in practice) she comprehends and dutifully accepts drudgery as her "peculiar institution." She pitches and strikes the tent, carries it from one encampment to another, gathers and chops the wood, and not only dresses and cooks the game which forms the family's food (when they have any) but goes into the woods and backs it home, when her lord returns with the tidings that he has killed something. Tanning or dressing hides, making tents, clothing, moccasins, etc., all devolve on her. Under such a dispensation, it is not difficult to believe that she often willingly accepts a rival in the affections of her sullen master, as promising a mitigation rather than an aggravation of the hardships of her lot.

And yet even the Indian women are idle half their time, from sheer want of any thing to do. They will fetch water for their white neighbors, or do any thing else whereby a piece of bread may be honestly earned; and they would be ten times more than they do, if they could find work and be reasonably sure of even a meager reward for it.

I urge, therefore, that in future efforts to improve the condition of the Indians, the women be specially regarded and appealed to. A conscientious, humane, capable Christian trader, with a wife thoroughly skilled in household manufactures and handicraft, each speaking the language of the tribe with whom they take up their residence, can do more good than a dozen average missionaries. Let them keep and sell whatever articles are adapted to the Indians' needs and means, and let them constitute and maintain an Industrial School, in which the Indian women and children shall be freely taught how to make neatly and expeditiously not only moccasins, but straw hats, bonnets, and (in time) a hundred other articles combining taste with utility. Let a farm and garden be started so soon as may be, and vegetables, grain, fruits given therefrom in exchange for Indian labor therein, at all times when such labor can be made available. Of course, the school, though primarily industrial, should impart intellectual and religious instruction also, wisely adapted in character and season to the needs of the pupils, and to their perception of those needs. Such an enterprise, combining trade with instruction, thrift with philanthropy, would gradually mold a generation after its own spirit—would teach them to value the blessings of civilization before imposing on them its seeming burdens; and would, in the course of twenty years, silently transform an indolent savage tribe into a civilized Christian community. There may be shorter modes of effecting this transformation, but I think none surer.

Doubtless, such an enterprise demands rare qualities in its head—that of patience prominent among them. The vagrancy of the Indians would prove as great an obstacle to its success as their paltry but interminable wars. Very often, in the outset, the apostle of industry and civilization would find himself deserted by all his pupils, lured away by the hope of success elsewhere in marauding or hunting. But let him, having first deliberately chosen his location, simply persevere, and they will soon come round again, glad enough to find food that may be had even for solid work; for all I can learn impels me to believe that hunger is the normal state of the Indian, diversified by transient interludes of gluttony. Meat is almost his only good; and this, though plentiful at seasons, is at others scarcely obtainable in the smallest quantities, or dried to the toughness of leather. The Indian likes bread as well as the white; he must be taught to prefer the toil of producing it to the privation of lacking it. This point gained, he will easily be led to seek shelter, clothing, and all the comforts of civilized life, at their inevitable cost; and thus his temporal salvation will be assured. Otherwise, his extermination is inexorably certain, and cannot long be postponed.

ANN SOPHIA STEPHENS

(1813–1886)

One of the "damned mob of scribbling women" Hawthorne vilified, Ann Sophia Stephens capitalized on the social and moral conventionalities of her day. Like her popular contemporaries, she is worth reading for her transparent record of mid-nineteenth-century American values. What was pulp fiction in 1860 is fascinating documentation today.

Mrs. Stephens was a magazine editor as well as a writer of fiction, and could be expected to know how to appeal to popular tastes. Her novel, *Malaeska; or, the Indian Wife of the White Hunter* (1860), was chosen as the first title in Beadle's Dime Novel series. To a circulation of half a million people, the publisher presented the series' purpose: "to answer to the popular demand for works of romance, but also to instill a pure and elevating sentiment in the hearts and minds of the people."

"Sentiment," the key word, is quickly reduced to sentimentalism; Mrs. Stephens offers a plot that requires the characters to endure sudden death, abandonment, betrayal, separation of mother and child, suicide. The emotions of motherhood, however, are those on which she elaborates most —certainly because the majority of her readers could be expected to enrich the story by providing their own contexts.

Malaeska, the Indian princess secretly married to a white hunter, represents pure, natural womanhood. She is a female "noble savage," and when her husband is killed, she innocently takes her son to his Indian-hating grandparents in Manhattan. There she is reduced to the position of servant, and bound to keep her identity a secret from her growing child. He, in turn, is taught to treat her contemptuously, as a nurse of inferior race. Mrs. Stephens, thoroughly understanding her audience, remarks on Malaeska's "woman's destiny"—to deny herself for the sake of others. "Civilization," she remarks, "does not always reverse this mournful picture of womanly self-abnegation."

But if the reader's sympathies are wholly with the suffering mother, the author punishes her thoroughly for having committed interracial marriage. Her child grows to manhood unaware of his relationship to her and filled with the "haughty hate" for Indians taught him by the whites. In the novel's denouement, he learns his mother's identity (compare a similar scene in Mark Twain's *Pudd'nhead Wilson*) and commits suicide in shame, leaving his mother heartbroken and his lovely bride-to-be committed to a "lonely useful life." The sins of the fathers are visited unremittingly on the sons, and the innocent daughters suffer with them.

In the passage reprinted below, Malaeska and her baby travel to Manhattan. The idealized character of the Indian wife, the romantic treatment of nature, and the appeal to female readers are exhibited in these paragraphs.

From *Malaeska; or the Indian Wife of the White Hunter,* 1860

Night and morning, for many successive days, that frail canoe glided down the current, amid the wild and beautiful scenery of the Highlands, and along the park-like shades of a more level country. There was something in the sublime and lofty handiwork of God which fell soothingly on the sad heart of the Indian. Her thoughts were continually dwelling on the words of her dead husband, ever picturing to themselves the land of spirits where he had promised that she should join him. The perpetual change of scenery, the sunshine playing with the foliage, and the dark, heavy masses of shadow, flung from the forests and the rocks on either hand, were continually exciting her untamed imagination to comparison with the heaven of her wild fancy. It seemed, at times, as if she had but to close her eyes and open them again to be in the presence of her lost one. There was something heavenly in the solemn, perpetual flow of the river, and in the music of the leaves as they rippled to the wind, that went to the poor widow's heart like the soft voice of a friend. After a day or two, the gloom which hung about her young brow, partially departed. Her cheek again dimpled to the happy laugh of her child, and when he nestled down to sleep in the furs at the bottom of the canoe, her soft, plaintive lullaby would steal over the waters like the song of a wild bird seeking in vain for its mate.

Malaeska never went on shore, except to gather wild fruit, and occasionally to kill a bird, which her true arrow seldom failed to bring down. She

Ann Sophia Stephens, *Malaeska; or, The Indian Wife of the White Hunter* (New York, 1929), pp. 67–72.

would strike a fire and prepare her game in some shady nook by the riverside, while the canoe swung at its mooring, and her child played on the
fresh grass, shouting at the cloud of summer insects that flashed by, and
clapping his tiny hands at the humming-birds that came to rifle honey
from the flowers that surrounded him.

The voyage was one of strange happiness to the widowed Indian. Never
did Christian believe in the pages of Divine Writ with more of trust than
she placed in the dying promise of her husband, that she should meet him
again in another world. His spirit seemed forever about her, and to her
wild, free imagination, the passage down the magnificent stream seemed a
material and glorious path to the white man's heaven. Filled with strange,
sweet thoughts, she looked abroad on the mountains looming up from the
banks of the river—on the forest-trees so various in their tints, and so richly
clothed, till she was inspired almost to forgetfulness of her affliction. She
was young and healthy, and every thing about her was so lovely, so grand
and changing, that her heart expanded to the sunshine like a flower which
has been bowed down, but not crushed beneath the force of a storm. Part
of each day she spent in a wild, dreamy state of imagination. Her mind was
lulled to sweet musings by the gentle sounds that hovered in the air from
morning till evening, and through the long night, when all was hushed save
the deep flow of the river. Birds came out with their cheerful voices at
dawn, and at midday she floated in the cool shadow of the hills, or shot into
some cove for a few hours' rest. When the sunset shed its gorgeous dyes
over the river—and the mountain ramparts, on either side, were crimson
as with the track of contending armies—when the boy was asleep, and the
silent stars came out to kindle up her night path, then a clear, bold melody
gushed from the mother's lips like a song from the heart of a nightingale.
Her eye kindled, her cheek grew warm, the dip of her paddle kept a liquid
accompaniment to her rich, wild voice, as the canoe floated downward on
waves that seemed rippling over a world of crushed blossoms, and were
misty with the approach of evening.

Malaeska had been out many days, when the shady gables and the tall
chimneys of Manhattan broke upon her view, surrounded by the sheen of
its broad bay, and by the forest which covered the uninhabited part of the
island. The poor Indian gazed upon it with an unstable but troublesome
fear. She urged her canoe into a little cove on the Hoboken shore, and her
heart grew heavy as the grave, as she pondered on the means of fulfilling
her charge. She took the letter from her bosom; the tears started to her
eyes, and she kissed it with a regretful sorrow, as if a friend were about to
be rendered up from her affections forever. She took the child to her heart,
and held him there till its throbbings grew audible, and the strength of her
misgivings could not be restrained. After a time she became more calm.

She lifted the child from her bosom, laved his hands and face in the stream, and brushed his black hair with her palm till it glowed like the neck of a raven. Then she girded his little crimson robe with a string of wampum, and after arranging her own attire, shot the canoe out of the cove and urged it slowly across the mouth of the river. Her eyes were full of tears all the way, and when the child murmured, and strove to comfort her with his infant caress, she sobbed aloud, and rowed steadily forward.

HENRY DAVID THOREAU

(1817–1862)

Alone among major American writers of the nineteenth century, Thoreau made an extensive study of Indian history and culture. Preserved in eleven manuscript volumes now in the Pierpont Morgan Library, his notes and extracts from over two hundred books offer evidence that he was planning to write on the subject. At his deathbed, friends recorded that his last words were "Indians" and "moose."

In his first book, Thoreau indicated that Indians were an early interest as well as a late one. *A Week on the Concord and Merrimack Rivers* (1849) is, in its author's metaphor, a basket woven of comments on moral and natural facts, suggested by the landscape of his native region and enriched by wide reading and knowledge of local history. In the "Wednesday" chapter, Thoreau recalls the friendship of Wawatam and Alexander Henry; in "Thursday," he retells the story of Hannah Duston's captivity. The volume is full of his meditations on past dwellers on the land. The first selection below is excerpted from "Sunday," and offers an admirable exposition of the facts of Indian-white contact.

In his second book, *Walden,* Thoreau commented on the superiority of Indian wigwams over the more expensive, less efficient housing of the whites. He is pleased to note that "in the savage state every family owns a shelter as good as the best." In this book Indians in history and legend are frequently cited, and the general theme is well represented by this remark: "The customs of some savage nations might, perchance, be profitably imitated by us."

Thoreau's fullest portrait of Indians occurs in *The Maine Woods,* the record of three trips to Maine taken between 1846 and 1857; the book was published posthumously in 1864. On the third voyage, Thoreau was accompanied by Joe Polis, a Penobscot guide, who offered him his richest firsthand experience of contemporary Indian gifts and manners. The second selection below is from "Allegash and East Branch," the record of this third trip. Earlier in the book Thoreau generalizes about the degraded state of the contemporary Maine Indian: in this last piece, he contents himself with close observation of an Indian who is at home in the woods, but has also assimilated some of the white man's commercial values.

From *A Week on the Concord and Merrimack Rivers,* 1849

In this Billerica solid men must have lived, select from year to year; a series of town clerks, at least; and there are old records that you may search. Some spring the white man came, built him a house, and made a clearing here, letting in the sun, dried up a farm, piled up the old gray stones in fences, cut down the pines around his dwelling, planted orchard seeds brought from the old country, and persuaded the civil apple tree to blossom next to the wild pine and the juniper, shedding its perfume in the wilderness. Their old stocks still remain. He culled the graceful elm from out the woods and from the riverside, and so refined and smoothed his village plot. He rudely bridged the stream, and drove his team afield into the river meadows, cut the wild grass, and laid bare the homes of beaver, otter, muskrat, and with the whetting of his scythe scared off the deer and bear. He set up a mill, and fields of English grain sprang in the virgin soil. And with his grain he scattered the seeds of the dandelion and the wild trefoil over the meadows, mingling his English flowers with the wild native ones. The bristling burdock, the sweet-scented catnip, and the humble yarrow planted themselves along his woodland road, they too seeking "freedom to worship God" in their way. And thus he plants a town. The white man's mullein soon reigned in Indian cornfields, and sweet-scented English grasses clothed the new soil. Where, then, could the Red Man set his foot? The honey-bee hummed through the Massachusetts woods, and sipped the wild-flowers round the Indian's wigwam, perchance unnoticed, when, with prophetic warning, it stung the Red child's hand, forerunner of that industrious tribe that was to come and pluck the wild-flower of his race up by the root.

The white man comes, pale as the dawn, with a load of thought, with a slumbering intelligence as a fire raked up, knowing well what he knows, not guessing but calculating; strong in community, yielding obedience to authority; of experienced race; of wonderful, wonderful common sense; dull but capable, slow but persevering, severe but just, of little humor but genuine; a laboring man, despising game and sport; building a house that endures, a framed house. He buys the Indian's moccasins and baskets, then buys his

Henry David Thoreau, *A Week on the Concord and Merrimack Rivers* (Boston, 1849), pp. 56–60.

hunting grounds, and at length forgets where he is buried and ploughs up his bones. And here town records, old, tattered, time-worn, weather-stained chronicles, contain the Indian sachem's mark perchance, an arrow or a beaver, and the few fatal words by which he deeded his hunting grounds away. He comes with a list of ancient Saxon, Norman, and Celtic names, and strews them up and down this river—Framingham, Sudbury, Bedford, Carlisle, Billerica, Chelmsford—and this is New Angleland, and these are the New West Saxons whom the Red Men call, not Angle-ish or English, but Yengeese, and so at last they are known for Yankees.

When we were opposite to the middle of Billerica, the fields on either hand had a soft and cultivated English aspect, the village spire being seen over the copses which skirt the river, and sometimes an orchard straggled down to the waterside, though, generally, our course this forenoon was the wildest part of our voyage. It seemed that men led a quiet and very civil life there. The inhabitants were plainly cultivators of the earth, and lived under an organized political government. The schoolhouse stood with a meek aspect, entreating a long truce to war and savage life. Every one finds by his own experience, as well as in history, that the era in which men cultivate the apple, and the amenities of the garden, is essentially different from that of the hunter and forest life, and neither can displace the other without loss. We have all had our daydreams, as well as more prophetic nocturnal vision; but as for farming, I am convinced that my genius dates from an older era than the agricultural. I would at least strike by spade into the earth with such careless freedom but accuracy as the woodpecker his bill into a tree. There is in my nature, methinks, a singular yearning toward all wildness. I know of no redeeming qualities in myself but a sincere love for some things, and when I am reproved I fall back on to this ground. What have I to do with ploughs? I cut another furrow than you see. Where the off ox treads, there is it not, it is farther off; where the nigh ox walks, it will not be, it is nigher still. If corn fails, my crop fails not, and what are drought and rain to me? The rude Saxon pioneer will sometimes pine for that refinement and artificial beauty which are English, and love to hear the sound of such sweet and classical names as the Pentland and Malvern Hills, the Cliffs of Dover and the Trosachs, Richmond, Derwent, and Winandermere, which are to him now instead of the Acropolis and Parthenon, of Baiae, and Athens with its sea-walls, and Arcadia and Tempe.

> Greece, who am I that should remember thee,
> Thy Marathon and thy Thermopylae?
> Is my life vulgar, my fate mean,
> Which on these golden memories can lean?

We are apt enough to be pleased with such books as Evelyn's Sylva, Acetarium, and Kalendarium Hortense, but they imply a relaxed nerve in the reader. Gardening is civil and social, but it wants the vigor and freedom of the forest and the outlaw. There may be an excess of cultivation as well as of anything else, until civilization becomes pathetic. A highly cultivated man—all whose bones can be bent! whose heaven-born virtues are but good manners! The young pines springing up in the cornfields from year to year are to me a refreshing fact. We talk of civilizing the Indian, but that is not the name for his improvement. By the wary independence and aloofness of his dim forest life he preserves his intercourse with his native gods, and is admitted from time to time to a rare and peculiar society with Nature. He has glances of starry recognition to which our saloons are strangers. The steady illumination of his genius, dim only because distant, is like the faint but satisfying light of the stars compared with the dazzling but ineffectual and short-lived blaze of candles. The Society-Islanders had their day-born gods, but they were not supposed to be "of equal antiquity with the *atua fauau po,* or night-born gods." It is true, there are the innocent pleasures of country life, and it is sometimes pleasant to make the earth yield her increase, and gather the fruits in their season, but the heroic spirit will not fail to dream of remoter retirements and more rugged paths. It will have its garden-plots and its *parterres* elsewhere than on the earth, and gather nuts and berries by the way for its subsistence, or orchard fruits with such heedlessness as berries. We would not always be soothing and taming nature, breaking the horse and the ox, but sometimes ride the horse wild and chase the buffalo. The Indian's intercourse with Nature is at least such as admits of the greatest independence of each. If he is somewhat of a stranger in her midst, the gardener is too much of a familiar. There is something vulgar and foul in the latter's closeness to his mistress, something noble and cleanly in the former's distance. In civilization, as in a southern latitude, man degenerates at length, and yields to the incursion of more northern tribes:

> Some nation yet shut in
> With hills of ice.

There are other, savager, and more primeval aspects of nature than our poets have sung. It is only white man's poetry. Homer and Ossian even can never revive in London or Boston. And yet behold how these cities are refreshed by the mere tradition, or the imperfectly transmitted fragrance and flavor of these wild fruits. If we could listen but for an instant to the chant of the Indian muse, we should understand why he will not exchange his savageness for civilization. Nations are not whimsical. Steel and blankets are strong temptations; but the Indian does well to continue Indian.

From **The Maine Woods,** *1864*

Immediately below these falls was the Chesuncook dead-water, caused by the flowing back of the lake. As we paddled slowly over this, the Indian told us a story of his hunting thereabouts, and something more interesting about himself. It appeared that he had represented his tribe at Augusta, and also once at Washington, where he had met some Western chiefs. He had been consulted at Augusta, and gave advice, which he said was followed, respecting the eastern boundary of Maine, as determined by highlands and streams, at the time of the difficulties on that side. He was employed with the surveyors on the line. Also he had called on Daniel Webster in Boston, at the time of his Bunker Hill oration.

I was surprised to hear him say that he liked to go to Boston, New York, Philadelphia, etc., etc.; that he would like to live there. But then, as if relenting a little, when he thought what a poor figure he would make there, he added, "I suppose, I live in New York, I be poorest hunter, I expect." He understood very well both his superiority and his inferiority to the whites. He criticized the people of the United States as compared with other nations, but the only distinct idea with which he labored was, that they were "very strong," but, like some individuals, "too fast." He must have the credit of saying this just before the general breaking down of railroads and banks. He had a great idea of education, and would occasionally break out into such expressions as this, "Kademy—a-cad-e-my—good thing—I suppose they usum Fifth Reader there. . . . You been college?"

. . . .

It was very exhilarating, and the perfection of travelling, quite unlike floating on our dead Concord River, the coasting down this inclined mirror, which was now and then gently winding, down a mountain, indeed, between two evergreen forests, edged with lofty dead white pines, sometimes slanted halfway over the stream, and destined soon to bridge it. I saw some monsters there, nearly destitute of branches, and scarcely diminishing in diameter for eighty or ninety feet.

Henry David Thoreau, *The Maine Woods* (Boston and New York, 1891), pp. 201–202, 258–259, 300–301.

As we thus swept along, our Indian repeated in a deliberate and drawling tone the words "Daniel Webster, great lawyer," apparently reminded of him by the name of the stream, and he described his calling on him once in Boston, at what he supposed was his boardinghouse. He had no business with him, but merely went to pay his respects, as we should say. In answer to our questions, he described his person well enough. It was on the day after Webster delivered his Bunker Hill oration, which I believe Polis heard. The first time he called he waited till he was tired without seeing him, and then went away. The next time, he saw him go by the door of the room in which he was waiting several times, in his shirt-sleeves, without noticing him. He thought that if he had come to see Indians, they would not have treated him so. At length, after very long delay, he came in, walked toward him, and asked in a loud voice, gruffly, "What do you want?" and he, thinking at first, by the motion of his hand, that he was going to strike him, said to himself, "You'd better take care, if you try that I shall know what to do." He did not like him, and declared that all he said "was not worth talk about a musquash."

. . . .

We passed the Passadumkeag River on our left and saw the blue *Olamon* mountains at a distance in the southeast. Hereabouts our Indian told us at length the story of their contention with the priest respecting schools. He thought a great deal of education and had recommended it to his tribe. His argument in its favor was, that if you had been to college and learnt to calculate, you could "keep 'em property—no other way." He said that his boy was the best scholar in the school at Oldtown, to which he went with whites. He himself is a Protestant, and goes to church regularly in Oldtown. According to his account, a good many of his tribe are Protestants, and many of the Catholics also are in favor of schools. Some years ago they had a schoolmaster, a Protestant, whom they liked very well. The priest came and said that they must send him away, and finally he had such influence, telling them that they would go to the bad place at last if they retained him, that they sent him away. The school party, though numerous, were about giving up. Bishop Fenwick came from Boston and used his influence against them. But our Indian told his side that they must not give up, must hold on, they were the strongest. If they gave up, then they would have no party. But they answered that it was "no use, priest too strong, we'd better give up." At length he persuaded them to make a stand.

The priest was going for a sign to cut down the liberty pole. So Polis and his party had a secret meeting about it; he got ready fifteen or twenty stout young men, "stript 'em naked, and painted 'em like old times," and told them that when the priest and his party went to cut down the liberty pole, they were to rush up, take hold of it and prevent them, and he assured them that there would be no war, only a noise, "no war where priest is." He kept his men concealed in a house nearby, and when the priest's party were about to cut down the liberty pole, the fall of which would have been a death-blow to the school party, he gave a signal, and his young men rushed out and seized the pole. There was a great uproar, and they were about coming to blows, but the priest interfered, saying, "No war, no war," and so the pole stands, and the school goes on still.

We thought that it showed a good deal of tact in him, to seize this occasion and take his stand on it; proving how well he understood those with whom he had to deal.

RALPH WALDO EMERSON

(1803–1882)

Emerson's work exhibits the great difficulty even the most sensitive
American might have in understanding the Indian predicament. Transcendentalist and sage, he was able to see beyond the uses of Nature as commodity to its spiritual meanings. Yet he was a thorough believer in the idea
of progress. Though he expressed confidence in natural, unencumbered
man, advising Americans to accept two maxims—"Know thyself" and
"Study Nature"—he thought human beings were perfectible. This view
encouraged an optimism which failed to take the whole measure of troublesome events. The doctrine of Compensation, in which every seeming evil
moves toward the triumph of good, enabled Emerson to turn his eyes from
injustice and deceit.

On one rare occasion, when he made public objection to an outrage, he
revealed a heavily paternalistic attitude toward Indians. In an open letter
to President Martin Van Buren, dated April 23, 1838, he protested the
Removal of the Cherokee people:

In common with the great body of the American people, we have witnessed
with sympathy the painful labors of these red men to redeem their own race
from the doom of eternal inferiority, and to borrow and domesticate in the
tribe the arts and customs of the Caucasian race.

Although he goes on to demand justice and to lament the "unaccountable
apathy" of Americans with regard to Indian affairs, the terms of his praise
reveal the limitations of his sympathy. The following passage, the first five
pages of the essay "Civilization," provides an indispensable statement of
the ideology of nineteenth-century America. The material was originally
prepared as a lecture and delivered in April, 1861; it was later revised for
publication in *Society and Solitude*.

From *Civilization, 1870*

A certain degree of progress from the rudest state in which man is found—
a dweller in caves, or on trees, like an ape—a cannibal, and eater of pounded
snails, worms, and offal—a certain degree of progress from this extreme is
called Civilization. It is a vague, complex name, of many degrees. Nobody
has attempted a definition. Mr. Guizot, writing a book on the subject, does
not. It implies the evolution of a highly organized man, brought to supreme
delicacy of sentiment, as in practical power, religion, liberty, sense of honor,
and taste. In the hesitation to define what it is, we usually suggest it by
negations. A nation that has no clothing, no iron, no alphabet, no marriage,
no arts of peace, no abstract thought, we call barbarous. And after many
arts are invented or imported, as among the Turks and Moorish nations, it
is often a little complaisant to call them civilized.

Each nation grows after its own genius, and has a civilization of its own.
The Chinese and Japanese, though each complete in his way, is different
from the man of Madrid or the man of New York. The term imports a
mysterious progress. In the brutes is none; and in mankind today the savage
tribes are gradually extinguished rather than civilized. The Indians of this
country have not learned the white man's work; and in Africa, the negro of
today is the negro of Herodotus. In other races the growth is not arrested;
but the like progress that is made by a boy "when he cuts his eye-teeth,"
as we say—childish illusions passing daily away, and he seeing things really
and comprehensively—is made by tribes. It is the learning the secret of
cumulative power, of advancing on one's self. It implies a facility of
association, power to compare, the ceasing from fixed ideas. The Indian is
gloomy and distressed when urged to depart from his habits and traditions.
He is overpowered by the gaze of the white, and his eye sinks. The occasion of one of these starts of growth is always some novelty that astounds
the mind, and provokes it to dare to change. Thus there is a Cadmus, a
Pythias, a Manco Capac at the beginning of each improvement—some
superior foreigner importing new and wonderful arts, and teaching them.
Of course, he must not know too much, but must have the sympathy, language, and gods of those he would inform. But chiefly the seashore has

Ralph Waldo Emerson, *Society and Solitude: Twelve Chapters* (Boston, 1876),
pp. 21–26.

been the point of departure to knowledge, as to commerce. The most advanced nations are always those who navigate the most. The power which the sea requires in the sailor makes a man of him very fast, and the change of shores and population clears his head of much nonsense of his wigwam.

Where shall we begin or end the list of those feats of liberty and wit, each of which feats made an epoch of history? Thus, the effect of a framed or stone house is immense on the tranquillity, power, and refinement of the builder. A man in a cave or in a camp, a nomad, will die with no more estate than the wolf or the horse leaves. But so simple a labor as a house being achieved, his chief enemies are kept at bay. He is safe from the teeth of wild animals, from frost, sun-stroke, and weather; and fine faculties begin to yield their fine harvest. Invention and art are born, manners and social beauty and delight. 'T is wonderful how soon a piano gets into a log-hut on the frontier. You would think they found it under a pine stump. With it comes a Latin grammar—and one of those tow-head boys has written a hymn on Sunday. Now let colleges, now let senates take heed! for here is one who, opening these fine tastes on the basis of the pioneer's iron constitution, will gather all their laurels in his strong hands.

When the Indian trail gets widened, graded, and bridged to a good road, there is a benefactor, there is a missionary, a pacificator, a wealth-bringer, a maker of markets, a vent for industry. Another step in civility is the change from war, hunting, and pasturage to agriculture. Our Scandinavian forefathers have left us a significant legend to convey their sense of the importance of this step. "There was once a giantess who had a daughter, and the child saw a husbandman ploughing in the field. Then she ran and picked him up with her finger and thumb, and put him and his plough and his oxen into her apron, and carried them to her mother, and said, 'Mother, what sort of a beetle is this that I found wriggling in the sand?' But the mother said, 'Put it away, my child; we must begone out of this land, for these people will dwell in it.' " Another success is the post-office, with its educating energy augmented by cheapness and guarded by a certain religious sentiment in mankind; so that the power of a wafer or a drop of wax or gluten to guard a letter, as it flies over sea, over land, and comes to its address as if a battalion of artillery brought it, I look upon as a fine meter of civilization.

The division of labor, the multiplication of the arts of peace, which is nothing but a large allowance to each man to choose his work according to his faculty—to live by his better hand—fills the State with useful and happy laborers; and they, creating demand by the very temptation of their productions, are rapidly and surely rewarded by good sale: and what a police and ten commandments their work thus becomes. So true is Dr. Johnson's remark that "men are seldom more innocently employed than when they are making money."

The skillful combinations of civil government, though they usually follow natural leadings, as the lines of race, language, religion, and territory, yet require wisdom and conduct in the rulers, and in their result delight the imagination. "We see insurmountable multitudes obeying, in opposition to their strongest passions, the restraints of a power which they scarcely perceive, and the crimes of a single individual marked and punished at the distance of half the earth."

Right position of woman in the State is another index. Poverty and industry with a healthy mind read very easily the laws of humanity, and love them: place the sexes in right relations of mutual respect, and a severe morality gives that essential charm to woman which educates all that is delicate, poetic, and self-sacrificing, breeds courtesy and learning, conversation and wit, in her rough mate; so that I have thought a sufficient measure of civilization is the influence of good women.

Another measure of culture is the diffusion of knowledge, overrunning all the old barriers of caste, and, by the cheap press, bringing the university to every poor man's door in the newsboy's basket. Scraps of science, of thought, of poetry, are in the coarsest sheet, so that in every house we hesitate to burn a newspaper until we have looked it through.

The ship, in its latest complete equipment, is an abridgment and compend of a nation's arts: the ship steered by compass and chart—longitude reckoned by lunar observation and by chronometer—driven by steam; and in wildest sea-mountains, at vast distances from home,

> The pulses of her iron heart,
> Go beating through the storm.

No use can lessen the wonder of this control, by so weak a creature, or forces so prodigious. I remember I watched, in crossing the sea, the beautiful skill whereby the engine in its constant working was made to produce two hundred gallons of fresh water out of salt water, every hour— thereby supplying all the ship's want.

The skill that pervades complex details; the man that maintains himself; the chimney taught to burn its own smoke; the farm made to produce all that is consumed on it; the very prison compelled to maintain itself and yield a revenue, and, better still, made a reform school, and a manufactory of honest men out of rogues, as the steamer made fresh water out of salt— all these are examples of that tendency to combine antagonisms, and utilize evil, which is the index of high civilization.

MARK TWAIN
(1835-1910)

   Although Mark Twain's skepticism increasingly led him to question American pieties, he remained a child of the frontier in his most memorable treatments of the Indian. In his first book, *Innocents Abroad* (1869), he showed that he could muster critical detachment; describing Moorish prisoners in Tangiers, who must make mats and baskets, he comments: "This thing of utilizing crime savors of civilization." Yet, in another mood, he speaks irritably of Syrians and their sore-eyed children, who remind him of Indians: "These people about us had other peculiarities which I had noticed in the noble red man, too: they were infested with vermin, and the dirt had caked on them till it amounted to bark." He calls the Bedouins "Digger Indians," a mythical tribe invented by Americans to give full expression to their contempt.

   The selection excerpted below, from *Roughing It,* Mark Twain's account of his western adventures, presents an image of the Indian that powerfully and explicitly challenges the literary "noble savage." Its tone of intense bitterness, relieved only at the end by a bit of literary criticism and an amusing swipe at railroad employees, shocks the reader, who knows that Mark Twain here is expressing attitudes on which his countrymen were acting. A more sustained piece of literary criticism can be found in "Fenimore Cooper's Literary Offenses" (1895). In a broadly comic sketch, "Niagara" (1871), Mark Twain exhibits a naive narrator speaking to "Indian" souvenir hawkers (really Irish immigrants) in language learned from fiction.

   Mark Twain's inheritance of frontier prejudice is perfectly clear in *The Adventures of Tom Sawyer* (1876). The Indian blood of the half-breed, Injun Joe, is made to account for his vicious vengeance on young Dr. Robinson. He stands for evil in the boys' world; when he dies, in a cave triple-locked by the judge, an enormous "weight of dread" drops from Tom, and the author mocks those "sappy women" who would have had Joe pardoned.

   Three years later, in a passage eliminated from the published version of *A Tramp Abroad* (1879), Mark Twain returns to a more skeptical use of Indian material. In "The French and the Comanches," he satirizes the

highly civilized Europeans and their religion, by showing how they outdid
the Indians in refinements of brutality. One American prejudice vanquished
the other.

From *Roughing It,* 1872

On the morning of the sixteenth day out from St. Joseph we arrived at
the entrance of Rocky Canyon, two hundred and fifty miles from Salt Lake.
It was along in this wild country somewhere, and far from any habitation
of white men, except the stage stations, that we came across the wretchedest type of mankind I have ever seen, up to this writing. I refer to the
Goshoot Indians. From what we could see and all we could learn, they are
very considerably inferior to even the despised Digger Indians of California;
inferior to all races of savages on our continent; inferior to even the Tierra
del Fuegans; inferior to the Hottentots, and actually inferior in some respects
to the Kytches of Africa. Indeed, I have been obliged to look the bulky
volumes of Wood's *Uncivilized Races of Men* clear through in order to find
a savage tribe degraded enough to take rank with the Goshoots. I find but
one people fairly open to that shameful verdict. It is the Bosjesmans
(Bushmen) of South Africa. Such of the Goshoots as we saw, along the
road and hanging about the stations, were small, lean, "scrawny" creatures;
in complexion a dull black like the ordinary American negro; their faces
and hands bearing dirt which they had been hoarding and accumulating for
months, years, and even generations, according to the age of the proprietor;
a silent, sneaking, treacherous looking race; taking note of everything,
covertly, like all the other "Noble Red Men" that we (do not) read about,
and betraying no sign in their countenances; indolent, everlastingly patient
and tireless, like all other Indians; prideless beggars—for if the beggar instinct
were left out of an Indian he would not "go," any more than a clock without a pendulum; hungry, always hungry, and yet never refusing anything
that a hog would eat, though often eating what a hog would decline; hunters,
but having no higher ambition than to kill and eat jackass rabbits, crickets
and grasshoppers, and embezzle carrion from the buzzards and cayotes;

Samuel Langhorne Clemens, *Roughing It* (Hartford, 1872), pp. 146–149.

savages who, when asked if they have the common Indian belief in a Great Spirit show a something which almost amounts to emotion, thinking whisky is referred to; a thin, scattering race of almost naked black children, these Goshoots are, who produce nothing at all, and have no villages, and no gatherings together into strictly defined tribal communities—a people whose only shelter is a rag cast on a bush to keep off a portion of the snow, and yet who inhabit one of the most rocky, wintry, repulsive wastes that our country or any other can exhibit.

The Bushmen and our Goshoots are manifestly descended from the self-same gorilla, or kangaroo, or Norway rat, whichever animal-Adam the Darwinians trace them to.

One would as soon expect the rabbits to fight as the Goshoots, and yet they used to live off the offal and refuse of the stations a few months and then come some dark night when no mischief was expected, and burn down the buildings and kill the men from ambush as they rushed out. And once, in the night, they attacked the stage-coach when a District Judge, of Nevada Territory, was the only passenger, and with their first volley of arrows (and a bullet or two) they riddled the stage curtains, wounded a horse or two and mortally wounded the driver. The latter was full of pluck, and so was his passenger. At the driver's call Judge Mott swung himself out, clambered to the box and seized the reins of the team, and away they plunged, through the racing mob of skeletons and under a hurtling storm of missiles. The stricken driver had sunk down on the boot as soon as he was wounded, but had held on to the reins and said he would manage to keep hold of them until relieved. And after they were taken from his relaxing grasp, he lay with his head between Judge Mott's feet, and tranquilly gave directions about the road; he said he believed he could live till the miscreants were outrun and left behind, and that if he managed that, the main difficulty would be at an end, and then if the Judge drove so and so (giving directions about bad places in the road, and general course) he would reach the next station without trouble. The Judge distanced the enemy and at last rattled up to the station and knew that the night's perils were done; but there was no comrade-in-arms for him to rejoice with, for the soldierly driver was dead.

Let us forget that we have been saying harsh things about the Overland drivers, now. The disgust which the Goshoots gave me, a disciple of Cooper and a worshiper of the Red Man—even of the scholarly savages in *The Last of the Mohicans,* who are fittingly associated with backwoodsmen who divide each sentence into two equal parts: one part critically grammatical, refined and choice of language, and the other part just such an attempt to talk like a hunter or a mountaineer, as a Broadway clerk might make after eating an edition of Emerson Bennett's works and studying frontier life at the Bowery Theatre a couple of weeks—I say that the nausea which the

Goshoots gave me, an Indian worshiper, set me to examining authorities, to see if perchance I had been over-estimating the Red Man while viewing him through the mellow moonshine of romance. The revelations that came were disenchanting. It was curious to see how quickly the paint and tinsel fell away from him and left him treacherous, filthy and repulsive—and how quickly the evidences accumulated that wherever one finds an Indian tribe he has only found Goshoots more or less modified by circumstances and surroundings—but Goshoots, after all. They deserve pity, poor creatures; and they can have mine—at this distance. Nearer by, they never get anybody's.

There is an impression abroad that the Baltimore and Washington Railroad Company and many of its employees are Goshoots; but it is an error. There is only a plausible resemblance, which, while it is apt enough to mislead the ignorant, cannot deceive parties who have contemplated both tribes. But seriously, it was not only poor wit, but very wrong to start the report referred to above; for however innocent the motive may have been, the necessary effect was to injure the reputation of a class who have a hard enough time of it in the pitiless deserts of the Rocky Mountains, Heaven knows! If we cannot find it in our hearts to give those poor naked creatures our Christian sympathy and compassion, in God's name let us at least not throw mud at them.

FRANK HAMILTON CUSHING
(1857–1900)

Although Frank Cushing had no formal scientific training, his lifelong interest in Indians led to his appointment in the Bureau of Ethnology of the Smithsonian Institute. The department was newly created in the 1880s, and one of Cushing's earliest assignments was to travel among the tribes of the Southwest. He went to Zuñi for an expected stay of several months, but remained for four and a half years. In the course of those years, he survived the suspicions of his hosts and their dislike of his persistent note-taking and sketching. As much as Cushing respected Zuñi beliefs, he would not accede to demands that he stop recording sacred ritual; his tough-mindedness and physical courage strike the reader who turns the drying pages of the *Century Illustrated Monthly* to read three installments of Cushing's vigorous account. The magazine articles have been reprinted recently, with an introduction by Oakah L. Jones, Jr., by the American West Publishing Company.

Cushing was recalled from his work among the Zuñi through the influence of Senator John A. Logan; this politician was retaliating for Cushing's powerful opposition to a land scheme designed to cheat the Indians. Although his work was brought to a premature close, Cushing left valuable monographs on the people of the Southwest; because he was a writer interested in human behavior, he preserved unforgettable images of the Zuñi.

In the passage that follows, Cushing tells the story of his initiation in straightforward, concrete language. His prose drew the praise of Edmund Wilson, who called Cushing's work to the attention of students of American literature.

From *My Adventures in Zuñi*, 1882–1883

During the evening of the last day, just as I was sitting down with the rest around the family supper bowl, Colonel and Mrs. Stevenson came in to bid me goodbye. And on the following morning, long before daylight, their train passed over the lava hills, and I was once more alone in Zuñi.

During the day I told the Governor that I would follow my friends before two months were over. With great emphasis and a smile of triumph, he replied, "I guess not."

On the evening of the second day he beckoned me to follow, as he led the way into the mud-plastered little room, whither he had unearthed my head-band. In one corner stood a forge, over which a blanket had been spread. All trappings had been removed, and the floor had been freshly plastered. A little arched fireplace in the corner opposite the forge was aglow with piñon, which lighted even the smoky old rafters and the wattled willow ceiling. Two sheepskins and my belongings, a jar of water and a wooden poker, were all the furnishings. "There," said he, "now you have a little house, what more do you want? Here, take these two blankets—they are all you can have. If you get cold, take off all your clothes, and sleep next to the sheepskins, and *think* you are warm, as the Zuñi does. You must sleep in the cold and on a hard bed; that will harden your meat. And you must never go to Dust-eye's house (the Mission), or the Black-beard's (the trader's) to eat; for I want to make a Zuñi of you. How can I do that if you eat American food?" With this he left me for the night.

I suffered immeasurably that night. The cold was intense, and the pain from my hard bed excruciating. Although next morning, with a mental reservation, I told the Governor I had passed a good night, yet I insisted on slinging my hammock lengthwise of the little room. To this the Governor's reply was: "It would not be good for it to hang in a smoky room, so I have packed it away." I resigned myself to my hard fate, and harder bed, and suffered throughout long nights of many weeks rather than complain or show any unwillingness to have my "meat hardened."

An old priest, whom I had seen at the head of one of the dances, and whose fine bearing and classic, genial face had impressed me, used to come and chat occasionally of an evening with the Governor, in the other room.

Frank Hamilton Cushing, "My Adventures in Zuñi," *The Century Illustrated Monthly Magazine* 25:4 (Feb. 1883), pp. 509–11.

Often, as he sat in the firelight, his profile against the blazing background made me wonder if the ghost of Dante had not displaced the old Indian for a moment, so like the profile of the great poet was the one I looked upon. He had conceived a great affection for me, and his visits became more and more frequent, until at last one day he told me his name was Laí-ju-ah-tsai-lun-kia, but that I must forget his name whenever I spoke to him, and call him "father." Now that I wore the head-band and moccasins of his people, his attentions were redoubled, and he insisted constantly that I should dress entirely in the native costume, and have my ears pierced. That would make a complete Zuñi of me, for had I not eaten Zuñi food long enough to have starved four times, and was not my flesh, therefore, of the soil of Zuñi?

I strongly opposed his often repeated suggestions, and at last he so rarely made them that I thought he had altogether given up the idea.

On day, however, the Governor's wife came through the doorway with a dark blue bundle of cloth, and a long, embroidered red belt. She threw the latter on the floor, and unrolled the former, which proved to be a strip of diagonal stuff about five feet long by a yard in width. Through the middle a hole was cut, and to the edges, either side of this hole, were stitched, with brightly colored strips of fabric, a pair of sleeves. With a patronizing smile, the old woman said,

"Put this on. Your brother will make you a pair of breeches, and then you will be a handsome young man."

Under her instructions I stuck my head through the central hole, pushed my arms down into the little blanket sleeves, and gathered the ends around my waist, closely securing them with the embroidered belt. The sudden appearance of the Governor was the signal for the hasty removal of the garment. He folded it up and put it away under the blanket on the forge. Long before night he had completed a pair of short, thin, black cotton trousers, and secured a pair of long, knitted blue woolen leggins.

"Take off that blue coat and rag necklace," said he, referring to my blue flannel shirt and a tie of gray silk. "What! *another* coat under that. Take it off."

I removed it.

"There, now! Go over into that corner and put these breeches on. Don't wear anything under them."

Then the coarse woolen blanket shirt was again put on as before, only next to my skin. There were no seams in this remarkable garment, save where the sleeves were attached to the shoulders and from the elbows down to the wrists. The sides, a little below the armpits, and the arms inside down to the elbow, were left entirely exposed. I asked the Governor if I could not wear the under-coat.

"No," said he. "Didn't I say you must have your meat hardened?"

Fortunately, however, a heavy gray **serape**, striped with blue and black, and fringed with red and blue, was added to this costume. One of the young men gave me a crude copper bracelet, and the old priest presented me with one or two strings of black stone beads for a necklace.

The first time I appeared in the streets in full costume the Zuñis were delighted. Little children gathered around me; old women patronizingly bestowed compliments on me as their "new son, the child of Wa-sin-to-na." I found the impression was good, and permitted the old Governor to have his way. In fact, it would have been rather difficult to have done otherwise, for, on returning to my room, I found that every article of civilized clothing had disappeared from it.

During my absence for several days on an expedition to the Valley of the Pines in search of mines which had formerly been worked by the Zuñis, the old Governor and his wife industriously plastered my room, whitewashed the walls and even the rafters, spread blankets over the floor, and furnished it in Indian style more luxuriously than any other room in Zuñi. On the wall at one end, the Governor, in recollection of the pictures in officers' quarters which he had seen, had pasted bright gilt and red prints, which no one knows how many years past had been torn from bales of Mexican *bayeta*. Above, carefully secured by little pegs, was a photograph of Colonel Stevenson, which the latter had given the Governor before leaving, and which the Indians had designed as my companion. On my return I was so cordially greeted that I could no longer doubt the good intentions of the Zuñis toward me.

My foster father and many other of the principal men of the tribe now insisted that my ears be pierced. I steadily refused; but they persisted, until at last it occurred to me that there must be some meaning in their urgency, and I determined to yield to their request. They procured some raw Moqui cotton, which they twisted into rolls about as large as an ordinary lead-pencil. Then they brought a large bowl of clear cold water and placed it before a rug in the eastern part of the room. K'iawu presently came through the doorway, arrayed in her best dress, with a sacred cotton mantle thrown over her shoulders and abundant white shell beads on her neck. I was placed kneeling on the rug, my face toward the east. My old father, then solemnly removing his moccasins, approached me, needle and cotton in hand. He began a little shuffling dance around me, in time to a prayer chant to the sun. At the pauses in the chant he would reach out and grasp gently the lobe of my left ear. Each time he grasped, I braced up to endure the prick, until finally, when I least expected it, he ran the needle through. The chant was repeated, and the other ear grasped and pierced in the same way. As soon as the rolls of cotton had been drawn through, both the old man and K'iawu dipped their hands in the water, prayed over them, and, at the close of the prayer, sprinkled my head, and scattered the water about like rain-drops on the floor, after which they washed my hands and face, and dried them with the cotton mantle.

I could not understand the whole prayer; but it contained beautiful passages, recommending me to the gods as a "Child of the Sun," and a "Son of the Coru people of earth" (the sacred name for the priests of Zuñi). At its close, the old man said—"And thus become thou my son, Té-na-tsa-li," and the old woman followed him with, "This day thou art made my younger brother, Té-na-tsa-li." Various other members of the little group then came forward, repeating the ceremonial and prayer, and closing with one or the other of the above sentences, and the distinct pronunciation of my new name.

When all was over, my father took me to the window, and, looking down with a smile on his face, explained that I was "named after a magical plant which grew on a single mountain in the west, the flowers of which were the most beautiful in the world, and of many colors, and the roots and juices of which were a panacea for all injuries to the flesh of man. That by this name—which only one man in a generation could bear—would I be known as long as the sun rose and set, and smiled on the Coru people of earth, as a *Shi wi* (Zuñi)."

HELEN HUNT JACKSON
(1830–1885)

Among all of the nineteenth-century writers represented in this collection, Helen Hunt Jackson had the sharpest sense of Indian suffering. By the end of her life she had played a role in drawing public notice to Indian affairs analogous to that of her New England contemporary, Harriet Beecher Stowe, in the antislavery movement.

Born in Amherst, Massachusetts, a contemporary of Emily Dickinson, Helen Hunt Jackson was influenced by the New England penchant for moral and intellectual questioning. She began her literary career as a romantic poet; highly praised by Emerson, her place in post-Civil War genteel literary circles seemed secure. She began to write travel pieces, stories, novels, and children's books. Although she had never been identified with reform causes, in 1879 she found herself deeply moved by a lecture on Ponca troubles. Trips to California and her second marriage (to a Colorado banker, William Sharpless Jackson) confirmed this interest, which culminated in her preparation of a full indictment of United States government policy.

A Century of Dishonor: A Sketch of the United States Government's Dealings with Some of the Indian Tribes (1881) summarizes the experience of seven tribes with broken agreements; a separate section describes three massacres of Indians by whites. In a lengthy appendix, Jackson provides some of the documentation for her book in letters and government papers. *A Century of Dishonor* stands out among nineteenth-century accounts of Indian affairs for its vigor, its unsentimental firmness, the clarity with which it points to the failures of the present as well as the past. Helen Hunt Jackson concludes that "the United States government breaks promises now as deftly as then."

Despite its readability, *A Century of Dishonor* did not have the mobilizing effect for which its author had hoped. She travelled through California, did careful research into the old Spanish and Mexican families, and tried to absorb enough local color to compose a novel dramatizing the destruction of the Mission Indians. *Ramona,* published in 1884, resembles *Uncle Tom's Cabin* in its use of the conventions of sentimental fiction to frame moral and political issues. In the chapter reprinted below, the Christianized

Indian, Alessandro, son of a chief of the Mission Indians, is murdered by a white at the end of a long series of dispossessions and bereavements. He leaves Ramona, his half-Indian wife, and their surviving child to be rescued by Felipe, a young Spaniard; Felipe and Ramona marry and move to Old Mexico to escape the ruthless greed of white Americans. Jackson portrays a group of Indians who have already adapted their own sedentary, agricultural civilization to Christian values. Hardworking believers in tradition and community, they come to represent a tortured remnant, tragically destroyed.

From *Ramona,* *1884*

There was no real healing for Alessandro. His hurts had gone too deep. His passionate heart, ever secretly brooding on the wrongs he had borne, the hopeless outlook for his people in the future, and most of all on the probable destitution and suffering in store for Ramona, consumed itself as by hidden fires. Speech, complaint, active antagonism, might have saved him; but all these were foreign to his self-contained, reticent, repressed nature. Slowly, so slowly that Ramona could not tell on what hour or what day her terrible fears first changed to an even more terrible certainty, his brain gave way, and the thing, in dread of which he had cried out the morning they left San Pasquale, came upon him. Strangely enough, and mercifully, now that it had really come, he did now know it. He knew that he suddenly came to his consciousness sometimes, and discovered himself in strange and unexplained situations; had no recollection of what had happened for an interval of time, longer or shorter. But he thought it was only a sort of sickness; he did not know that during those intervals his acts were the acts of a madman; never violent, aggressive, or harmful to any one; never destructive. It was piteous to see how in these intervals his delusions were always shaped by the bitterest experiences of his life. Sometimes he fancied that the Americans were pursuing him, or that they were carrying off Ramona, and he was pursuing them. At such times he would run with maniac swiftness for hours, till he fell exhausted on the ground, and slowly regained

Helen Hunt Jackson, *Ramona* (Boston, 1886), pp. 422–429.

true consciousness by exhaustion. At other times he believed he owned vast flocks and herds; would enter any enclosure he saw, where there were sheep or cattle, go about among them, speaking of them to passers-by as his own. Sometimes he would try to drive them away; but on being remonstrated with, would bewilderedly give up the attempt. Once he suddenly found himself in the road driving a small flock of goats, whose he knew not, nor whence he got them. Sitting down by the roadside, he buried his head in his hands. "What has happened to my memory?" he said. "I must be ill of a fever!" As he sat there, the goats, of their own accord, turned and trotted back into a corral nearby, the owner of which stood, laughing, on his doorsill; and when Alessandro came up, said goodnaturedly, "All right, Alessandro! I saw you driving off my goats, but I thought you'd bring 'em back."

Everybody in the valley knew him, and knew his condition. It did not interfere with his capacity as a worker, for the greater part of the time. He was one of the best shearers in the region, the best horse-breaker; and his services were always in demand, spite of the risk there was of his having at any time one of these attacks of wandering. His absences were a great grief to Ramona, not only from the loneliness in which it left her, but from the anxiety she felt lest his mental disorder might at any time take a more violent and dangerous shape. This anxiety was all the more harrowing because she must keep it locked in her own breast, her wise and loving instinct telling her that nothing could be more fatal to him than the knowledge of his real condition. More than once he reached home, breathless, panting, the sweat rolling off his face, crying aloud, "The Americans have found us out, Majella! They were on the trail! I baffled them. I came up another way." At such times she would soothe him like a child; persuade him to lie down and rest; and when he waked and wondered why he was so tired, she would say, "You were all out of breath when you came in, dear. You must not climb so fast; it is foolish to tire one's self so."

In these days Ramona began to think earnestly of Felipe. She believed Alessandro might be cured. A wise doctor could surely do something for him. If Felipe knew what sore straits she was in, Felipe would help her. But how could she reach Felipe without the Señora's knowing it? And, still more, how could she send a letter to Felipe without Alessandro's knowing what she had written? Ramona was as helpless in her freedom on this mountain eyrie as if she had been chained hand and foot.

And so the winter wore away, and the spring. What wheat grew in their fields in this upper air! Wild oats, too, in every nook and corner. The goats frisked and fattened, and their hair grew long and silky; the sheep were already heavy again with wool, and it was not yet midsummer. The spring rains had been good; the stream was full, and flowers grew along its edges thick as in beds.

The baby had thrived; as placid, laughing a little thing as if its mother had never known sorrow. "One would think she had suckled pain," thought Ramona, "so constantly have I grieved this year; but the Virgin has kept her well."

If prayers could compass it, that would surely have been so; for night and day the devout, trusting, and contrite Ramona had knelt before the Madonna and told her golden beads, till they were wellnigh worn smooth of all their delicate chasing.

At midsummer was to be a fête in the Saboba village, and the San Bernardino priest would come there. This would be the time to take the baby down to be christened; this also would be the time to send the letter to Felipe, enclosed in one to Aunt Ri, who would send it for her from San Bernardino. Ramona felt half guilty as she sat plotting what she should say and how she should send it—she, who had never had in her loyal, transparent breast one thought secret from Alessandro since they were wedded. But it was all for his sake. When he was well, he would thank her.

She wrote the letter with much study and deliberation; her dread of its being read by the Señora was so great, that it almost paralyzed her pen as she wrote. More than once she destroyed pages, as being too sacred a confidence for unloving eyes to read. At last, the day before the fête, it was done, and safely hidden away. The baby's white robe, finely wrought in open-work, was also done, and freshly washed and ironed. No baby would there be at the fête so daintily wrapped as hers; and Alessandro had at last given his consent that the name should be Majella. It was a reluctant consent, yielded finally only to please Ramona; and, contrary to her wont, she had been willing in this instance to have her own wish fulfilled rather than his. Her heart was set upon having the seal of baptism added to the name she so loved; and, "If I were to die," she thought, "how glad Alessandro would be, to have still a Majella!"

All her preparations were completed, and it was yet not noon. She seated herself on the veranda to watch for Alessandro, who had been two days away, and was to have returned the previous evening, to make ready for the trip to Saboba. She was disquieted at his failure to return at the appointed time. As the hours crept on and he did not come, her anxiety increased. The sun had gone more than an hour past the midheavens before he came. He had ridden fast; she had heard the quick strokes of the horse's hoofs on the ground before she saw him. "Why comes he riding like that?" she thought, and ran to meet him. As he drew near, she saw to her surprise that he was riding a new horse. "Why, Alessandro!" she cried. "What horse is this?"

He looked at her bewilderedly, then at the horse. True; it was not his own horse! He struck his hand on his forehead, endeavoring to collect his thoughts. "Where is my horse, then?" he said.

"My God! Alessandro," cried Ramona. "Take the horse back instantly. They will say you stole it."

"But I left my pony there in the corral," he said. "They will know I did not mean to steal it. How could I ever have made the mistake? I recollect nothing, Majella. I must have had one of the sicknesses."

Ramona's heart was cold with fear. Only too well she knew what summary punishment was dealt in that region to horse-thieves. "Oh, let me take it back, dear!" she cried. "Let me go down with it. They will believe me."

"Majella!" he exclaimed, "think you I would send you into the fold of the wolf? My wood-dove! It is in Jim Farrar's corral I left my pony. I was there last night, to see about his sheep-shearing in the autumn. And that is the last I know. I will ride back as soon as I have rested. I am heavy with sleep."

Thinking it safer to let him sleep for an hour, as his brain was evidently still confused, Ramona assented to this, though a sense of danger oppressed her. Getting fresh hay from the corral, she with her own hands rubbed the horse down. It was a fine, powerful black horse; Alessandro had evidently urged him cruelly up the steep trail, for his sides were steaming, his nostrils white with foam. Tears stood in Ramona's eyes as she did what she could for him. He recognized her good-will, and put his nose to her face. "It must be because he was black like Benito, that Alessandro took him," she thought. "Oh, Mary Mother, help us to get the creature safe back!" she said.

When she went into the house, Alessandro was asleep. Ramona glanced at the sun. It was already in the western sky. By no possibility could Alessandro go to Farrar's and back before dark. She was on the point of waking him, when a furious barking from Capitan and the other dogs roused him instantly from his sleep, and springing to his feet, he ran out to see what it meant. In a moment more Ramona followed—only a moment, hardly a moment; but when she reached the threshold, it was to hear a gun-shot, to see Alessandro fall to the ground, to see, in the same second, a ruffianly man leap from his horse, and standing over Alessandro's body, fire his pistol again, once, twice, into the forehead, cheek. Then with a volley of oaths, each word of which seemed to Ramona's reeling senses to fill the air with a sound like thunder, he untied the black horse from the post where Ramona had fastened him, and leaping into his saddle again, galloped away, leading the horse. As he rode away, he shook his fist at Ramona, who was kneeling on the ground, striving to lift Alessandro's head, and to stanch the blood flowing from the ghastly wounds. "That'll teach you damned Indians to leave off stealing our horses!" he cried, and with another volley of terrible oaths was out of sight.

With a calmness which was more dreadful than any wild outcry of grief, Ramona sat on the ground by Alessandro's body, and held his hands in hers. There was nothing to be done for him. The first shot had been fatal, close to his heart—the murderer aimed well; the after-shots, with the pistol, were from mere wanton brutality. After a few seconds Ramona rose, went into the house, brought out the white altar-cloth, and laid it over the mutilated face. As she did this, she recalled words she had heard Father Salvierderra quote as having been said by Father Junipero, when one of the Franciscan Fathers had been massacred by the Indians, at San Diego. "Thank God!" he said, "the ground is now watered by the blood of a martyr!"

INDEX OF AUTHORS

Anonymous, 21

Barker, James Nelson, 149
Bartram, William, 114
Bird, Robert Montgomery, 191
Brown, Charles Brockden, 138
Bryant, William Cullen, 214

Child, Lydia Maria, 166
Cook, Ebenezer, 71
Cooper, James Fenimore, 250
Crèvecoeur, Michel Guillame Jean
 de, 95
Cushing, Frank Hamilton, 280

DeVries, David Pieterzen, 32

Emerson, Ralph Waldo, 272

Franklin, Benjamin, 101
Freneau, Philip, 120, 122
Fuller, Margaret, 209

Greeley, Horace, 257

Hawthorne, Nathaniel, 185
Henry, Alexander, 156

Irving, Washington, 161

Jackson, Helen Hunt, 285
Jefferson, Thomas, 107

Lawson, John, 74
Longfellow, Henry Wadsworth,
 236

Mather, Cotton, 56, 64
Melville, Herman, 222
Morton, Thomas, 28

Parkman, Francis, 218
Penn, William, 49
Poe, Edgar Allen, 197

Rogers, Robert, 79
Rowlandson, Mary, 40

Sigourney, Lydia Huntley, 205
Simms, William Gilmore, 176
Smith, Captain John, 14
Stephens, Ann Sophia, 261
Stone, John Augustus, 172

Thoreau, Henry David, 265, 269
Tompson, Benjamin, 36
Twain, Mark, 276

Whitman, Walt, 243, 245, 247
Woolman, John, 89

INDEX OF TITLES

Civilization, 272
Confidence-Man, His Masquerade,
 The, 225
Conspiracy of Pontiac and the
 Indian War after the Conquest of
 Canada, The, 218

Decennium Luctuosum, 64
Description of Pennsylvania, A, 49
Duston Family, The, 185

Edgar Huntly; or, Memoirs of
 a Sleep-Walker, 138

Decennium Luctuosum, 64
Description of Pennsylvania, A, 49
Duston Family, The, 185

Edgar Huntly; or, Memoirs of a Sleep-Walker, 138

Generall Historie of Virginia, New-England, and the Summer Isles, The, 14

Half-Breed: A Tale of the Western Frontier, The, 245
History of New York, A, 161
Hobomok: A Tale of Early Times, by an American, 166

Indian Bureau Reminiscence, An, 247
Indian Princess; or, La Belle Sauvage, The, 149

Journall of the Beginning and Proceedings of the English Plantation settled at Plymoth in New England, A Retation of, The, 21
Journal of John Woolman, The, 89
Journal of Julius Rodman, The, 197

Lawson's History of North Carolina,
Leaves of Grass, 243
Letters From an American Farmer, 95
Lines Occasioned by a Visit to an Old Indian Burying Ground, 120

Magnalia Christi Americana, 56
Maine Woods, The, 269
Malaeska; or the Indian Wife of the White Hunter, 261
Metamora, or the Last of the Wampanoags, 172
Moby Dick; or the Whale, 222
My Adventures in Zuñi, 1882–1883, 280

Narrative of the Captivity and Restoration of Mrs. Mary Rowlandson, A, 40
National Gazette, The, 122
New England's Crisis, 36
New Voyage to Carolina, A, 74
New English Canaan, 28
Nick of the Woods; or the Jibbenainosay, A Tale of Kentucky, 191
Notes on the State of Virginia, 107

Overland Journey from New York to San Francisco in the Summer of 1859, An, 257

Pocahontas, and Other Poems, 205
Poetical Works, 214
Ponteach; or the Savages of America, 79

Ramona, 285
Remarks Concerning the Savages of North America, 101
Roughing It, 276

Song of Hiawatha, The, 236
Sot-Weed Factor, The, 71
Summer on the Lakes, 209

Travels and Adventures in Canada and the Indian Territories, between the Years 1760 and 1776, 156
Travels Through North and South Carolina, Georgia, East and West Florida, 114

Voyages from Holland to America, 1632–1644, 32

Week on the Concord and Merrimack Rivers, A, 265
Wept of Wish-ton-Wish, The, 250
Writing of Benjamin Franklin, The, 102

Yemassee: A Romance of Carolina, The, 177